Norman Larry Eugene
Hemmerling - Christensen

COMPARATIVE STUDIES IN REPUBLICAN LATIN IMAGERY

PHOENIX

JOURNAL OF THE CLASSICAL ASSOCIATION

OF CANADA

REVUE DE LA SOCIETE CANADIENNE

DES ETUDES CLASSIQUES

SUPPLEMENTARY VOLUME X

TOME SUPPLEMENTAIRE X

Comparative Studies in Republican Latin Imagery

ELAINE FANTHAM

UNIVERSITY OF TORONTO PRESS

© University of Toronto Press 1972
Toronto and Buffalo
Printed in Canada
ISBN 0-8020-5262-2
Microfiche ISBN 0-8020-0130-0
LC 77-185710

DIS MANIBUS PIISSIMAE MATRIS

ROSAMUND CROSTHWAITE

REFERENCES AND ABBREVIATIONS

The abbreviations used in the text are, for Latin authors, those of the Oxford Latin Dictionary. Greek authors are abbreviated as in Liddell and Scott (9th ed.). Quotations are taken from the Oxford Classical Texts, where not otherwise specified. I have cited Menander from Koerte-Thierfelder (vol. I, ed. 3; Leipzig 1957) and Koerte (vol. II, ed. 2; Leipzig 1953), and the Oxford Classical text of *Dyskolos*; the fragments of Middle and New Comedy are cited from Kock (indicated as KII or KIII), whom I have found more convenient for use and verification than Meineke. Since I have referred often to modern works for minor points, and have made repeated use only of well-known studies, it seemed superfluous to add to the bulk of the book by a misleadingly large bibliography. I have therefore omitted a bibliography, giving full references in the first citation of each work or article consulted.

Contents

Preface

The title of this monograph calls for an apology, which may perhaps serve as an explanation of the book itself. I have used the word "Republican" merely as a time-indicator in the hope that students of Augustan and Silver Latin will not reach for the book and be disappointed. My interest is prose – spoken and written – and I believe that Latin prose can be said to have reached maturity by the end of the Republic; this is the reason for my time-limit. The word "imagery" can also be misleading; readers familiar with studies of imagery in English literature or Latin epic may be led to expect a discussion of image as symbol or leit-motif; but prose-imagery is more limited in intent and application, and my sights must be set lower than either C. Day Lewis's in *The Poetic Image* or Viktor Pöschl's in *Virgils Poetische Dichtkunst*. Like others I have resorted to "imagery" as a shorthand for all forms of figurative language which arise in my chosen field. These are predominantly *metaphor*, in which a word or words from another sphere of activity are substituted for the literal word of the context, and *analogy*, in which statements drawn from another sphere are used comparatively to explain and animate the literal statement of the writer. These overlap in the form of the metaphor κατὰ τοῦ ἀνάλογον: we can say either "in the race of life the old man has run his last lap and is approaching the finishing post," or "as a runner when he races his last lap draws near to the finishing post, so the old man draws near to the end of life." The former is a metaphor, the latter a comparison or analogy.

Simile is rare in Latin prose; the simplest form, Aristotle's "he rushed like a lion," is too weak to be effective, and is used in Latin chiefly where the identification implied by metaphor is felt to be too bold or embarrassing: the full Homeric form, which adds decorative context to the simile, is inappropriate to prose. The only common form of simile is the formal comparison illustrated above. I could not call this work "Studies in *Prose* Imagery," since the comic dramatists wrote in verse: yet they are the only extensive evidence for the figurative language of good colloquial Latin. For this reason I have attempted to relate the practice of Terence, and to some extent Plautus, to that of Cicero in familiar, rhetorical, and literary prose. The questions I want to ask are:

From what physical or social contexts is Latin imagery commonly derived?

To what extent is the choice of context influenced by the primacy of Greek as a cultural language and the derivation of the earliest Latin drama from Greek models?

How are the metaphors expressed in terms of syntax, through verb, noun, adjective, or a combination of syntactical forms?

How is the choice of imagery and its content related to the literary genre?

How is the form of imagery – the development of its expression – related to the literary genre?

I hope to establish by this approach some of the limitations which govern figurative language in Latin speech and prose.

I have read and benefited from several studies of metaphor as an element of English style, but their value to me has been chiefly indirect, in suggesting questions to be asked. I hope the authors will forgive a lack of specific acknowledgment. I am conscious of an immense debt to scholars in my own field. From Eduard Fraenkel I learned, as an undergraduate, how to read and appreciate Latin, although I know how far I must fall short of the standards he required. Gordon Williams taught me when I was a naïve new graduate, and has helped and sustained me ever since with a generosity that only his colleagues and pupils can fully appreciate. In particular, he has patiently read and advised on the manuscript at two different stages in its growth. I have also profited greatly from helpful and stimulating discussions with Neville Collinge and George Grube, and would like to thank them, as much for their patience as for their erudition. Any errors or perversities in the text are my own. Since I approached Alexander Dalzell with my manuscript he has constantly shown the greatest kindness in giving his advice and technical assistance. Finally, Miss Jean Jamieson and the staff of the University of Toronto Press have made it a pleasure for an inexperienced author to work with them.

This book was published with the help of grants from the Humanities Research Council, using funds provided by the Canada Council, and from the Publications Fund of the University of Toronto Press, to whom I wish to express my thanks.

E.F.

Toronto, 1971

PART I The imagery of Terence

Introduction
Metaphor and imagery in Terence

A student of the use of imagery in Latin authors might be excused if he considered the plays of Terence scarcely relevant to his interest: fully developed imagery of beauty and artistry will be found in lyric and epic poetry; exuberant and colourful imagery at the popular level, in the uninhibited language of Plautus and Petronius; the elaborate imagery of rhetoric in the speeches, rhetorical and philosophical works of Cicero and in Seneca. By comparison one would expect the naturalistic *purus sermo*[1] of Terence's dramas to reveal only the simplest and most conventional similes and metaphors, as restricted in range as those admitted in the relatively unadorned prose of Cicero's correspondence or the narrative passages of his speeches and other works.

Paradoxically the very restriction of range is one feature which makes the investigation of imagery and figurative language in Terence rewarding: he is the first source for those who are interested in *sermo familiaris*, and who

1 *Terence's Elocutio in the light of Republican rhetorical theory.* It is still disputed whether Terence's claim in the prologue to *Hautontimorumenos* (46) "in hac est *pura oratio*," is moral or stylistic; but no doubt attaches to Caesar's description *"puri sermonis* amator" (Don. *Vita Terenti*). In this context *purus* brings Terence into line with the *genus attenuatum* of e.g. *Rhet. Her.* 4.11; "attenuata (sc. oratio) est quae demissa est usque ad usitatissimum *puri sermonis* consuetudinem"; from a plain stylist such as Caesar, then, *purus sermo* is praise of the highest order. For Cicero, *purus* is associated, at a level of relative praise, with the good spoken Latin of the aristocrat (cf. *Brut.* 213; patrio fuisse instituto *puro sermone* adsuefactam domum), characterized by *elegantia* (cf. *Brut.* 211, and 252, referring back to 211, 213) and with the plain style of Caesar; cf. *Brut.* 261, on Caesar's speeches; consuetudinem vitiosam et corruptam *pura* et incorrupta *consuetudine* emendat ... ad hanc *elegantiam* verborum Latinorum ... adiungit illa oratoria ornamenta (etc.) and 262 on the *commentarii*; nihil est enim in historia *pura* et inlustri brevitate dulcius. The *elegantia* which Cicero praises in Caesar and other exponents of the plain style expresses the same standards as the word which Cicero applies in verse (where ēlēgāntī sermōne would be impossible) to Terence's language; "*lectus* sermo." This then is naturalistic writing; an artistic representation of natural educated speech.

wish to form an idea of the imagery and metaphor acceptable in the daily speech of the educated Roman. From this point of view the comparison of metaphorical language in Terence with that found in Cicero's correspondence is illuminating, since the categories of metaphor at home both in Terence and in the considerably larger body of Cicero's letters may be considered as characteristic of educated Roman speech and thought, although the level of their treatment naturally reveals artistry beyond the reach of the average educated Roman. With this in mind I have tried to combine with the Terentian examples a comprehensive account of the figurative use of the same words or concepts in Cicero's correspondence. Some of these images are also attested in another genre nearer to prose than to poetic usage, that is in satire: both the fragments of Lucilius, who wrote for the same public a generation after Terence, and Horace's *Satires* and *Epistles* illustrate the metaphorical practice of familiar writing.

But if the main interest of this analysis is a study of *sermo familiaris*, two objections seem to arise: first, why not base such an investigation on the far richer material available in Plautus? This seemed less profitable as a focus for inquiry because Plautus' special genius produced too many images which are purely comic or "scurrilous," verbal exuberance for its own sake, for the sake of its sound, or for sheer absurdity; comic exaggeration or abuse, as well as mock-tragic pomp far removed from normal speech. Plautus' figurative language must often have been alien to the vocabulary and thought of the educated Roman, and deliberately so: countless colourful and splendid images, especially in the mouths of slaves and parasites, have been created for their comic power, not their naturalism. It would be short-sighted to exclude the figurative language of Plautus altogether, since much of it, particularly in the dialogue of young men or their respectable fathers, is clearly comparable to the language of Terence's citizens and Cicero's acquaintances, but I have felt justified in selecting from Plautus' Cornucopia only the material which is closest to everyday speech: this involves a measure of a priori discrimination and selection, but most cases chosen are confirmed by parallel usage in both Terence and Cicero.[2]

2 In this respect it will be seen that my approach differs from that of one of the most recent articles touching on the imagery of Terence (P.B. Corbett, "Vis Comica," *Eranos*, vol. 62, 1964, 52–69), which concentrates on an important category of imagery in Plautus and Terence, imagery expressing violence (*vis*) through the syntactical medium which is most common in both writers and dominant in Terence, i.e. the verb. Corbett states (52) that "while Plautus and Terence, especially the former, are poets of sufficient creative power and originality to be able to devise imagery of their own, nor is there any doubt

The second objection to the study of Terence as a source for the imagery of educated Roman speech lies in the word *Roman*. Terence was famed for his fidelity to the ethos of Menander, in characterization and hence in the representation of his dialogue. How can we call Terence's imagery Roman? Or in what sense is it Roman, and not Greek? I have assumed that Terence's figurative use of language often represents similar figures in the Greek of Menander and Apollodorus. How far this is true can be gauged partly by comparing surviving examples of imagery from Menander and New Comedy as a whole; but since this material is so limited in quantity, and since its survival has been prejudiced by the specialist interests of those who quote the fragments – grammarians, glossarists, collectors of ἀποφθέγματα and students of social habit like Athenaeus – I have thought it worthwhile to compare material from the far greater body of Plato's works (and occasionally from other fourth-century sources). This often coincides in the choice of imagery with surviving examples in New Comedy; in view of the known influence of the philosophical schools on the writers of New Comedy, it is perhaps not unreasonable to conclude that a metaphor appearing both in the Platonic dialogues and in Terence, may have passed through the intermediate stage of New Comedy.

Plautus, too, is a witness for the imagery of Menander, but because of his sweeping originality, one far less reliable. I have compared the imagery of four Menander-based plays of Plautus: *Aulularia*, *Bacchides*, *Cistellaria*, and *Stichus*. Certain scenes and passages in each of these plays offer figurative language so close to that of Terence that they seem valid evidence for the practice of Menander himself – evidence that is in some cases confirmed from his extant plays and fragments. The *Trinummus* and *Mercator*, based on the Θησαυρός and Ἔμπορος of Philemon, also contain so much figurative language which can be paralleled from Terence or Menander, that they serve here as

that on occasions they do this, it is reasonable to suppose that the bulk of the imagery used by them belongs to a common fund of *sermo cottidianus* already in existence in their day, and which they have most felicitously adopted." Study of the figurative language of Plautus, Terence, and Cicero, in the letters, has convinced me that there is far more in common, and genuinely representative of dignified *sermo cottidianus* (or *familiaris*) to Terence and Cicero, than to Terence and Plautus.

Corbett's article provides a nearly comprehensive list of verbs expressing "violence ... other forms of aggressiveness ... forceful or energetic action" (55) in both Plautus and Terence, but there is no discussion of individual passages, and he is not interested in considering the influence on their language of the Greek imagery in the New Comedies which they adapted; I hope to show that this *can* be identified, and is of considerable importance for Terence's imagery.

further illustration of the practice of New Comedy as a whole. From these different sources, I believe it is possible to create a reasonably faithful picture of the extent to which Terence's imagery represents that of his originals.

But to say that a metaphor in Terence represents or echoes one in Menander or Apollodorus is not to prove that it is un-Roman. The elegant speech of the Roman aristocrats owed much to the Hellenization of the early second century B.C., and the Greek inspiration of much of Terence's imagery and expression was only part of the general education of the Roman intellectual élite, derived from their contact with the Greek world. If this language was in some sense foreign and new to Rome in Terence's generation, it was the beginning of the ideal cultivated by spoken Latin of the classical epoch; insofar as any Roman living in the first half of that century was educated, he would have spoken in an idiom close to that of Pamphilus or Chaerea, Chremes or Micio. The language of the Gracchi, of Catulus and Caesar Strabo, of Crassus and Antonius, and that of Cicero's generation did not cease to acquire new colouring from their own Greek educational background, and yet in imagery, as in other respects, there is a real continuity and consistency of practice from Terence to Cicero and later to Seneca and Pliny in their letters.

I hope, then, to provide through this catalogue raisonné of figurative language and metaphor in Terence, a picture both of the Greek inspiration behind the imagery of Roman educated speech, and of the range and application of the imagery itself. Thus for any individual figurative usage, where Greek precedents exist but Roman parallels are lacking at the level of *sermo familiaris*, we may make a presumption that Terence's imagery derives from that of the original; where Greek precedents are lacking in New Comedy and Attic prose but Roman parallels are fairly numerous, the image may fairly be considered as Roman in origin and part of Terence's resources from contemporary *sermo familiaris*; in the many cases where both Greek and Roman parallels exist in reasonable quantity, it is possible that the same metaphor has arisen naturally and independently in each language. However, I would like to argue for the possibility that Terence is himself responsible for the incorporation and naturalization of at least some Greek imagery into the tradition of educated Latin speech.

I

The main categories of metaphorical allusion

Certain categories of metaphor, for instance those based on fire, on heat and cold, on sickness and health, on navigation, or on war and single combat, are relatively common. Those images will be considered first, grouped under separate headings. For each group I shall provide comparative material from Greek New Comedy and related literature, and illustrate the growth of these metaphors in Latin *sermo familiaris* from Cicero's letters, where parallels are available.

I FIRE

An.

308   quo mage lubido frustra *incendatur* tua.

Hau.

367   ut illius animum cupidum inopia *incenderet*.

Eu.

67–9   haec verba una mehercle falsa lacrimula ... /*restinguet*.

72   et taedet et amore *ardeo*.

84–5   tremo horreoque postquam aspexi hanc: : bono animo es.
        accede *ad ignem hunc*, iam *calesces* plus satis.

274   *uro* hominem. (cf. 438; te ut male *urat*.)

Ph.

82   hanc *ardere* coepit perdite.

107–8   ut ni vis boni
        in ipsa inesset forma, haec formam *exstinguerent*.

186   loquarne? *incendam*; taceam? instigem; purgem me? laterem
                                             lavem.

974–5   hisce ego illam dictis ita tibi *incensam* dabo
        ut ne *restinguas* lacrimis si exstillaveris.

Hec.

562   quam ob rem *incendor* ira

Ad.

310   me miserum, vix sum compos animi, ita *ardeo* iracundia.

With the exception of *Eu.* 84–5 all these metaphors are expressed through verbs, perhaps the most economical and compressed form of imagery. *Incendor* and *ardeo* are virtually synonymous in their two fields of reference, except that their differing syntax makes *ardeo* more convenient in providing an adjectival present participle, and in being more suited for situations where no ablative of cause is specified. Both can denote a state of burning anger; this is their function in *Ph.* 186, 974, *Hec.* 562, and *Ad.* 310. Compare their usage in Plautus, *As.* 420, qui semper me *ira incendit*; *Ps.* 201, *ira incendor*; and in Cicero's letters, *Att.* 2.19.5, *ardet dolore et ira* noster Pompeius; *Att.* 6.2.2, saepe *incensum ira vidi*.[3] In *Fam.* 1.9.9, ab eoque in me esset *incensus*; and *Att.* 14.10.4, *ardentes* in eum litteras, the verbs alone are sufficient to imply anger.

Both verbs are associated with desire, especially *ardere*, which implies passion in Plautus *Epid.* 555, *pectus ardens*; *Mer.* 600, *pectus ardet*, as in *Eu.* 72 and *Ph.* 82. *Ph.* 82 is a special case. The transitive use of *ardere* is vouched for by Arruntius Celsus according to Charisius, but the Mss read simply *amare*. We should surely respect a grammarian's deliberate citation, but this is a licence avoided by most later authors.[4] The use of *deperire* in the same sense at *Hau.* 525 is easier since we are dealing with a compound verb, and it has parallels in *Am.* 517, *Cas.* 470, *Epid.* 482, *Mil.* 1026 (compare the synonymous use of transitive *demori* at *Mil.* 970, 1040), and *Ps.* 528. Transitive *ardere* may be explained partly as formed by analogy with *deperire*, and partly, I think, as a usage intended by Terence to reflect vulgar idiom. *Ph.* 82 is spoken by a slave, Geta, and it is interesting that Terence's only use of *deperire* is likewise spoken by a slave. But whereas transitive *deperire* was used freely by Plautus and Catullus (35, 12), the transitive use of *ardere* did not become current.

In Cicero's letters the association of these verbs with desire, enthusiasm, and love is conventional; cf. *Fam.* 9.14.4, tuis factis sic *incensus sum* ut nihil umquam *in amore fuerit ardentius*; *Q.fr.* 3.1.18, *amore* sum *incensus*; ad *Brut.* 23.4, his *ardentibus ... cupiditate*; *Att.* 13.28.2, *incensum cupiditate*; 16.13b.2, *ardeo studio historiae*.

---

3 Add the similar use of *ardeo* with *invidia*, *Q.fr.* 2.15.4; *dolore*, *Att.* 9.6.4; 11.9.2; *furore et scelere*, *Att.* 10.4.2.

4 Perhaps only in Verg. *Ecl.* 2.1; formosum pastor Corydon *ardebat* Alexim; Horace and Ovid use the verb with an ablative (of the instrument?) or in + the ablative.

Terence's instances of *urere* in *Eu.* 274 and 438 cover a different range, resentment and jealousy; thus they barely differ from his use of *mordeo* in *Eu.* 445. Donatus comments on 274, *uro pro eo quod est dolere cogo*; it implies the causing of pain or anger, as does *urere* in Pl. *Bac.* 1091, *Poen.* 770, and *Per.* 801a–b, *uritur cor mi./: : da illi cantharum, exstingue ignem, si/cor uritur, caput ne ardescat*, where the literal meaning of the metaphor is exploited for comedy. *Urere* is not used figuratively in Cicero's correspondence, and he expresses jealousy, etc. by *dolore/invidia ardere* (see n.3).

One final figurative use of these "burning" verbs associates them with shame or scandal;[5] cf. Pl. *Cas.* 937, maxumo ego *ardeo flagitio*; and Cic. *Att.* 4.17.2, consules *flagrant infamia*. This is not found in Terence.

I have suggested economy of language as Terence's motive for compressing the metaphor into a single verb, but a noun-metaphor would admit equal compression. The advantage of verbs, from Terence's point of view, seems to be their unobtrusiveness. Since they create less of a physical image, the audience is not distracted from the psychological content of the metaphor by visualizing its physical or concrete meaning. The exception in this group, *Eu.* 85, *hunc ignem*, is a daring identification of the courtesan Thais (called *nostri fundi calamitas* in 79 by the same kind of reverse personification) as the fire which inflames Phaedria with passion; the speaker is the witty and cynical slave Parmeno, and his retort, exploiting the literal sense of *tremo horreoque*, offers a touch of fantasy more characteristic of Plautus than Terence. However, like several other images in the opening scene of *Eunuchus* it seems to parody and reflect conventional lovers' language such as reappears in the *sermo amatorius* of the Elegists. Since the metaphors of love are to some extent a sub-language, needing separate analysis, they will be discussed in the Appendix to this section.

Plautus has no identifications comparable with *Eu.* 85; *Mer.* 590–1 (below) and *As.* 919, *ex amore tantum est homini incendium*, are more conventional.

Cicero develops the use and application of these noun-metaphors. He employs *ardor* of enthusiasm, *Fam.* 11.8.2; *Att.* 12.13.1; *ad Brut.* 5.1; once, in *Att.* 12.13.1, it describes the pain of his mourning for Tullia. In *Fam.* 6.12.4, *cum hic ardor restinctus esset*, it stands for the fever of political hatred and vengeance. In neither of these last examples is the word assisted by the context. *Incendium* symbolizes political ruin in *Fam.* 4.13.2; 9.3.1; 10.33.5, and *Att.* 4.6.1.

---

5 On the connection of *flagitium* with *flagrare*, and its association with the vocabulary of fire, see Usener, *Kleine Schriften*, vol. 4, p. 368.

The deprecatory *igniculus* occurs in intimate letters (*Fam.* 15.20.2; *Att.* 15.26.2) applied to personal affection or spirit.

Cicero adds to *ardere* and *incendere* the verbs *exardescere*, always of indignation (with *dolore*, *Q.fr.* 2.3.2; *ad Brut.* 2.3; with *iracundia*, *Fam.* 1.9.20; cf. also *Att.* 2.21.1, following a reference to *iracundia*), *flagrare* (*Att.* 4.17.2, above; 5.11.1; 7.4.1 and 17.4; 13.21a.2), and *inflammari* (*Fam.* 1.7.9; 2.4.2; 11.21.1; *Att.* 5.21.5) as an intensive equivalent of *ardere*, to convey enthusiasm or love of glory. Finally, an idiom of Pl. *Trin.* 678, *ne scintillam quidem relinques*, recurs in *Fam.* 10.14.2, *ut ne quae scintilla teterrimi belli relinquatur*.

This image of quenching fire is a source of metaphor in *Ph.* 974–5, and more subtly in *Eu.* 67–9, *haec verba una ... lacrimula/ ... restinguet*: "she will quench those angry (burning) words of yours with one little faked tear." But Terence carries the metaphor furthest from its prosaic application in *Ph.* 108, *haec formam exstinguerent*; "these disfigurements would have obliterated her beauty." What assists the image here is *vis boni*, which suggests that her beauty is a flame or burning light. For this, Plautus has no parallel; it is perhaps too Platonic in its poetry. But he often combines the metaphor of love's fire with a facetious reference to its quenching by water or tears; such allusions, coming from cynical slaves, are similar to *Eu.* 67–69 or 84–5, which are exceptional in Terence. Compare Pl. *Epid.* 554–5, *Per.* 801a–b above, and *Mer.* 590–1,

> ita mi in pectore atque in corde facit amor *incendium*
> ni ex oculis *lacrimae* defendant, iam *ardeat* credo caput.

The tone is more serious, when the guardian speaks in *Trin.* 675–6,

> si istuc, ut conare, facis†indicium†, tuom incendes genus
> tum tibi aquai erit cupido genu' qui restinguas tuom.

This is based on shame, conceived as a fire (cf. *Cas.* 937 above) which will consume the honour of the offender's whole family.

Cicero too uses *restinguere* and *exstinguere*, conventionally in metaphors based on *lumen* (*Fam.* 4.3.2) or *ardor* (*Fam.* 6.12.4; *ad Brut.* 5.1) and more freely with various concepts: *bellum*, *Fam.* 10.23.5; 11.12.1; and 28.2 (this is traditional, cf. Pl. *Per.* 754); *gratiam*, *Fam.* 1.1.4; *odia*, *Att.* 9.1.3; *rumorem*, *Att.* 15.1.5; *sermunculum*, *Att.* 13.10.3. In his literary works he develops more elaborate play on this image in such passages as *Fin.* 4.7, quid? ille *incendat*? (sc. audientem) *restinguet* citius si *ardentem* acceperit.

Imagery based on fire is hard to find in the surviving works of Menander, and is extremely rare in New Comedy as a whole. Menander has no instance of fire-words used in erotic contexts: with *incendere* of provoking to anger, compare *Dysk.* 899:

κόπτωμεν οὕτω τὰς θύρας, αἰτῶμεν, ἐπιφλέγωμεν;

In *Perikeiromene* 42–3, πάντα δ' ἐξεκάετο/ταῦθ' ἕνεκα τοῦ μέλλοντος, ἐκκάειν is used of the eruption of a crisis, a use paralleled by that of *ardescere/exardescere* in Latin. The only other figurative use of a word associated with *fire* is that of διάπυρος, *Dysk.* 183, applied to the inventive fire of a clever slave (see under *calidus* in the next section).

Such metaphors are relatively infrequent in Plato also; men are kindled (ἐξάπτεσθαι) by enthusiasm for philosophy: *Resp.* 498b, *Ep.* 7.340b, ἐξημμένος ὑπὸ φιλοσοφίας ὥσπερ πυρός: an evil bursts into flame; *Resp.* 556e, τοιοῦτον κακὸν ἐκκαόμενον (cf. Men. *Pk.* 42); φλέγεσθαι is used of erotic excitement in *Charmides* 155d, but is absent from similar passages in *Symposium* and *Phaedrus*, despite its frequency in tragedy. The few instances gathered by Louis, *Les Metaphores de Platon* (Paris: Les Belles Lettres, 1945), pp. 117–18, 190, show that this is not an important category of imagery in Plato's works.

However, the metaphorical use of σβέννυμι and its compounds is fairly widespread: cf. *Resp.* 411c, 498a, 556e, etc., and occurs once in Menander: *Sikyonios* 198 Kassel: κύκλῳ πάλιν κατεσβέσθη π[όλυς] ἦχος.

Thus the evidence available suggests that this category of metaphor was not found by Terence in his originals, but was introduced as an idiom natural to spoken Latin.

Ia HEAT AND COLD

Hau.

349 *Concaluit.*

Eu.

85 Accede ad *ignem* hunc, iam *calesces* plus satis.

380 Ne nimium *calidum* hoc sit modo.

Ad.

152 Sperabam iam *defervisse* adulescentiam.

534 Quom *fervit* maxume, tam placidum quam ovem reddo.

Eu.

268 Nimirum hic homines *frigent.*

517 Ubi *friget* ...

Ph.

994   Si non totus *friget*, me enica.

Ad.

233   *Refrixerit* res.

When Syrus in *Hau.* 349 says of Clitipho, *concaluit*, he is describing the young man's excitement and tension. So, too, in *Eu.* 85 (see above) *calesces* expresses the excitement of passion. This element of excitement or eagerness seems present in the only instances of *caleo* in Plautus. (*Concalesco* and *calesco* do not occur.) Both *Ps.* 1127: dum recens est/, dum *calet* dum datur devorari decet iam, and *Poen.* 914: nihil est, nisi dum *calet* hoc agitur, urge immediate action, but whereas *Ps.* 1127 is culinary, comparing the dupe to hot food, in *Poen.* 914, *calet* seems to be impersonal, applied to the circumstances themselves. In Cicero's correspondence, *calere* is used both of persons (*Fam.* 7.10.2; cf. Caelius, *Fam.* 8.6.5, Hirtius, *Att.* 15.6.2), and abstractions (*iudicia*, *Att.* 4.18.3; *rumores*, Caelius, *Fam.* 8.1.2). Cicero also introduces the verb *calefacere* colloquially for "putting a man in a hot spot" (*Fam.* 16.18.2, *Q.fr.* 3.2.1; cf. Caelius, *Fam.* 8.6.4). In a letter to Quintus (3.7.3, *Hortensi calor multum valebit*) *calor* seems to describe the fire of political eloquence. All these examples occur in intimate correspondence – with Atticus, Quintus, Trebatius – and mark the metaphor as conversational rather than literary. The adjective *calidus* seems to undergo considerable change of meaning; in Plautus, the alliterative *calidum consilium* (*Epid.* 256, and *Mil.* 226) seems to imply speed and effectiveness; possibly the source of the image, like that of others in Plautus, is culinary; a "piping hot" plan. In *Mos.* 609, the impersonal *calidum* hoc est: etsi procul abest, *urit* male, like Ter. *Eu.* 380, connotes danger. The idea is expressed more fully in *Epid.* 673–4, of the cunning slave, *Volcani* iratist filius/quaqua tangit, omne *amburit*, si astes, *aestu calefacit*. In the letter of Hirtius quoted in *Att.* 15.6.2, ne quod *calidius* ineant consilium, the adjective has the same implications of rashness and danger, but this may be due to the use of the comparative, since his use of *calere* in the same letter merely implies laudable courage and energy.

    With *calidus* in the sense of quick-witted, inventive, cf. Men. *Dyskolos* 183 of the slave Geta: ἔχει ⟨τι⟩ διάπυρον. For the other sense, hotheaded or dangerous, compare Amphis. κιι, p. 246, fr. 33: ἡ δὲ διὰ τὸ μὴ σαφῶς/τί ποτ' ἀφ ἑκάστου πράγματος συμβήσεται/διαλελογίσθαι δρᾷ τι κἀὶ νεανικὸν/καὶ θερμόν, which speaks for a use of θερμός in New Comedy very similar to that of *calidus* in *Eu.* 380. These are however the *only* extant parallels in Middle and New Comedy.

I have included *fervere*, with its allusion to seething, boiling liquid, under this heading.[6] Terence's use of *fervere* with the connotation of excited anger in *Ad.* 534 is close to that of Caelius in *Fam.* 8.8.2, *ferventer* loqui est coeptum, and 8.6.4, scripsi Curionem valde *frigere*, iam *calet*; nam *ferventissime* concerpitur; cf. *Rhet. Her.* 4.21, in re *frigidissima cales*; in *ferventissima friges*. The verb is absent from Cicero's own letters, and occurs only once in Plautus, *Am.* 1030, faciam *ferventem* flagris, applied alliteratively to the heat of physical pain, but for the metaphor cf. *Mer.* 959, mea uxor ... *in fermento iacet*.

The use of *defervisse* in *Ad.* 152 is very close to the detailed analogy drawn by Alexis, κ11, p. 313, 45, between the growth of man and wine.

ὁμοιότατος ἄνθρωπος οἴνῳ τὴν φύσιν
τρόπον τιν᾽ ἐστί· καὶ γὰρ οἶνον τὸν νέον
πολλή ᾽στ᾽ ἀνάγκη, καὶ τὸν ἄνδρ᾽ ἀποζέσαι
πρώτιστον, ἀφυβρίσαι τε ...

and suggests the possibility that Terence is presenting in concentrated form an image of this type in Menander's 'Αδελφοί β. The metaphor has a continued existence in Latin; cf. Cic. *Cael.* 43, cum adulescentiae *cupiditates defervissent*, which may, however, be a reminiscence of *Adelphoe*, since Cicero quotes from the same scene of *Adelphoe* (act 1, sc. 2), in *Cael.* 38. Cicero uses *defervere* of rhetorical style in *Orat.* 107, *Brut.* 316; from the letters, cf. *Fam.* 2.8.1 (to Caelius), dum *effervescit* haec gratulatio.

Terence seems to be the first to use *frigeo*, *frigesco* of failure and indifference. Neither word is found in Plautus, and there is no equivalent idiom in Menander or other New Comedy. The Terentian usage, applied to persons who are coldly received (*Eu.* 268, 517), and to an affair which is allowed to die of indifference (*Ad.* 233) is paralleled from Cicero's letters, *Fam.* 7.11.3 and 18.2; 9.10.3; 1.14.1; *Q.fr.* 2.5.3; 3.2.3, and 6.3 and 4; *Att.* 1.14.1; 2.1.6; 4.17.3, both of persons and situations. Contrast the quotation in *Rhet. Her.* 4.21 above, where *frigere* implies apathy. In Cicero, *refrigescere* can be associated with the similar metaphor *iacere* (*Q.fr.* 3.2.3; *Att.* 4.17.3). The image has become conventional; hence the flamboyant variation of Caelius, *Fam.* 8.6.4; Curioni nostro tribunatus *conglaciat*, answered by Cicero, *Fam.* 2.13.3; *congelasse* nostrum amicum laetabar otio.

Ph. 994 conforms to none of these categories: Chremes, who "totus friget," is terrified (cf. 997, *delirat miser timore*). Phormio's invitation to test

6 On this verb and its culinary associations in metaphor, see West, *Reading Horace*, pp. 65–8, discussing Hor. *Carm.* 1.13.4: meum/*fervens* difficili bile tumet iecur; cf. also *macerare* as used in Terence, p. 59 below.

this statement by touch suggests that the image here is of one stiff with the paralysis of fear. We can contrast the portrayal of fear in Men. *Epitr.* 581 (cf. *Perik.* 163), πέφρικ' ἐγὼ μέν, αὖός εἰμι τῷ δέει, in terms of shivering and a dry throat.

The metaphor of cold, like that of heat, seems to be as popular in Latin as it is rare in Greek.[7]

II SICKNESS AND CURE

An.

193   animum *aegrotum* ad deteriorem partem plerumque adplicat (cf. *An.* 559, *Hau.* 100).

468   quod *remedium* nunc huic malo inveniam?
       (cf. *Ph.* 185, 200, 617, for *remedium invenire*).

831   eiu' labore atque eiu' dolore gnato ut *medicarer* tuo.

944   quom ego possim in hac re *medicari* mihi.

Hau.

539   magnarum saepe id *remedium* aegritudinumst.

Eu.

225-6 di boni quid hoc *morbist*? adeone homines immutarier
       ex amore ut non cognoscas eundem esse.

439   id ut ne fiat haec res solast *remedio.*

Ph.

575   senectus ipsast *morbus.*

695   quid minus utibilest quam *hoc ulcus tangere*?

821-2   cupiditates
       quas ... paullo *mederi* possis.

824   ego nullo possum *remedio* me evolvere ex his turbis.

Hec.

239   tuos esse illi mores *morbum* mage quam ullam aliam rem arbitror.

Ad.

294   solu' mearum miseriarumst *remedium.*

This class of metaphors is strongly represented in Menander and New Comedy. The imagery that presented emotional, moral, or political disturbance in

7 Neither in this nor succeeding categories have I attempted to differentiate examples of Terentian imagery according to metre, since I have concluded from a study of the examples and a statistical analysis that there is no correlation between the quantity or development of imagery and the different stylistic levels of *senarii* and long-verse in Terence. In Plautus, by contrast, there is a perceptible elaboration of the language and extent of individual images in long-verse and canticum.

terms of sickness was an old established tradition already elaborately developed
in Sophocles and exploited extensively in Euripides and the Platonic dialogues;
cf. Goheen, *The Imagery of Sophocles' Antigone* (Princeton 1951), p. 41:
"disease and cure images ... have a traditional basis going back to Homer.
The expression of almost any adverse condition as a νόσος can be found in
Greek poetry."

However, these metaphors seem to be absent from the relatively complete plays, so that their frequency in the fragments may be due to an unrepre-
sentative selection in our sources. I give what I believe to be a full list:

Menander
Kith.
fr. 2   πενία. τί γὰρ τοῦτ' ἐστίν; ἧς γένοιτ' ἂν εἰς
         φίλος βοηθήσας ἰατρὸς ῥᾳδίως
Vol. IIK
fr. 80   ἐκφυγοῦσα δ' ἣν εἶχεν νόσον
         οὐκ ἔσχε τοὺς ῥηθέντας ἀναθέσθαι λόγους.
200   πολλοῖς ὑπέκκαυμ' ἐστ' ἔρωτος μουσική.
518   οὐκ ἔστιν ὀργῆς, ὡς ἔοικε, φάρμακον
         ἀλλ' ἢ λόγος σπουδαῖος ἀνθρώπου φίλου.
568   ἕτερος ⟨δ⟩'ἀπόλωλε. καιρός ἐστιν ἡ νόσος
         ψυχῆς. ὁ πληγεὶς δ' εἴσεθ' ᾗ τιτρώσκεται.
571   ἕν ἐστ' ἀληθὲς φίλτρον εὐγνώμων τρόπος
         τούτῳ κατακρατεῖν ἄνδρος εἴωθεν γυνή.
642   τῷ μὲν τὸ σῶμα ⟨γὰρ⟩ διακειμένῳ κακῶς
         χρεία' στ' ἰατροῦ, τῷ δὲ τὴν ψυχὴν φίλου.
         λύπην γὰρ εὔνους οἶδε θεραπεύειν λόγῳ.
652   πάντων ἰατρὸς τῶν ἀναγκαίων κακῶν/χρόνος ἐστίν.
718   νόσων χαλεπώτατος/φθόνος.
782   ἰατρός ἐστιν ὁ λόγος ἀνθρώποις νόσων.

The same distribution of imagery is found in the fragments of Middle
and New Comedy. Compare the use of νόσος as a metaphor for anxiety
(Antiphanes, KII, p. 54.107), love (Euboulus, KII, p. 178.41), and poverty
(Diphilus KII, p. 574.105). νοσεῖν is used of moral sickness by Diphilus (KII,
p. 547.24, αἱ κρίσεις δ' ἡμῶν νοσοῦσιν) and Theognetus (KIII, p. 364.1). For the
use of φάρμακον compare Antiphanes, KII, p. 46.86 and Philemon KII,
p. 497.73. But by far the most common symbol is the ἰατρός: cf. Antiphanes,

κιι, p. 121, fr. 259; Philemon, κιι, p. 481, fr. 11 and p. 509, fr. 98 (the plot ot land is a doctor treating a feverish patient: it provides only a very light diet); p. 513, fr. 108 (men are cheered by the sight of a friend as patients recover when they see the doctor); Diphilus, κιι, p. 570, fr. 88 and p. 576, fr. 117 λύπης δὲ πάσης γίνετ' ἰατρὸς χρόνος, echoed by Philippides, κιιι, p. 310, fr. 32 (cf. Men. fr. 652 above).

There are obvious coincidences between Menander and Terence: the metaphors on νόσος/morbus (e.g., Men. fr. 568 is similar to Ter. Ph. 575) and φάρμακον/remedium (fr. 518 is a near equivalent of Ph. 185). In the case of Ph. 575, we have from Donatus the original Greek text of Menander's follower Apollodorus: κιιι, p. 286, fr. 20, τὸ γῆράς ἐστιν αὐτὸ νόσημα. The most noticeable difference is the predominance of ἰατρός in the Greek dramatists, where medicus is entirely absent from Terence, and the absence of verb-based metaphors in Menander to correspond with mederi and medicari in Terence. In this respect Pl. Cist. 73–4, presumably based on Menander, is significant,

> erit isti morbo melius : : confidam fore
> si medicus veniat qui huic morbo facere medicinam potest,

in that Plautus has used medicus, whereas we may suspect that Terence has consciously avoided this as he avoids other personal metaphors (cf. also Mer. 489).

The images of Men. fr. 200 (caustic surgery), 538 (wasting-away, cf. consumption?), and 568 (the wound of love's arrow) are perhaps too conspicuous to have pleased Terence. The first two involve technical terms, the last seems a cliché of the lover's vocabulary, which will find its parallels not in Terence, but in later elegists (see Appendix). Cicero, on the other hand, uses in his letters many detailed metaphors based on surgery, bloodletting, dieting, etc.,[8] and metaphors based on wounds, entirely absent from Terence,

---

8 Cf. Fam. 1.1.4, rebus ... clam exulceratis; 1.9.15, vellem non solum salutis meae quem ad modum medici, sed ut aliptae etiam virium et coloris rationem habere voluisset; 5.13.3 (omnia membra rei publicae) ... nullum reperies profecto quod non fractum debilitatumve sit; Att. 1.16.11, missus est sanguis invidiae sine dolore; 2.1.7, medicina quae sanaret vitiosas partes rei publicae quam quae exsecaret; 4.3.3, ego diaeta curare incipio: chirurgiae taedet; 6.1.2, ut si medicus cum aegrotus alio medico traditus sit irasci velit ei medico qui sibi successerit si quae ipse in curando constituerit mutet ille, sic Appius cum ... provinciam curarit, sanguinem miserit ... mihi tradiderit enectam, προσανατρεφομένην eam a me non libenter videt; 9.10.3, ut aegroto dum anima est, spes esse dicitur.

are common; cf. *Fam.* 4.6.2, *hoc tam gravi vulnere* etiam illa quae *consanuisse videbantur recrudescunt*; 15.4.14: ad *sanandum vulnus* iniuriae; *Att.* 1.17.3: ut nihil *a domesticis vulneris* factum sit, illud quidem quod erat, eos certe *sanare* potuisse; and 5.17.6: *in sanandis vulneribus* quae sunt imposita provinciae.

Perhaps the point of *vulnus* rather than *morbus* is that the harm has been deliberately inflicted by enemies. Thus in Cicero's political life the metaphor is essential, but it has no natural place in Terence's comedies. The one more specific metaphor at Ter. *Ph.* 690, *hoc ulcus tangere*, finds an approximate equivalent in Cicero's *vulnus refricare*, *Att.* 5.15.2, 12.18.1 or at *Att.* 3.15.2, sed non faciam ut ... *meis vulneribus* saepius *manus adferam*.

How far does Terence differ from Plautus in his use of medical metaphor? I have mentioned Plautus' use of *medicus*, but in both *Cistellaria* and *Mercator* the point of the metaphor lies in the person who is to heal the illness, and to have eliminated *medicus* would have destroyed the meaning required. Plautus' vocabulary is different: he does not use either *mederi* or *sanare*, or even *remedium*, but has several similar metaphors based on *medicina* and *mederi*. These are, however, relatively fewer than in Terence. We may compare with *Cist.* 74–5 above,

Cur.

160   viden ut anu'tremula *medicinam* facit?
           eapse merum condidicit bibere, foribus dat aquam quam bibant.

Men.

98–9   homines non alit, verum educat
           recreatque. nullus melius *medicinam facit*.

Mer.

951   hic homo non sanust : : *medicari* amicus quin properas mihi?

Mos.

387   istum lepide *medicabo* metum.

In Cicero the metaphors based on *remedium* and *medicina* can be distinguished. He uses *remedium* only in the context of personal grief: *Fam.* 5.15.1, illius tanti *vulneris* quae *remedia* esse debebant ... *Att.* 12.21.5, ab his me *remediis* noli in istam turbam vocare. *Medicina* is more general, of national and personal ills: important are *temporis medicina Fam.* 5.16.6 (cf. ἰατρὸς χρόνος) and the combination of *medicina* with *morbus* in *Fam.* 9.3.2, gravitas *morbi* facit ut *medicinae* egeamus, *Att.* 2.20.3, novo quodam *morbo* civitas moritur ... tamen nulla *medicina* adferatur; 10.14.2, nescioquo modo imbecillior est *medicina* quam *morbus*.[9]

Plautus' use of *morbus, aegrotus*, and *aegrotare* is similar to that of Terence. Add to *Cist.* 74–5:

Trin.

28–30   nam hic nimium *morbus* mores invasit bonos
        ita plerique omnes iam sunt intermortui
        sed dum illi *aegrotant* ...

Trin.

75–6   omnibus amicis *morbum* tu incuties gravem
        ut te videre audireque *aegroti sient*

Truc.

465–6   male quod mulier facere incepit nisi id ecficere perpetrat,
        id illi *morbo*, id illi seniost ...

The abundant medical metaphors in the surviving fragments of Philemon suggest that *Trin.* 28 ff. and 75 ff. are a close translation of the Greek (cf. also Diphilus fr. 24, αἱ κρίσεις δ' ἡμῶν νοσοῦσιν), but the word play on *mores/morbum* is clearly Roman, both in Plautus and Terence *Hec.* 239.

Both Plautus (*Cist.* 74–5) and Terence associate *morbus* with the sickness of love, but what is exceptional in Plautus (add perhaps *Mer.* 489, 951, but here the keynote is *madness*, not sickness) is very common in Terence and will become more so in the elegiac poets. *Aegrotus* (*An.* 193, 557, *Hau.* 100) is used only of the lovesick; so also *morbus, Eu.* 225; *medicari, An.* 831, 944; *mederi, Ph.* 821–2. This probably reflects Menander's treatment of love as a sickness which appears at fr. 200 (cf. Euboulus fr. 41ĸ) although Terence gives no parallel for love as a wound, a cliché which is to become dominant in the elegists.

Terence is most attracted to the noun *remedium* (six instances) and in his later plays uses it with some boldness, at *Ph.* 824 in combination with another metaphor (ex turbis *evolvere*) and at *Ad.* 294 applied to an actual person – the man, who alone has power to cure Sostrata's troubles. As in Cicero, *remedium* is not associated with *morbus* but with misfortunes and grief; its medical origin is already forgotten and the figurative sense has become its normal use.

9 *Medicina*; cf. also *Fam.* 5.15.4; *Q.fr.* 2.16.2; *Att.* 2.1.7; 2.23.2; 3.7.2; 12.21.5; 16.15.5. For *mederi*; cf. *Att.* 1.17.1 (suspiciones) quibus ego *mederi* cum cuperem ... 3.12.2, cui *vulneri* ut scribis *medere* si quid potes, 10.11.1, ea tempora nostra sunt ut ego eis *mederi* non possim, 13.9.2 haec res *mederi* potest.

III NAUTICAL METAPHORS: WIND AND STORMS

An.

446   animum ad uxorem *appulit*

        (Donatus: quasi ab iactatione fluctuum et aestus marini.)

480   nunc huius periclo fit, ego *in portu navigo*.

562   dehinc facile ex illis sese *emersurum* malis

845   omni' res est iam *in vado*.

Eu.

1046   an fortunam conlaudem, quae *gubernatrix* fuit.

*Ph.

689   huic mandes, *qui te ad scopulum e tranquillo auferat*.

        (Reading of F² and E only.)

Hec.

311   qui eos *gubernat* animus eum infirmum gerunt.

Ad.

302   tot res repente circumvallant se ... unde *emergi* non potest.

This group is very common in Menander and later Greek comedy.

Menander

Epit.

396   καὶ νῦν χαριέντως ἐκνενευκέναι δο[κῶ
       τῷ μὴ δι' ἐμοῦ ταῦτι κυκᾶσθαι.

Pk.

380   ἐφόλκια
       ἡγησ]άμην δὴ πτωχὸν ὄντα παιδία
       τρέφειν.

Dysk.

398   κατακέκομμ' ἐ[γὼ
       ὁ μάγειρος ὑπὸ τούτου νεωλκῶν τὴν ὁδ[όν

KII

fr. 59   νῦν ἀληθινὸν
       εἰς πέλαγος αὐτὸν ἐμβαλεῖς γὰρ πραγμάτων
       ... οὗ τῶν τριάκοντ' οὐκ ἀπόλλυται τρία
       πλοιάρια· γήμας δ' οὐδὲ εἷς σέσωσθ' ὅλως.

fr. 205 ὁ δεύτερος πλοῦς ἐστι δήπου λεγόμενος
       ἂν ἀποτυχών τις οὐρίου κώπαις πλέῃ.

417   ὁ τῆς τύχης
... τοῦτ ἔστι τὸ κυβερνῶν ⟨ἅπαντα⟩ καὶ στρέφον
καὶ σῷζον.

616   ὅ τε πλοῦτος ἐξώκειλε τὸν κεκτημένον
εἰς ἕτερον ἦθος.

656   εἰκόν' οὐκ ἔχω
⟨εὑρεῖν⟩ ὁμοίαν τῷ γεγονότι πράγματι·
... ἀλλ' ἐν πελάγει συγκλυσμός; ἀναπνοὴν ἔχεις
"Ζεῦ σῶτερ' εἰπεῖν 'ἀντέχου τῶν σχοινίων''
ἐτέραν περιμεῖναι χἀτέραν τρικυμίαν.
ναυαγίου δ'ἂν ἐπιλάβοι, ἐγὼ δ'ἅπαξ
ἀψάμενός εἰμι καὶ φιλήσας ἐν βυθῷ.

                    Greek Middle and New Comedy

Anaxandrides
KII, p. 137
fr. 4   τὸν γὰρ οἴακα στρέφει
δαίμων ἑκάστῳ.

Euboulus
KII, p. 192
fr. 76   ὡς εὖ νεναυάγηκεν ἐπὶ τοῦ τηγάνου.

Xenarchus
KII, p. 468
fr. 2   ἡ τοῦ δὲ Σωτῆρος Διὸς τάχιστά γε
ἀπώλεσε ναύτην καὶ κατεπόντωσέν μ' ὁρᾷς.

Theophilus
KII, p. 475
fr. 6   οὐ συμφέρον νέα' στὶ πρεσβύτῃ γυνή.
ὥσπερ γὰρ ἄκατος οὐδὲ μικρὸν πείθεται
ἐνὶ πηδαλίῳ τὸ πεῖσμ' ἀπορρήξασα δὲ
ἐκ νυκτὸς ἕτερον λιμέν' ἔχουσ' ἐξευρέθη.

Philemon
KII, p. 533
fr. 213   οὔτε γὰρ ναυαγός, ἂν μὴ γῆς λάβηται φερόμενος
οὔποτ' ἂν σώσειεν αὐτόν, οὔτ' ἀνὴρ πένης γεγὼς
μὴ οὐ τέχνην μαθὼν δύναιτ' ἂν ἀσφαλῶς ζῆν τὸν βίον.
κἂν μὲν ὁρμισθῇ τις ἡμῶν εἰς λιμένα τὸν τῆς τέχνης

ἐβάλετ' ἄγκυραν καθάψας ἀσφαλείας εἵνεκα.
ἂν δ' ἀπαιδεύτου μετάσχῃ πνεύματος φορούμενος,
τῆς ἀπορίας εἰς τὸ γῆρας οὐκ ἔχει σωτηρίαν.

(With this developed analogy, compare Philemon fr. 28 below, and perhaps Plautus, *Mer.* 875–880 (p. 25 below).)

STORMS

Menander
Sam.
210–11   στρόβιλος ⟨ἢ⟩
σκη[πτός, οὐκ ἀ]νθρωπός ἐστι.
Flor.
58   σκηπτός τις εἰς τὴν οἰκίαν
ῥαγδαῖος ἐμπέπτωκεν.
fr. 162   μὴ θεομάχει, μηδὲ προσαγόυ τῷ πράγματι
χειμῶνας ἑτέρους.
335   ἀλλ' ἐν ἀκαλύπτῳ κὰι ταλαιπώρῳ βίῳ
χειμαζόμενος ζῇ.
656   εἰκόν' οὐκ ἔχω
⟨εὑρεῖν⟩ ὁμοιάν τῷ γεγονότι πράγματι,
ζητῶν πρὸς ἐμαυτόν, τί ταχέως ἀπολλύει
στρόβιλος; ἐν ὅσῳ συστρέφεται, προσέρχεται,
προσέβαλεν, ἐξήρειψεν, αἰὼν γίνεται.

(There follows the separate nautical image of the συγκλυσμός quoted above.)

Middle and New Comedy

Alexis
κπ, p. 364
fr. 178   χείμων ὁ μειρακίσκος ἐστὶ τοῖς φίλοις.
Philemon
κπ, p. 485
fr. 28   οὐ τοῖς πλέουσι τὴν θαλατταν γίνεται
μόνοισι χειμών, ὡς ἔοικε ...
χοὶ μὲν πλέοντες ἐνίοθ' ἡμέραν μίαν
ἢ νύκτα χειμασθέντες, εἶτ' ἐκ τοῦ κακοῦ

σωτηρίας ἐπέτυχον· ἢ τὸ πνεῦμα γὰρ
αὐτοὺς τὸ σῷζον ἧκεν, ἢ 'φάνη λιμήν·
ἔμοι δὲ τοῦτ' οὐκ ἔστιν. οὐκ εἰς ἡμέραν
χειμάζομαι μίαν γὰρ, εἰς τὸ ζῆν δ' ὅλον.

I have considered nautical and meteorological imagery together, because
in Menander and in Cicero's letters metaphors of wind, hurricane, and storm
are either combined or associated with distress at sea. As in our examination
of medical metaphors, we see that those used by Terence are more simple
and less technical than the Greek imagery. In particular, there are no extended
analogies. No doubt such terms as ἐφόλκια and νεωλκεῖν had no meaningful
equivalents for a Roman audience. Only in the use of *guberno* and *gubernatrix*
(*fortuna*), Hec. 311, Eu. 1046, is there a close parallel to Greek usage (cf. Men.
fr. 417, Anaxandrides fr. 4 above).

Strangely, the metaphors used by Terence are almost totally absent in
Plautus, despite his abundance of casual nautical imagery. *Emergere* is not
used,[10] *gubernare* occurs only once, *Mil.* 1091, iam ex sermone hoc *gubernabunt*
doctius porro.[11] *Portus* features in a metaphor at *As.* 158, quam magis te in
altum capessis, tam aestus te in portum refert. However, *Aul.* 803, propemodum
iam esse *in vado salutis*, supplies a close parallel and a guarantee of the interpretation for *An.* 845. Since *Aulularia* is based on Menander, this may suggest that
both instances have a common origin in a Menandrian image.[12]

The reference to shipwreck at the hands of *Amor* in *Cist.* 221–2, *maritumis
moribus mecum expetitur;/ita meum frangit* amantem animum, is almost

10 *Emergere* is probably intended to represent ἐκνεῖν (as at *Epitr.* 396) in *An.* 562, *Ad.*
302. The Terentian use of *portus* in *An.* 480, however, is simpler than any use of λιμήν
in Greek comedy quoted above, although naturally the associations are similar. Storm,
wind, and whirlwind do not feature at all.

11 On this metaphor, common in Greek since Aeschylus and Pindar, see Fraenkel,
Horace, pp. 154–5. Ter. *Hec.* 311 – the mind as steersman – goes back to many instances
in Plato; cf. *Phaedr.* 247ᵉ, ψυχῆς κυβερνήτῃ ... νῷ. The *Hecyra* passage is initially con-
fusing because Terence is speaking of the hot-tempered nature of children; *animus*, however, should not be taken as θυμός but, as so often in Terence, for the mind or intelligence as a whole.

12 That *vadum* is here a symbol of safety is confirmed by its literal occurrence in *Rud.*
170, in vadost; iam facile enabit. See also G. Williams, *JRS* 47, 1957, 243 (reviewing
Propertiana by D.S. Shackleton Bailey) for the best interpretation of *Prop.* 2.14.29–30,
veniat mea litora navis/servata, an sidat onusta vadis. *Vada* are mentioned here not as
dangers, but as lying within sight of harbour, at a stage in the voyage where safe arrival
could normally be expected; cf. *Mer.* 197, quoted in n. 13 below.

certainly an adaptation of Menander, cf. fr. 656 above. In *Bac.* 797, *Epid.* 74,
Mos. 738–42, slaves use a ship as the symbol of themselves and their intrigues.
The Philemon-based plays are particularly rich in nautical imagery; cf.
Mer. 197[13] (the ship driven onto the rocks); 695–6 (the bosun's shouting);
875–80 quoted below; *Mos.* 677 (similar to *Mer.* 197); 738–42; 751; 918;
Trin. 1026 (cf. *Mer.* 875) *cape vorsoriam* of changing course.

All these naval metaphors are fully exploited by Cicero, often in extended
analogies involving several terms. The most common context is that of
steering the ship of state and the highly elaborate analogy of *Fam.* 1.9.21 may
serve as the fullest example available in the letters:

> numquam enim in praestantibus in re publica *gubernanda* viris laudata
> est in una sententia perpetua permansio. sed ut in *navigando tempestati*
> obsequi artis est, etiam si *portum tenere* non queas, cum vero id possis
> mutata *velificatione* adsequi, stultum est eum *tenere* cum periculo *cursum*
> quem coeperis.

Other extended metaphors are:

Fam.

9.15.3   *sedebamus* enim *in puppi et clavum tenebamus*, nunc autem vix est
          in *sentina* locus.

12.25.5   *conscende ... ad puppim.* Una *navis* est iam bonorum omnium
          quam ... damus operam ut *rectam teneamus*, utinam *prospero*
          cursu ... sed quicunque *venti* erunt ...

16.27.1   qui nisi *a gubernaculis recesserint*, maximum ab universo *nau-*
          fragio periculum est.

Att.

2.7.4   iam pridem *gubernare* me taedebat ... nunc vero cum cogar
          exire de navi non abiectis sed ereptis gubernaculis cupio istorum
          naufragia ex terra intueri.

---

13 *Equidem me iam censebam esse in terra atque in tuto loco/verum video me ad saxa ferri*
saevis fluctibus. The metaphor of driving onto the rocks (found in Men. fr. 616, ὅ τε
πλοῦτος ἐξώκειλε τὸν κεκτημένον, occurs in Ter. *Ph.* 689, if we accept the alternative reading of F[2] and E, *qui te ad scopulum e tranquillo auferat*, as genuine. Compare *ad*
scopulum appellere, Cic. *de Orat.* 2.154. The use of *Tranquillum, tranquilla res* alone,
although derived from the same nautical context, seems to evoke no specific imagery at,
for example, *An.* 620, *qui me hodie ex tranquillissima re coniecisti in nuptias* (see section VII).
Cf. also *Eu.* 1038, *Ph.* 479; Plautus *Am.* 478, *Mos.* 414, 417.

Indeed in many Ciceronian occurrences of *gubernare*[14] the word has become a dead metaphor. Perhaps the extreme instance is *Att.* 6.1.2:

> nunc autem *domus* mehercle *nulla* tanto consilio aut tanta disciplina *gubernatur* ... quam tota nostra provincia.

It may be that many of these images derive ultimately from Greek rhetoric. Certainly Quintus, quoted in *Q.fr.* 1.2.13, ὀρθὰν τὰν ναῦν, uses a Greek proverb, and Cicero himself, *Att.* 7.3.5, *mihi* σκάφος *unum erit quod a Pompeio gubernabitur*, chooses a Greek word to convey his nautical imagery.

Of the metaphors found in Terence, *portus* and *emergere* are common in Cicero. *Portus* is especially associated with the refuge of philosophy and literature (*Fam.* 5.15.3; 7.30.2; 9.6.4; *Att.* 4.6.2), but also with political safety (*Fam.* 13.66.2; *ad Brut.* 13.2; *Att.* 3.19.1; 6.13.2). *Emergere* is more colourless; Cicero does not associate it with other nautical vocabulary,[15] but neither does Terence. Indeed in *Ad.* 302, Terence combines it with the military metaphor *circumvallare*; cf. Cic. *Att.* 5.8.1, incommoda valetudo e qua iam *emerseram*; 5.10.3, ex hoc negotio *emerserim*; 6.2.4, incredible est quantum civitates *emerserint*. *Obrui*, the opposite of *emergere*, is perhaps more formal; its metaphorical use is found only in *Q.fr.* 1.1.4, neve te *obrui* tamquam fluctu ... sinas, and 5, dormientem gubernatorem *obruere*.

Shipwreck, featured in several of the Greek metaphors quoted, and implicit in Pl. *Cist.* 222, *Mer.* 197, *Mos.* 677, 742, is a favourite Ciceronian image for political disaster. To *Fam.* 16.27.1, and *Att.* 2.7.4 above, add *Fam.* 4.13.2; 13.5.2; *Att.* 3.15.7, and 4.19.2, with an additional detail, *haec enim me una ex hoc naufragio tabula delectat*. The occurrence of such metaphors in even the most spontaneous letters shows to what extent they had passed from political rhetoric into private idiom.

---

14 *Gubernare* is visualized fully as a metaphor at *Fam.* 1.9.21 above, *Att.* 2.7.4 above, 2.9.3; 7.3.5 above. At *Fam.* 2.7.1; 2.17.1; *ad Brut.* 18.3; *Att.* 3.8.4; 4.18.2; 6.1.2; 6.3.3; 10.8.6; 12.25.1; 13.25.2; 14.11.1; at 15.9.1 and 16.2.2 it is colourless, a mere synonym for *moderari*.

The other forms from this root are usually true metaphors; cf. *gubernator*, *Q.fr.* 1.1.5 (twice); as a synonym of *moderator* in *Att.* 8.11.1; *Fam.* 2.6.4; *gubernatio*, *Fam.* 10.1.2; *ad Brut.* 22.2; and *gubernacula*, *Fam.* 16.27.1; *ad Brut.* 1.2; *Att.* 2.7.4, above.

15 Compare with *An.* 562, Cicero, *Cael.* 28; qui totam adulescentiam voluptatibus dedidissent, *emersisse* aliquando et *se* ad frugem bonam ... *recepisse*, and 75: *emersit totumque se eiecit atque extulit*.

WIND AND STORM

In Menander weather is a source of imagery, usually with maritime associations; nothing similar is found in Terence. *Men.* fr. 162 above is particularly revealing; Koerte (vol. 2, 67) equates it with Ter. *Eu.* 76-8.

et ne te adflictes ...
neque praeter quam quas ipse amor molestias
habet addas, et illas quae habet recte feras.

Without economizing in verses, Terence has eliminated Menander's χειμῶνας, substituting the literal *molestias*; at the same time he has rejected the deification of love implied by θεομάχει and the inevitability of ἀναγκαίους. The whole tone is more subdued, and it is perhaps legitimate to assume that he found *tempestates* or *procellae* too melodramatic for his taste. What has been rejected here may well have been rejected in adapting other plays.

Plautus is more at ease with such metaphors. Twice he quotes the nautical proverb *utquomque in alto ventust, exim velum vortitur (Epid.* 49, *Poen.* 754; cf. Cic. *de Orat.* 2.187, *ad id unde aliquid flatus ostenditur, vela do*) and in *Mer.* 875-80 he expands a poetic contrast of storm and calm in an allegorical speech introduced by a remoulding of the same proverb, and almost certainly based in Philemon;

huc ventus secundus nunc est; cape modo vorsoriam:
hic favonius serenust, istic auster imbricus,
hic facit tranquillitatem, iste omnis fluctus conciet.
recipe te ad terram, Charine, huc ex advorso vide sis
nubis ater imberque instat – aspicin? – ad sinisteram
caelum ut est spendore plenum nonne ex advorso vides?[16]

Cicero introduces the conventional metaphor of favourable wind in *Att.* 2.1.6, Caesarem ... cuius nunc *venti* valde sunt *secundi*. An innovation

16 The metaphorical use of *tempestas* in Plautus is virtually confined to the Philemon-based plays. Cf. *Mos.* 137, 162 (where the storm is not in a marine context) and *Trin.* 399, suae senectuti is acriorem *hiemem* parat/quom illam importunam *tempestatem* conciet. Here the resemblance to Philemon fr. 213K above seems to guarantee that Plautus is adapting the image of his original. Since Menander compares a violent man to a hurricane or thunderbolt (σκηπτός, στρόβιλος) we might have expected to find this application of *tempestas* in Plautus; indeed such a metaphor is presupposed in Latin usage by Cicero's deprecation of *tempestas comissationis* in *de Orat.* 3.164. Instead we have (*Capt.* 911) *clades calamitasque, intemperies modo in nostram advenit domum*, violence conveyed by sound rather than image.

seems to be his use of *ventus* in describing the shifts of political favour; cf. from the correspondence, *Fam.* 2.6.4, eorum *ventorum* quos proposui moderator quidam et quasi gubernator, and Caelius' racy allusion, *Fam.* 8.8.2, *quo vento* proicitur Appius minor, which recall Cicero's use in the speeches of *aura* (*Mur.* 36; *Sest.* 101) in the context of a sea metaphor.

Finally *tempestas*, in Plautus a source of metaphor without explicit maritime associations, takes on a new life in Cicero.

Fam.

4.3.1   multo enim ante, *tamquam ex aliqua specula*, prospexi *tempestatem* futuram.

ad Brut.

23.4   quantamque impendere rei publicae *tempestatem* (cf. *Att.* 9.9.4).

Att.

2.21.2   si homines *transitum tempestatis* exspectare voluissent ...

7.13.2   ut *e portu sine gubernaculis egressi tempestati nos traderemus.*

With *Att.* 2.21.2 compare *Att.* 15.9.2, sed hunc quidem *nimbum* cito *transisse* laetor. At *Q.fr.* 1.1.5 Cicero contrasts *vis tempestatis* with *summa tranquillitas*. Of these, certainly *Fam.* 4.3.1, *Att.* 7.13.2, and *Q.fr.* 1.1.5 are explicitly tempests *at sea*, and the predominance of the ship of state as an ingredient in metaphor serves to explain these images, as it is also the basis for so many of the examples quoted in this section. To this extent the nautical metaphors of Cicero's correspondence should not be considered typical of normal Roman colloquial usage, but rather of political rhetoric, for which there is no natural place in Terence. In general, however, nautical, like medical imagery was accepted from the Greek and taken over with enthusiasm by all Roman prose writers influenced by Greek literature and rhetoric.

IV WARFARE AND SINGLE COMBAT:

GLADIATORIAL ALLUSIONS: LOVE AS WAR

This section includes a large number of varied metaphors. I have distinguished (A) general references to warfare, strategy, and battle, (B) references suggestive of single combat, whether in the field or in the arena, and (C) metaphors specifically dealing with the conflicts of love.

A

An.

180-2   id voluit nos sic ...

        sperantis iam amoto metu, interoscitantis *opprimi.*

227   ne de hac re pater imprudentem *opprimat.*

Hau.

669 ff.   ita hac re *in angustum oppido nunc meae coguntur copiae*:

        ... *triumpho* si licet me *latere tecto* abscedere.

757   cesso hunc *adoriri* (cf. *Ad.* 404, *adortust* ... fratrem)

Ph.

229-30   ego *in insidiis* hic ero

      succenturiatus, si quid deficias.

321   cedo senem: iam *instructa sunt mi* in corde consilia omnia.

346   *prima coitiost acerrima.*

      si eam *sustinueris,* postilla iam ut lubet ludas licet.

      (Donatus: *a proelio*; nam et congredi milites et coire dicuntur)

Ad.

302   tot res repente *circumvallant* se unde emergi non potest.

718-9   nunc vero domi

      certum *obsidere* est usque donec redierit.

Ad.

773-5   in ipsa turba atque in peccato maxumo,

      quod vix sedatum satis est, potatis, scelus

      quasi *re bene gesta.*

B

Eu.

Prol. 16-18   (cf. also 6, *laesit prior*)

      is ne erret moneo, et desinat *lacessere*

      habeo alia multa quae nunc condonabitur,

      quae proferentur post si perget *laedere.*

417   *iugularas* hominem.

420   quo pacto Rhodium *tetigerim* in convivio.

899   *dabit hic pugnam aliquam denuo.*

1060   *Adcingar.* (Cf. *Ph.* 318, *accingere.*)

Ph.

Prol. 11–13   (cf. also 19–20)

> minu' multo audacter quam nunc *laedit laederet.*
> nunc siquis est qui hoc dicat aut sic cogitet:
> "vetu' si poeta non *lacessisset prior* ..."

46–7   Geta
> *ferietur* alio munere ubi era pepererit.

964   hi *gladiatorio animo* ad me adfectant viam.

Ad.

958   suo sibi gladio hunc *iugulo.*

C *(see also Appendix,* pp. 83, 85f.)

These occur in two scenes: *Eunuchus,* act 1, scene 1, where a slave instructs his master on the folly of love, and *Hecyra,* act 1, scene 1, in which two courtesans present the opposite point of view.

Eu.

53–5   infecta pace, ultro ad eam venies indicans
> te amare et ferre non posse: actumst, ilicet
> peristi: *eludet ubi te victum senserit.*

59–61   in amore haec omnia insunt vitia: iniuriae
> *suspiciones, inimicitiae, indutiae,*
> *bellum, pax rursum*

74–5   quid agas, nisi *ut te redimas captum* quam queas
> minimo.

Hec.

64–5   hortor ne quoiusquam misereat
70   quin *spolies mutiles laceres* quemquam nacta sis.
> hiscin tu amabo non contra *insidiabere?*

73   aut qua via te *captent,* eadem ipsos *capi?*
> (cf. *Eu.* 74 above)

Some of the words considered here as metaphors had in Terence's time a common existence outside the realm of war or combat: *opprimere, adoriri, laedere, lacessere* were perhaps already largely deprived of their military associations. Nevertheless, I believe that these allusions would still be accepted by Terence's audience with their background of personal military experience; even in Cicero's time the colouring of *laedere* or *lacessere* is shown by their frequent combination with *provocare, oppugnare,* or other suggestive phrases.

They are the natural image for political controversy as they are for literary polemic in Terence's prologues to *Eunuchus* and *Phormio*. I quote two political examples:

Fam.

12.22.1 Nos hic cum homine *gladiatorio* ... Antonio *bellum gerimus*, sed non *pari condicione, contra arma* verbis. At etiam de te contionatur, nec impune, nam sentiet quos *lacessierit*.

cf. *Fam.*

1.9.19 in quo possem illorum animos mediocriter *lacessitus* leviter *repungere*,

and 20 non *lacessentem laesisset*

and one from the literary sphere:

Fam.

12.30.1 non enim te epistulis sed voluminibus *lacesserem*; quibus quidem me ante *provocari* oportebat.

The first group consists largely of metaphors uttered by the slave or parasite (*Ad.* 718 is the grim exception). They are similar to the prevailing type in Plautus which was definitively analysed by Fraenkel, *Elementi Plautini in Plauto*, (Florence 1960) ch.viii, pp. 223–41. Closest to the style of Plautus' examples are *Hau.* 669–71 (the slave as general, with his prospect of a triumph),[17] *Ph.* 229–30, with its jargon *succenturiatus*, and 321, in which the parasite's ingenious plots are represented as so many troops. Both elements can be found in a fragment of Caecilius, 229R, *nunc meae malitiae, Astutia, te opus est subcenturiari*, which shows that he had not deviated from this Plautine tradition.

As samples of this tradition compare the boasts of Pseudolus; 571–2 "concedere aliquantisper huc mi intro lubet/*dum concenturio in corde sycophantias*," and in the following scene; 579–83; "*nam ego in meo pectore prius ... ita paravi copias,/duplicis triplicis dolos perfidias*, ut ubiquomque hostibus congrediar/... facile ut vincam, facile ut spoliem meos perduellis meis perfidiis." Beside this, and the ensuing daydreams, Terence's, *iam instructa sunt mi in corde consilia omnia*, is revealed as a conscious toning down of language.

17 *Bacchides* act 4, sc. 9 and *Persa* act 5, sc. 1 are good examples of this theme. For the phrase *re bene gesta* (*Ad.* 755; *Per.* 754) and its association with triumphal inscriptions, cf. Fraenkel *op. cit.*, p. 229, and n. 3. Note, however, that Fraenkel (p. 224, n. 3) contrasts Terence's use of *triumphare* as a standard metaphor for *gaudere* in *Eu.* 394 and *Ph.* 543, with the full dramatization and development of the triumph image in Plautus.

For the pun on *latere tecto* (we might give "with my rear well-covered" as an equivalent) cf. Pl. *Per.* 28, *ulmeae catapultae* tuom ne *transfigant* latus, and *Poen.* 828, agere aetatem praepeditus *latere forti ferreo*. For *adorior* and *insidiae*[18] compare Pl. *Mil.* 1389–90.

> *paratae insidiae sunt*; in statu stat senex
> ut *adoriatur* moechum.

Obsidio provides metaphors similar to *Ad.* 718 at *As.* 280, erum *in obsidione* linquet; inimicum animos auxerit, and *Mos.* 1048, *ex obsidione* in tutum *eduxi manuplares meos*. It is worth noting that although Terence is using a Plautine type of metaphor (and one presumably absent from his original, see below), the actual phraseology in these passages is independent of any surviving instances in Plautus.

Not surprisingly, Cicero's use of military metaphors is confined to the most general aspects of warfare. From the correspondence I have gathered the following examples:

Fam.

5.16.2   omnibus *telis* fortunae *proposita* sit vita nostra.

9.20.1   In Epicuri nos, adversari nostri, *castra coniecimus*.

Q.fr.

3.2.2   homo undique † atius † (saucius? T-P) et, cum a me maxime *vulneraretur*, non tulit ...

Att.

1.16.1   sic ... vehementer *proeliatus sum*, ut *clamor concursusque* maxima cum mea laude fierent ... *quas ego pugnas* et *quantas strages edidi*! *quos impetus ... in totam illam manum feci* ... (te) spectatorem *pugnarum* mirificarum desideravi.

1.20.2   neque sine *nostris copiis* intra alterius *praesidia* veniendum.

10.15.2   *vexillo* opus est. convolabunt.

In the second group the language of the soldier and parasite provide three unusual metaphors. *Iugularas*, *Eu.* 417, of verbal slaughter is unparalleled. But for the sword at the throat in *Ad.* 958, cf. *Mer.* 613, in which the lover receives bad news with the words: *demisisti gladium in iugulum*: iam cadam. *Ad.* 958 and *Mer.* 613 both suggest the final despatch of the fallen gladiator by

---

18 *Insidiae* is a common metaphor in Plautus: cf. *Bac.* 1206, lepide ipsi hi sunt *capti*, suis qui filiis *fecere insidias*; *Cas.* 436, hinc *ex insidiis* hisce ego *insidias dabo*; *Aul.* 662, *Bac.* 286, *Mil.* 303, *Ps.* 593, 1239, and 1245. So too the only instance of *insidiari* "to lie in wait for," *Ps.* 1241 in the same sense as *insidias dare*: ubi cum stimulis et flagris *insidiantur*.

his opponent, but the allusion cannot be proved.[19] The use of *tangere* (*Eu.* 420) of scoring a verbal point has not been commented upon. Plautus' use of *tangere* approaches this idea only at *Per.* 634, "*tactus* lenost, qui rogaret ubi nata esse diceret," and Ps. 1308, sed Simo ut probe/tactu' Ballio est. In *Eunuchus* it is close to the use of *mordere*, later in the same scene (445, see p. 60 s.v.). So too in Cicero's letters, *Att.* 2.19.1, minae Clodi ... modice me *tangunt*, is close to the figurative use of *mordere* in *Fam.* 3.12.2; *Att.* 6.2.8; 11.7.8; 13.12.1, and (*re-*) *pungere* in *Fam.* 1.9.19; 2.13.3; 7.15.1; *Att.* 2.16.1 and 17.2; 6.6.3; 13.45.3. This again is most naturally construed as an allusion to sword-play, the specific context of *pungere* in e.g. *Sest.* 24. The use of *ferire* in *Ph.* 47 is similar. Here, and at Pl. *Trin.* 245, ibi illa pendentem *ferit*, it refers to one stung, or touched, for money.[20] Neither Plautus nor Cicero offers a parallel for the mock-heroic *adcingar*, "I will gird myself up," used by the parasite Gnatho, *Eu.* 1060 (cf. Phormio in *Ph.* 318, where *accingere* is combined comically with another metaphor – of eating,[21] but *Q.fr.* 2.12.1, mihi crede, *in sinu est; neque ego discingor*, "I've taken him in my arms; but without un-buckling my weapon," shows that such imagery was common in light-hearted exaggeration.

Eu. 55 and *Ph.* 964 are definite allusions to the world of the gladiator. Although Cicero's own letters contain only two undoubted allusions; one literary (from the Satires of Lucilius) *Q.fr.* 3.4.2, cum Aesernino Samnite *Pacideianus comparatus viderer*; the other a reference to the trainer, in *Att.* 1.16.3 (cf. 1.16.1, p. 30 above), cum reus ... tamquam clemens *lanista* frugalissimum quemque secerneret, they were obviously commonplaces of political language. Thus he answers Lucceius, in *Fam.* 5.13.2, "*casus enim gladiatorii similitudinesque eae*, tum rationes in ea disputatione a te collectae, vetabant me rei publicae penitus diffidere." This features in Caelius' letters:

Servilius de repetundis *saucius* Pilio tradetur ... *recte hoc par habet.* (8.8.3)
Nec haec adhuc mihi videmini intelligere *qua nos pateamus* et qua simus imbecilli.[22] (8.17.2)

19 Cic. *Att.* 1.16.2 "cum illum *plumbeo gladio iugulatum iri* diceret," seems to be proverbial.
20 Compare a similar application of the metaphor: Prop. 4.5.44, Thais .../cum *ferit* astutos comica moecha Getas; also Prop. 4.3.50 and Rothstein *ad loc.* Horace (*Sat.* 2.7.99) uses the verb in a description of gladiatorial combat.
21 For the parasite, eating is often a kind of challenge to battle (e.g. Men. 107, 184–5), but here the meal is itself a metaphor for Phormio's legal duel.
22 This need not be gladiatorial, but suggests at least sword-play. Cf. *Off.* 1.21 in philosophorum vita minus multa *patent* quae fortuna *feriat* (but contrast *telis fortunae* proposita, *Fam.* 5.16.2 above).

Eu. 54–5, *actumst, ilicet/peristi: eludet ubi te victum senserit,* a metaphor from the conflict of love, is given three explanations by Donatus; his second comment, *eludere proprie gladiatoriumst cum vicerint,* is borne out by Cicero *Opt.Gen.* 17, *quasi rudibus eius eludit oratio. A me autem, ut cum maximis minima conferam, gladiatorum par nobilissimus inducitur,* Aeschines, *tamquam Aeserninus, ut ait Lucilius* ... and in the erotic sphere by Prop. 4.1.139–40 nam tibi *victrices* quascumque labore parasti/*eludit palmas* una puella tuas.

The imagery of love as warfare does not seem to feature in Plautus, largely because his plots favour unanimity of the lovers against a common foe; even *Truculentus,* in which the *meretrix* defeats her military admirer, fails to exploit its metaphorical potential. But metaphors from warfare and combat are equally rare in New Comedy, and I have found no examples related to slave-intrigue. In the extended domestic siege of the *Perikeiromene* (217 ff., prepared from 192 on) military language is freely used, especially in 198–9, 228–30 (a sexual double-entendre), and 233–4, but the officer Polemon and his retainers, like Thraso and his supporters in *Eunuchus* (act 4, sc. 7) are in deadly earnest, and do not see their words as metaphors. There is only one example of the erotic category of war-image; Polemon in 406–7 confesses he has been taken by storm; οἴμοι[Γλυκέριον]/ὡς κατὰ κράτος μ᾽ εἴληφας.

Outside Menander, Alexis, κιι fr. 98.1–3 τὸ συλᾶν τοὺς πέλας/... ῥάπτουσι δὲ/πᾶσιν ἐπιβουλάς, offers a parallel for the guerrilla warfare of *Hec.* 70 (p. 28 above) in describing the techniques and principles of *Hetaerae*: this type of image may well have been more frequent in the cruder psychology of comedy before Menander, who largely excludes the mercenary and aggressive roles from his plots. One fragment of Menander (568κ, p. 15 above) has already been mentioned in connection with the imagery of sickness and cure. The theme, that of Love's wound, is one that could be developed towards either combat-imagery, or that of sickness and healing; the opportunity for combat-imagery is not taken; instead, as we have seen the wound is combined with the νόσος-motif which is so popular in New Comedy.

From this material it is apparent that metaphors of warfare as well as those of the arena, are Roman, not Greek in inspiration. An alternative source of combat-imagery was available to the Greek dramatists, in the boxing and wrestling of the *palaestra.* This was a common source of analogy in Greek philosophy and rhetoric, and is found alongside Roman equivalents in Cicero's theoretical works, but it is lacking not only in Roman Comedy, but also in surviving Greek New Comedy. Yet since Roman Comedy had the option of drawing its language from the arena, with its national appeal, we may suspect that references to the *palaestra* did occur in the originals, and were replaced: this is confirmed by the preservation of the nouns *gymnasium* (*Aul.* 410) and *palaestra* (*Ph.* 484 and *Bac.* 66 f.) as metaphors in Plautus and Terence. There was no Roman substitute for the establishment; either the Greek noun had to stand, or the metaphor be abandoned (see p. 63 below, s.v. *palaestra*).

V THE DRAMA

Hau.

402   immo ut patrem tuum vidi esse habitum, diu etiam

duras dabit,[23]

(cf. *Eu.* 354 *duras* fratri' *partes* praedicas).

Hau.

709   huic equidem consilio *palmam do.*

Eu.

151-2   sine illum *priores partes* hosce aliquot dies
         apud me habere

Eu.

930   id verost quod ego mi puto *palmarium*
         me repperisse

Ad.

880   non *posteriores* feram

(Donatus: Translatio est a partibus histrionum in fabula.)

The metaphors which Terence draws from the theatre are limited to two: the *partes*, or role and the *palma* or prize of the contest. The transferred use of *partes* is established in Plautus' time: cf.

Mer. 276 metuo ne illaec simiae *partis ferat*

Mil. 811   actutum *partes* defendas *tuas*

The former identifies a stage character with the symbolic ape of a dream; the latter refers to a disguised role which the character must play, and is scarcely a metaphor. Both the reference to the "difficult" role and to the πρωταγωνιστής and δευτεραγωνιστής are likely to be Greek, but are used naturally by Cicero and his contemporaries. In the letter enclosed at *Att.* 10.8b (cf. also 10.10), M. Antonius writes, *duriores partes* mihi impositas esse (cf. *Eu.* 354). With *priores partes* (*Eu.* 151) compare Cicero's words; *Q.fr.* 3.4.4, tibi istius generis

23 On the ellipse of *partes* here see Löfstedt, *Syntactica* II, 253-4.

in scribendo *priores partes* tribuo quam mihi (cf. *Att.* 1.16.12, consul ... ille, *deterioris histrionis* similis). He also uses *persona*, not apparently metaphorical in Plautus or Terence:

Fam.

7.33.2 ... *deponere illam* iam *personam* in qua me saepe illi ipsi probavi.

Att.

10.15.3 nisi cuius gravioris *personae suscipiendae* spes erit ante oblata.

The *palma* or dramatic prize naturally occurs literally both in Plautus (*Am.* Prol. 69) and Terence, (*Ph.* Prol. 17), but Plautus also has a good example of the metaphorical use:

Mos.

32–3 is nunc in aliam partem *palmam possidet*
virtute id factum et magisterio tuo.

Here however it is quite possible that the *palma* is gladiatorial, not dramatic. At *Trin.* 706

palmam habes: hic victust, vicit tua *comoedia*
hic agit magis *ex argumento* et *versus meliores* facit,

we have the same allusion to a play within a play as at *Mil.* 811 above; at the same time literal and to be taken as a metaphor. On the other hand Terence has coined the use of *palmarius* (or is it a noun *palmarium?*) in the sense of prize-winning, and the image was apparently without later imitation.

We might expect the scope of Terence's (and Plautus') theatrical imagery to be more limited than either that of later Greek comedy or the urbane vocabulary of Cicero's letters. The Roman comic dramatists were not writing for an audience with literary or technical interests: even the concept of a theatre must have been new to the Romans of their times. In fact, the surviving fragments of later Greek comedy provide only one image of this category:

Amphis.

κΙΙ, p. 241

fr. 17   ἄστυ δὲ θέατρον ἀτυχίας σαφοῦς γέμον.

This is found several times in Cicero; at its most expanded in *Q.fr.* 1.1.42, *Theatrum* totius Asiae virtutibus tuis est datum, *vocesque referantur* (also at *Fam.* 12.29.1; 13.64.2; *Att.* 13.20.2).

Other theatrical metaphors are based on *scaena* (Caelius, *Fam.* 8.11.3, and *ad Brut.* 17.2, tibi nunc populo et *scaenae*, ut dicitur serviendum est) and *spectaculum*, which however is better referred to the gladiatorial entertainments. For the latter, cf. Caelius, *Fam.* 8.14.4, magnum et iucundum tibi Fortuna *spectaculum* parat and *Att.* 2.15.2, praeclarum *spectaculum* mihi propono, modo *te consessore spectare* liceat. *Q.fr.* 2.11.3, multa dixi in ignobilem regem, quibus est totus *explosus* refers to the hissing (or Roman equivalent) of a play or actor from the stage. Finally, the most "literary" or formal dramatic comparisons occur as special pleading in the famous letter to Lucceius (*Fam.* 5.12.2) and in the immense letter to Quintus (*Q.fr.* 1.1.46), tamquam *poetae boni* et *actores industrii* solent, sic tu in extrema parte et conclusione muneris ... diligentissimus sis, ut hic tertius annus imperi tui *tamquam tertius* ⟨*actus*⟩ perfectissimus atque ornatissimus fuisse videatur. Thus the dramatic or theatrical imagery of Cicero's correspondence seems to be reserved for the most elaborate letters. We may suspect that the metaphors addressed to Quintus were deliberately chosen to appeal to his special interests.

VI TEACHER, TUTOR, TRAINER, PUPIL

An.

192   tum siquis *magistrum* cepit ad eam rem inprobum ...

475-7   non sat commode
         divisa sunt temporibu' tibi, Dave, haec : : mihin?
         : : num immemores *discipuli*?

Ph.

144-5   quid *paedagogus* ille qui citharistriam?
         quid rei gerit?

Hec.

203-4   in eodemque omnes mihi videntur *ludo* doctae ad malitiam; et
         ei ludo, si ullus est, *magistram* hanc esse sati' certo scio.

Perhaps the only common feature of these passages, which distinguishes them from the surviving parallels in New Comedy, is that the metaphors are applied only to people, whereas the instances in New Comedy are personifications of inanimate or abstract nouns. Terence's usage largely coincides with that of Plautus: *An.* 192 and 477 assume the favourite Plautine motif of the clever slave who leads and controls others (especially his young master). Davus is the wicked teacher of 192,[24] and Mysis and her friend in 477 his alleged pupils, but 475–6, with their allusion to mistimed cues, suggest rather the dramatic repetiteur. In *Ph.* 144, as Donatus points out, Phaedria is called a *paedagogus* not because he is in any sense a tutor or guardian, but because his main activity is (86) in *ludum ducere et redducere*, to escort his favourite lyre-player. In fact, where Terence might have used the word *paedagogus* in a more general sense, he has preferred *magister*, both literally in *An.* 54, *dum aetas metus magister prohibebant*, and metaphorically in 192. Only in *Ph.* 144 is he forced to use the Greek word *paedagogus* because no Roman equivalent existed for this kind of escort.

Plautus seems to use *magister* for παιδαγωγός, without differentiation, while admitting *paedagogus* both literally (*Bac.* 138 and 142) and metaphorically. Thus in *Bac.* (act 1, sc. 2) Lydus is a *paedagogus* (138, 142), but his control is described as *magisterium* (148) and he calls himself *magister* and Pistoclerus *discipulus* in 152. The scene leads up to the metaphor of the wicked slave as *magister*; 163–4, peior *magister* te istaec docuit, non ego./nimio es ad istas res *discipulus docilior*/quam ad illa quae te *docui*, ubi operam perdidi. Similarly in *Pseudolus*, at 447, Pseudolus is described as the evil genius of his young master; hic *dux*, hic illist *paedagogus*; in 933 he is Simia's *magister*, and again in 1193 *praeceptor* tuo' qui te hanc fallaciam/*docuit*. However, in 933, as in *Epid.* 592, quae *didici* dixi omnia/Epidicus mihi fuit *magister* and *An.* 477, the allusion is to the dramatic διδάσκαλος.

The Latin word or title *magister* was used in so many different contexts, social, religious, and political, that it is not surprising that it represents several professions which would have distinct names in Greek. Besides the clear references to the dramatic repetiteur above, *Mos.* 32–3 is more ambiguous; is nunc in aliam partem *palmam* possidet/virtute id factum tua et *magisterio tuo*, could refer to the drama (cf the allusion to the *palma* in *Trin.* 706) or the gladiatorial school. If we attribute the imagery in both *Mostellaria* and *Trinummus* to Philemon, the latter is excluded, but either or both may be a Plautine creation. In *Trin.* 226, *magister* mihi *exercitor* animus nunc est, and

---

24 An alternative interpretation is suggested by the use of the verb *applicare* in the next line (193). If the nautical sense of *applicare* (q.v. p. 42 below) is intended by Terence, *magister* would then stand for *magister navis*, as in Verg. *Aen.* 5.176; 6.353; our image would then be that of the young man as a ship driven into harm by a wicked helmsman. However the context seems too indefinite to sustain this metaphor, and I am inclined to take *applicare* neutrally in 193 as in *Hau. Prol.* 23.

1015–16 huic, quisquis est/gurguliost *exercitor is hunc hominem cursuram docet*, the allusion is to the γυμναστής or παιδοτριβής. Neither occurs as an element of comparison in surviving New Comedy, but references to athletics are common, and a frequent source of imagery in Plato, so that we would assume such references as appear in Plautus (there are none in Terence) have a Greek rather than a Roman inspiration.

Hec. 203–4 depicts the *matrona* as *magistra* in a school for spite. Twice in Plautus a woman is treated as *magistra*: *St.* 105, *discipulus venio ad magistras* (a father speaks to his daughters), and *Truc.* 737, in an extended analogy in which the courtesan teaches the lover his letters; this picture of the lover as a child learning from his "mistress" recalls the elementary school of love in *Mer.* 303–5. There is no instance of διδάσκαλος applied to a woman in New Comedy (although it is applied to feminine abstracts) and the idea seems at first incompatible with the Athenian attitude to women. Yet it is unreasonable to assume four metaphors of Roman comedy all based on this concept, and each independently invented by Plautus and Terence. Probably the underlying Greek imagery relied on the verb διδάσκειν not on διδάσκαλος as the vehicle of the metaphor.[25]

The group of illustrations from New Comedy quoted below is so different from the Roman examples that some explanation seems to be required. It is difficult to believe that imagery based on διδάσκαλος, διδάσκειν, and παιδαγωγός was never applied to persons in Greek Comedy. The metaphors of *Bac.* 163–4, *Epid.* 592, *Mer.* 303–5, *St.* 105, or Ter. *An.* 475–7 are so well integrated with their context that they should be considered as adaptations of similar metaphors in the Greek plays. The absence of such examples in Greek is, I believe, a coincidence. On the other hand the absence of personifications like Men., fr. 338 below from Roman Comedy reflects a difference of taste, and it is more than likely that where Plautus and Terence found such solemn apophthegms in Greek comedy they deliberately omitted them, or modified their form.[26]

---

25 Compare for instance Men. fr. 338 and Antiphanes fr. 294 below with Men. fr. 229 χρεία διδάσκει, κἂν ἄμουσος ᾖ σόφον/Καρχηδόνιον, where the same image is expressed by the verb.

26 I am not suggesting that Plautus avoided personification as such. Comparisons between a given character or thing and a type or class of men are common (e.g. from *Trinummus* 226, 512, 1016); it is only the generalized identification which Plautus seems to dislike. For Terence's avoidance of personifying imagery as a whole, see the comparison of the two dramatists, p. 78.

Menander

fr. 338κ   ἆρ ἐστιν ἀρετῆς κἀι βίον διδάσκαλος
                ἐλευθέρου τοῖς πᾶσιν ἀνθρώποις ἀγρός.

Antiphanes

κπ, p. 127

fr. 294   πενία γάρ ἐστιν ἡ τρόπων διδάσκαλος.

Anaxandrides

κπ, p. 161

fr. 61   Ἔρως σοφιστοῦ γίνεται διδάσκαλος
                σκαιοῦ πολὺ κρείττων πρὸς τὸν ἀνθρώπων βίον.

cf. Alexis

κπ, p. 401

fr. 289   οὐκ ἔστι παιδαγωγὸς ἀνθρώποις ἄρα
                ἔρωτος οὐδεὶς ἄλλος ἐπιμελέστερος.

Cicero's metaphorical use of *magister* in the correspondence is more restricted. He twice refers to Dolabella as *magister*: in *Fam.* 9.7.2 to Varro, where the sense of *magister* is revealed by his comment πολλοὶ μαθηταὶ κρείσσονες διδασκάλων, and a year later in *Att.* 13.47.1. For this the latest editor, Shackleton Bailey, can give no explanation, but notes (vol. vi, p. 386) that Cicero applies the same metaphor to Caesar in *Fam.* 7.25.1 a few days later, "sed heus tu, manum de tabula: *magister* adest citius quam putaramus; vereor ne in Catomum Catonianos." Fadius Gallus had evidently been writing notes in class – in praise of Cato.

The remaining case, *Fam.* 9.16.7, contrasts Hirtius and Dolabella as dicendi *discipulos*, ... cenandi *magistros*, an easy and unambiguous image based on the literal use of *discipuli* (which is not used figuratively in the letters). *Magistra*, representing the Greek application of διδάσκαλος to abstracts, is absent from Cicero's correspondence, except in a fragmentary letter from Nepos; his use of *magistra philosophia* is similar to instances in Cicero's rhetorical and philosophical works; *de Orat.* 3, 57 vetus illa *doctrina* eadem videtur et recte faciendi et bene dicendi *magistra*, *Fin.* 1.71, *magistra ac duce natura*. The practice of Plautus, Terence, and Cicero in his private writings suggests that such personifications were not at ease in Roman *sermo* as they clearly were in Greek Comedy.

VII FOWLING, HUNTING AND FISHING

An.

602   in nuptias *conieci* erilem filium (cf. 620, 668)

733   repudio quod consilium primum *intenderam.*

Hau.

513   *intendenda* in senemst fallacia.

Eu.

247   hoc novomst *aucupium.*

Ph.

330–1   quia non *rete accipitri tennitur neque milvo*
           qui male faciunt nobis: illis qui nil faciunt *tennitur.*

382   proinde *expiscare* quasi non nosses.

Ad.

220   abi, nescis *inescare* homines, Sannio.

There is one interesting difference between Terence's use of this range of metaphor, and that of Plautus: in Plautus, imagery from hunting and snaring is largely associated with erotic themes – the *sermo meretricius* exemplified in *Asinaria, Bacchides, Truculentus*; none of the Terentian examples above are connected with love themes, but rather with more general intrigue. In this respect Plautus' practice has many parallels in Hellenistic erotic writing, if only one[27] from New Comedy.

First, let us consider *fowling*. In *Eu.* 247 and *Ph.* 330–1, the parasite compares his profession to bird-catching. The similar comparison in *As.* 215, hic noster quaestus *aucupi* simillimust, is spoken by a Lena in an erotic context, and is greatly enlarged by Plautus ... (220 f.), aedes nobis *area* est, *auceps* sum ego,/*esca* est meretrix, lectus *inlexest*, amatores *aves*. The same theme and context recur in *Bac.* 50, *viscus* meru' vostrast blanditia ... duae unum expetitis palumbem, peri, *harundo* alas verberat, and 1158, tactus sum vehementer *visco*,[28] whereas *Bac.* 792, nunc ab *transenna* hic turdus lumbricum petit, and *Rud.* 1237–8, si quis avidus poscit *escam* avariter/decipitur in *transenna*, apply to slave intrigue, and material greed. In this, *Ru.* 1237–8 is close to the spirit of *Ad.* 220. The frequency of fowling metaphors in *Bacchides* tends to support a

27 The reference to nets (παγίδες); *Amphis.* κιι, p. 242, fr. 23: cf. Plautus, *Epid.* 216.
28 On these metaphors in Greek erotic literature, see K. Preston, *Studies in the Diction of the Sermo Amatorius in Roman Comedy* (Chicago 1916), pp. 55–6; La Penna, "Note sul Linguaggio Erotico dell'Elegia Latina," *Maia* iv, 1951, 205, n. 2.

Menandrian origin for *Eu.* 247 and *Ad.* 220, but there are no parallels surviving in Menander or New Comedy as a whole. Plautus' use of *auceps, aucupium* as an image for eavesdropping (*Mil.* 990, venaturam facere atque *aucupium* auribus; cf. *St.* 102) is not found in Terence or later authors. With Terence's use of *inescare,* cf. Livy 22.41.4 and 41.23.8, nos caeci specie parvi beneficii *inescamur.* The Greek equivalents of *esca, inescare,* δέλεαρ, δελεάζειν seem to be a favourite metaphor of didactic ethics; Plato. *Tim.* 69a, ἡδονὴ κακοῦ δέλεαρ,[29] *Euthyd.* 272, d2, Xen. *Mem.* 2.1.4 (θήρια) ... τὰ μὲν γαστρὶ δελεαζόμενα ... τῇ ἐπιθυμίᾳ τοῦ φαγεῖν ἀγόμενα πρὸς τὸ δέλεαρ ἁλίσκεσθαι, τὰ δὲ πότῳ ἐνεδρεύεται, and especially of the Epicureans, Epic. *Sent. Vat.* 16, Philodemus, *Lib.* p. 14.o. From popular use in philosophy it would naturally enter the vocabulary of New Comedy.

If *Ph.* 330–1 is the only explicit reference in Terence to the use of nets in fowling, the vaguer use of *conicere* in the *Andria* examples seems to be modelled on snare and ambush metaphors; cf. Pl. *Per.* 796, ut me in tricas coniecisti, *Trin.* 237b (Amor) ... postulat se in plagas conicere. The latter recurs in Cicero, *Fam.* 12.25.4, conieci in Caesaris Octaviani plagas. Terence leaves the verb alone to convey the force of the image. His use of *intendere* in *An.* 733, *Hau.* 513, is similar. In grouping these examples under fowling and hunting I am following Donatus' first explanation of *An.* 733, verbum a venatoribus translatum, qui *retia intendunt* ad feras captandas. Compare with *rete tendere* in *Ph.* 330, the symbolic *retia* of the *meretrices* in Pl. *Epid.* 216, and retia tendere, Prop. 2.32.20; 3.8.37, Ovid. *Am.* 1.8.69, plagas tendere, Cic. *Off.* 3, 68.

However Pl. *Bac.* 709, de ducentis nummis primum intendam ballistam in senem, by its similarity of context with *Hau.* 513, seems to argue for taking *intendere* in both Terence passages of hurling a weapon (cf. also Cic. *Har.* 7, telum intendere). In the case of a careful artist like Terence, it is wiser to assume that the ambiguity is deliberate, and that he chose to avoid too specific associations by his use of the verb alone. There is a similar instance in Cicero's letters; *Att.* 2.19.1, iis periculis quae mihi ipsi intenduntur.

Terence's use of the verbs *evolvere* and *revolvere,* which seem originally to have been connected with the imagery of the hunting-net, is even less explicit, and I have therefore discussed the implications of these words separately, s.v. *evolvere* in the alphabetical list which follows.

29 Note, however, that Cicero, *Sen.* 44, "divine enim Plato 'escam malorum' appellat voluptatem quod ea videlicet homines capiantur *ut pisces,*" associates the image with fishing, not fowling.

Expiscari, the only metaphor derived from fishing in Terence, has no affinity with the many references to fishing as a symbol of plotting and intrigue in Plautus.[30] Donatus explains it as *diligentissime quaerere ubinam pisces lateant*: ergo tractum verbum a piscatoribus. The only other examples of *expiscari* in the classical period come from Cicero's intimate letters, with the same sense of *diligentissime quaerere*; *Att.* 2.17.3, velim ex Theophane *expiscere* quonam in me animo sit Arabarches (here the reading is due to an emendation), and to Paetus, *Fam.* 9.19.1, nescis me ab illo omnia *expiscatum*.[31]

---

30 Cf. *Piscatus, Bac.* 102; *hamus, rete* etc., *Truc.* 35-42, from erotic contexts. *Hamus* is used in slave intrigue at *Cur.* 431, *Mos.* 1070.

31 More frequent in the same sense is the hunting metaphor *odorari*, used only in letters to Atticus: *Att.* 4.8a.4 and 14.2; 6.4.3; 12.22.3; 14.3.2 and 22.1; 15.3.1.

2

Individual usages

I have arranged in alphabetical order the *key-words* of imagery which does not come under any of the preceding categories. This section represents only the more unusual or significant usages, and omits proverbial imagery. Where no Greek illustrations are given, this is because I know of nothing comparable in either New Comedy or related literary sources.

Abligurrire. Eu. 235   A more picturesque equivalent of *comedere*, q.v.

Arrigere aures. An. 933   So also Pl. *Rud.* 1293 *mihi ... arrexit aures*, Verg. *Aen.* 1, 152; 2, 303. The phrase is properly applied to animals. While Terence does not directly compare persons with animals (the exception is the abusive epithet *canis* used by the vulgar Gnatho in *Eu.* 803), he does transfer verbs from animal to human behaviour; cf. s.v. *gannire, ringi,* below.

Appellere and *Applicare*   It is possible that in Terence's use of both these verbs nautical imagery is intended. To take *appellere* first: on *An.* 446, animum ad uxorem *appulit*, Donatus comments, bene *appulit*, quasi ab iactatione fluctuum et aestus marini. The verb occurs only in the *Andria*; in 807, haud auspicato huc *me appuli*, the nautical sense is literal; "I have hardly put in to land under good omen." Prol. 1, poeta quom primum animum ad scribendum *appulit*, uses the same idiom as 446, and may have arisen from a reminiscence of 446 when Terence came to write the prologue. Neither here nor in 446 is there anything to make the nautical allusion explicit, and it is open to question whether Terence meant to convey any image by his use of the verb, but *Andria* is rich in sea metaphors (cf. 480, 562, 845), and the plot is preoccupied with voyage and shipwreck. We know that ὁρμίζειν is used by Philemon (κιι, p. 533, fr. 213) of returning to safety, "steering the ship of one's life into

harbour." Thus in 446, *appulit* may be a pale reflection of a more clearly
nautical idiom in Menander's Ἄνδρια. *Applicare (An.* 193, 924, *Hau.* 23, 393)
is a near synonym of *appellere*; is *An.* 193, "animum aegrotum ad deteriorem
partem plerumque *adplicat*," meant to depict the mind as a ship steered
towards disaster? If so, we must take *magister* in 192 in the sense of helmsman.
I have already suggested (p. 36 on *magister*) that I do not think this is intended
here, and it may be fairer to distinguish between the metaphorical vitality of
applicare and *appellere*, for Cicero uses *appellere* only of putting into land,
literally (e.g., *Att.* 13.21.3) and metaphorically; cf. *de Orat.* 2.154, "*tamquam
ad aliquem libidinis scopulum* sic tuam mentem ad philosophiam *appulisti*,"
whereas for him, as for Terence, *applicare* can be a synonym of *appellere*, but
has a wider range of reference; cf. *Inv.* 2.153, *navem applicare* (literal); *Tusc.*
1.115, *ad philosophiam applicare*, *de Orat.* 2.154 above; but also *de Orat.* 1.177,
ad aliquem quasi patronum applicare, a technical use found similarly in Ter.
An. 924. Thus of these two verbs, *appellere* may be a living nautical metaphor
in Terence; but there is little positive support for the figurative force of
applicare.

Auspicato. An. 807   Haud *auspicato* huc me appuli. It may be asked whether
this use of *auspicato* is strictly metaphorical, yet since there is no question of
formal religious activity, and this clearly stands out as a Roman element, its
presence in Terence deserves notice. There is a group of such allusions in
Plautus, where characters (only slaves or parasites) reflect on their good or
bad luck. Nearest is *Aul.* 447, *ne ego edepol veni huc auspicio malo*. Contrast the
good omens of *Epid.* 183, *liquido exeo foras auspicio, avi sinistera*, and *St.* 459,
auspicio hodie optimo exivi foras. The last instance is apparently a quotation
from Gelasimus' book of classic jokes (hence the hiatus due to reading aloud),
and argues for a long tradition of such comments. Plautus also uses *auspicato*
itself once: *Per.* 607, *vide ut ingrediare auspicato : : liquidumst auspicium, tace.*
What is significant is Terence's avoidance of such a "Roman" allusion after
his first play. Thus at *Ad.* 775, a situation parallel to *Aul.* 447 and *An.* 807,
Syrus' comment is *sane nollem huc exitum*.

Bolus. Hau. 673   Crucior *bolum* mihi ereptum tam desubito e faucibus. The
Greek word βόλος (√βάλλω) is used by Plautus of a cast of the dice (*Cur.* 611)
and hence predominantly of any successful trick (cf. French "coup"), or the
profit gained from it (*Per.* 658, *Poen.* 101, *Truc.* 724, 844). The idiom also
occurs in Lucil. 881M. quovis posse me emungi bolo. *Hau.* 673 follows a series

of military images, and itself involves a mixed metaphor (*e faucibus ereptum*) for comic effect. The confusion of images reflects the way in which Syrus' wit and his very versatility are running away with him. There are no examples of this use of βόλος in Greek literature, and it should probably be considered as sub-literary, soldier's Greek; cf. Tenney Frank, *Life and Literature of the Roman Republic* (Berkeley 1930), pp. 69–73.

Caedere. Hau. 242 dum *sermones caedimus*/illae sunt relictae. Syrus is again the speaker. The Thesaurus has no parallel for this use of *caedere*. The Greek idiom κόπτειν τὰ ῥήματα quoted by Priscian, Keil II, p. 323, is obviously close, but there is no example of this use of κόπτειν from New Comedy or related authors. For (κατα-)κόπτειν with a personal object in Menander v. sub *obtundere*.

Cantilena. Ph. 495 *Cantilenam eandem canis.* Both *cantilena* and *canere/cantare* (cf. *Hau.* 260) are used in Latin of repeated or trite sayings. Compare from Plautus, *Bac.* 985, metuo ne idem *cantent* (sc. tabellae) quod priores; *Trin.* 287, haec dies noctesque tibi *canto* ut caveas; and 350, sed civi inmuni scin quid *cantari* solet? The two instances frequently quoted from Cicero's letters are not strictly parallel: in *Att.* 1.19.8, vafer ille Siculus insusurret Epicharmus *cantilenam* illam suam, the sense is nearer to *incantation* or *formula*. *Q.fr.* 2.12.1, iam pridem istum *canto* Caesarem, implies rather singing Caesar's praises. But a comparable image is provided by *fabula* at *Att.* 4.2.4, ad suam veterem *fabulam* rediit, and *Att.* 13.34.1, haec *decantata* erat *fabula*. The Greek ὑμνεῖν is used both of repeated praises and of the constant refrain of advice or statement, e.g., Plato, *Resp.* 549e, οἷα φιλοῦσιν αἱ γυναῖκες περὶ τῶν τοιούτων ὑμνεῖν; *Prot.* 317a, 343b, etc. but is not found in New Comedy.

Circumspicere. Ad. 639 numquid *circumspexti*? numquid prospexti tibi? The article on *circumspicere* in Thesaurus shows that the metaphorical use of the verb, first attested in Terence, is surprisingly uncommon. With a dependent clause it is perhaps more natural: cf. Cic. *Q.fr.* 1.1.10 ... esse *circumspiciendum* diligenter ut ... omnes ministros ... rei publicae praestare videare. The absolute use of the verb occurs in the intimate elliptical style of *Att.* 16.5.3, etenim *circumspice*, sed ante quam erubesco.

Claudere. An. 573 nolo tibi ullum commodum in me *claudier*; *Eu.* 164, meam/benignitatem sensisti in te *claudier*; *Ad.* 607, propter suam impotentiam se semper credunt *claudier*. For *claudere* of favours cut off, add to McGlynn's parallels (vol. I, p. 87) Cic. *Fam.* 4.13.6, in ... consuetudinem quam adhuc meus pudor mihi *clausit* insinuabo. The construction of *Ad.* 607 makes the person subject of the verb, and comparison with *Hec.* 702, tot me nunc rebu' miserum *concludit* pater (see also s.v. *concludere*) suggests that in *Ad.* 607 *claudier* is used for *concludi(er)*, whereas in *An.* 573 and *Eu.* 164, the sense is nearer that of *intercludi(er)*. These three passages are the only instances of *claudere* in Terence, and the fact that is is confined to the archaizing -*ier* infinitive, combined with the total absence of the word from Plautus, suggests that it was not part of normal familiar speech at that time. It should be added that *intercludere* occurs nowhere in Terence, and in Plautus only in a pseudo-military context, *Mil.* 223.

The idioms of *Ad.* 607 and *Hec.* 702 may represent a use of συγκλεῖν similar to Men. fr. 628.

χρηστὸς τρόπος
εἰς χαλεπὸν ὅταν ᾖ συγκεκλεισμένος βίον.

Columen. *Ph.* 287 bone custos salve, *columen* vero familiae. The confusions of the Romans themselves about the meaning of *columen* are reflected in Donatus' text.

1 "columen" culmen. An "columen" columna, unde columellae apud veteres dicti servi maiores domus. Lucilius xxii (fr. 1 M) servus neque infidus domino neque inutilis quoiquam/Lucili columella hic situs Metrophanes ... 2 sustentatio vel decus, unde columnae dictae.

Donatus first identifies *columen* with *culmen*, the later form favoured especially in hexameters. The two coincide in literal meaning: ridgepole, roof, and in the transferred sense of "vault of heaven" (Pl. *Mos.* 765 columen; cf. *culmen,* Cic. *Aratea* 26, 307). His second equation is more problematic. Architecturally *columen* is a horizontal support element, *columna* a vertical column or pillar. J. Perrot, *Les dérivés latins en -men -mentum* (Paris 1961), pp. 171–2 believes the two words may have a common etymology from √colo (as in Latin colus, Greek πόλος, which coincides with *columen/culmen* in Pl. *Mos.* 765; Cic. *Aratea* 26, 307 above.) He suggests that the Romans, aware of the relationship, from the beginning used *columen* metaphorically in the sense of *columna,* parallel to the Greek figurative use of στῦλος in Aesch. *Ag.* 898, and Eur. *I.T.*57, στῦλοι γὰρ οἴκων παῖδές εἰσιν ἄρσενες, or of κίων, Pindar *Ol.* 2.82 (cf. ἔρεισμα, lat. *fulmen, Ol.* 2.6). This is certainly the sense of *columella* (diminutive of *columna*) in Lucilius, and the family name. It is possible that the Greek image of vertical support led to a misinterpretation in the Hellenized first century B.C. of the obsolescent Roman image. This would occur naturally once *columen* was displaced by *culmen* in its literal architectural role. The phrase *senati columen* seems to have been formalized before Plautus; cf. Fraenkel *El. Pl.*, p. 226 on *Epid.* 188, *senati qui columen cluent* and *Cas.* 536, *senati columen, praesidium* popli. Here a generalized interpretation on the lines of "sustentatio vel decus" is natural, but in *Am.* 367 *columen audaciae* the sense of peak or summit required is closer to the architectural origin. We may compare the use of θρίγκος in Eur. *Tr.* 489, θρίγκος ἀθλίων κακῶν and Plato *Resp.* 534e ὥσπερ θρίγκος τοῖς μαθήμασιν ἡ διαλεκτική ... ἐπάνω κεῖται. Closest to the context of Ter. *Ph.* 287 is a fragment by an unknown Palliata-writer Com. Inc: Pall. 38 Ribbeck; *tutamen familiae, domuique columen*, where the association with *domus* keeps the architectural motif alive; the sense of support is still compatible with the horizontal ridgepole. In the Ciceronian period the usage merely echoes the Plautine pattern: *Sest.* 19 *columen rei publicae*; *Phil.* 13, 26; *columen amicorum Antoni*, and in contrast, *Flacc.* 41 *istud columen* accusationis tuae Mithridates, cf. *Am.* 367, "summit"; Catullus' one example in 64.26 *Thessaliae columen Peleu*, though epic in colouring follows the same pattern as *senati columen*. In Livy 38.51.4, unum hominem *caput columenque imperi Romani esse*, and Hor. *Carm.* 2.17,3–4 *mearum grande decus columenque rerum*, the same traditional image appears without any detail to show specific awareness of the original sense.

But with Seneca *Tro.* 6, *columen eversum occidit/pollentis Asiae*, and 124–8, *columen patriae, mora fatorum/tu praesidium Phrygibus fessis/tu murus eras, umerisque tuis/stetit illa decem fulta per annos;/tecum cecidit*, the idea of a vertical column has taken over, and the use of *fulcire* in 128 confirms the use of *columen* for the Pindaric κίων (applied to Hector in *Ol.* 2.82) as *murus* echoes the Homeric πύργος.

Columna is very rare as a metaphor; besides Hor. *Carm.* 1.35.13–4, *ne pede proruas stantem columnam*, Donatus has preserved Enn. *Ann.* 348v, *regni versatum summam venere columnam*, which perhaps suggests a source in early tragedy for Sen. *Tro.* 6. Clearly, as a metaphor of support *columna* was ousted by *columen* early in the development of Latin, only to be avenged when *columen*, no longer fully understood, was reinterpreted in the first century A.D. as an alternative for *columna*.

See also chap. 5, p. 130 on *Sest.* 19, and p. 118 for related uses of *fulmen, fulcire.*

Comedere. Eu. 1087 hunc comedendum vobis propino et deridendum. *Comedere* with a person or his property as direct object is the prevalent image in comedy for wasting or squandering; cf. Pl. *Mos.* 12 and 14, (senex) quem absentem *comes*, *Ps.* 1126, illum *comessurus* es? followed by 1127; *devorari* decet iam (here the reference is to plundering rather than wasting). Terence uses two synonyms: *exedere*; *Hau.* 462, te ... quem adsidue *exedent* (perhaps merely a metrical convenience, but the effect is also more extreme than *comedere*) and *abligurrire*; *Eu.* 235, patria qui *abligurrierat* bona; cf. Pl. *Capt.* 84, parasites seek "homines ... quos *ligurriant*"; Lucil. 530M, publicitus vendis tamen et extrema *ligurris*. Cicero's letters contain both expressions, as also *devorare*; cf. *Fam.* 11.21.2, non quo veterem (sc. rem) *comederit* ... sed hanc ipsam recentem novam *devoravit*, and *ibid.* 5, cum ... agrariam curationem *ligurrirent*. *Att.* 6.1.25, putat enim suos nummos vos *comedisse*, is more conventional.

This is a very common metaphor in New Comedy; cf. κατεσθίειν, καταφαγεῖν, Antiphanes κιι, p. 16.239, Alexis κιι, p. 340.123; Anaxippus κιι, p. 297.32, and Men. *Epitr.* 707K, καταφαγεῖν τὴν προῖκά μου, fr. 325, δέκα τάλαντα καταφαγών. The more vivid καταβιβρώσκω occurs in Hegesippus κιιι, p. 313.30, οἱ καταβεβρωκάσ' ἕνεκ' ἐμοῦ τὰς οὐσίας.

Concludere. Ph. 744 *Conclusam* hic habeo uxorem saevam; here the image of the wife as a wild beast is suggested partly by *saevus*, but more effectively by the verb *concludere*, which is shown for example by Pl. *Cur.* 449–50, in cavea si forent/*conclusi*, itidem ut pulli gallinacei ... to be the vox propria for caging animals. The concept of woman as a wild beast is Menandrian; cf. fr. 422κ, κάκιστόν ἐστι θηρίον γύνη, but the form of the joke in *Phormio* is more suggestive of a Roman origin. On *An.* 386 and *Hec.* 702, tot nunc me rebu' miserum *concludit* pater, Donatus also suggests that the image is derived from the caging or hunting down of wild beasts but the contexts are neutral; see s.v. *claudere* above.

Conflare. An. 650 quantasque ... mihi *conflavit* sollicitudines; *Eun.* 874–5, magna familiaritas/*conflatast*. This verb is found in Plautus only in its literal sense of kindling a fire: *Ru.* 765, dabo ignem, si quidem in capite tuo *conflandi* copiast. The usage is close to the Greek συμφυσᾶν, at e.g., Ar. *Eq.* 468, ταῦτ' ἐφ' οἶσίν ἐστι συμφυσώμενα, where the context shows the metaphor to be one of forging with the bellows.

Conglutinare. An. 913 meretricios amores nuptiis *conglutinas*. Cf. in Plautus *Bac.* 693; finge quod lubet, *conglutina*, and a similar use of *adglutinare*, *Aul.* 801, mihi ad malum malae res plurumae se *adglutinant*, which may suggest a parallel image in the Menandrian originals of these plays. However, the Greek equivalent, συγκολλᾶν, found in Ar. *Vesp.* 1041 (cf. *Nub.* 446 ψευδῶν συγκολλητής) and similarly in Plato *Menex.* 236b, does not occur in surviving New Comedy. *Conglutinare* in Cicero's letters, *Fam.* 11.27.2, voluntates nostras consuetudine *conglutinari*, and *Att.* 1.17.10, *conglutinatam* concordiam, 7.8.1, *conglutinare* amicitias, offers close parallels to the usage in *An.* 913.

Conradere. Hau. 141, *Ph.* 40, *Ad.* 242   Terence uses this verb only of scraping together money; cf. Pl. *Poen.* 1363, credo *conradi* potest. (This, the only instance in Plautus, is from one of the alternative endings of the play, and rejected by Leo as post-Plautine. Lindsay, on the other hand, accepts this scene as genuine.) The word is not found after Lucretius (1.401, fidem dictis *corradere* nostris) and has no close equivalent in Greek comedy. Compare also the similar use of *abradere* in *Ph.* 333 in the sense of robbing or filching.

Crux. Eu. 383   Illis *crucibus* quae nos ... semper omnibus *cruciant* modis. The identification of the tormenting courtesans with *cruces* is on a pattern found earlier in the same play. In the first scene Thais is called both nostri fundi *calamitas* (79) and hunc *ignem* (85) because of her effect on her lover. This is distinct from the Plautine epithet *crux* "gallows-bird," *Mos.* 743, *Per.* 795. *Cruciare* is found here to explain the use of *crux*, also at *Hau.* 81, 1045, but *excruciare* is more common of tormenting anxiety or love (*An.* 886, *Hau.* 177, 413, *Eu.* 920, *Ph.* 187) as in Plautus. *Discruciare* used figuratively five times by Plautus, occurs in Terence only once, in Canticum: *Ad.* 610, *discrucior* animi, where Aeschinus is really torn *apart* by divided loyalties. The identical phrase occurs in the Menandrian *Aulularia* 105, but it is unlikely that this imagery, based on slave-punishment, represents a similar metaphor in the original. The relative frequency of the three synonymous forms is the same in Cicero's letters; *excruciare* occurs eleven times (always in intimate letters), *cruciare* four times, plus three instances in letters from Caelius, Balbus, and Caesar, and *discruciare* only once (*Att.* 14.6.1), and once in Caelius' letter, *Fam.* 8.3.1, both times in the form *discrucior*. Catullus' usage is similar: *excruciare* three times in the shorter poems, 76.10, 85.2 and 99.12; *discruciare* only once in the form *discrucior*, in the highly artificial style of the *Coma Berenices*, 66.76, but *cruciare* is not found. (For a discussion of these verbs, see Heusch, *Das Archaische in der Sprache Catulls*, pp. 75-6.)

Excarnificare, *Hau.* 813, is a similar metaphor, confined to this one instance in Terence, and absent from Plautus. It is used literally of physical torture in Cic. *N.D.* 3.82. (For the imagery of torture in Lyric and Elegy, see Appendix.)

Debacchari. Ad. 184   Si sati' iam *debacchatus* es. Terence uses this in a context quite divorced from actual Bacchanals. It is not found in Plautus, who uses *bacchari*, but only of actual Bacchic orgies (*Am.* 703) or alcoholic revelry (*Mil.* 856, applied to a drinking vessel). By Cicero's time *bacchari* can be used as a metaphor for raging vandalism (*Har.* 39), but *debacchari* is found only once after Terence, in Horatian lyric (*Carm.* 3.3.55, qua parte *debacchentur* ignes). A near parallel in Greek is the use of ἐκβακχεύεσθαι in Plato, *Resp.* 561a; speaking of the young man's wild oats, he qualifies, ἂν εὐτυχῆς ᾖ, καὶ μὴ πέρα ἐκβακχευθῇ. The verb is also used of poetic frenzy in *Phaedr.* 245a. Plato's usage suggests a Terentian coinage of *de-bacchari* to render ἐκβακχεύεσθαι in the text of Diphilus' Συναποθνῄσκοντες, the original of this scene of the *Adelphoe*, but there are no examples of (ἐκ)-βακχεύεσθαι in New Comedy.

Delibuere. Ph. 856   Satine est si te *delibutum* gaudio reddo? On this Donatus comments "ad animum transtulit quod est corporis, nam delibutus unctus dicitur." From *Ph.* 339, "ten asymbolum venire unctum et lautum e balineis," we can see how being perfumed with oil was associated with a feeling of luxury and confort, just as this practice lies behind the use of *nitidus* and *nitor* in praise of sleek grooming and elegant style (see p. 172 below). But the metaphor here is far more bold, and I have found nothing approaching it in Greek.

Depectere. Hau. 950–1   egone si vivo adeo exornatum dabo/adeo *depexum* ut dum viverit mei semper meminerit. For *depectere* as a symbol of a beating, cf. Plaut. *Capt.* 896, fusti *pectito*; *Rud.* 661, leno pugnis *pectitur*. The ironic use of *exornare* here in association with *depectere* suggests grooming, in contrast with the neutral usage of *ornare* at *Ad.* 176, *ornatus* esses ex tuis virtutibus, or Plaut. *Rud.* 183, 488, ad hoc exemplum *ornatum* "in this condition," and 730, ita ego te hinc *ornatum* mittam tu ipsus te ut non noveris.

Deperire. Hau. 525   Minimeque miror Clinia hanc si *deperit*. This is the only example from Terence of *deperire* used in the sense of *amare*, a colloquialism common in Plautus: cf. *Am.* 517, hic te exflictim *deperit*; *Bac.* 470, meretricem indigne *deperit*; *Cas.* 107, istam ... quam tu *deperis*, etc. Plautus, but not Terence, uses *perire* in the same sense, more often intransitively "to die of love," but for the transitive use, cf. *Poen.* 96, 1075, earum hic alteram *ecflictim perit*. Heusch, *op. cit.*, pp. 74–5, shows that active *deperire* is colloquial in its use by Catullus (35.12; 100.2), whereas the passive and intransitive *deperditus esse* is acceptable in the epic style of 64 (119). Compare Terence's use of the adverb *perdite* with *amare* (*ardere*?) in *Hau.* 97 and *Ph.* 82 with Catullus 45.3; 104.3. It may be significant that his only example of *deperire* is spoken by a slave. (See also p. 8 for a discussion of *ardere* in *Ph.* 82.)

Derivare. Ph. 322   in me omnem iram *derivem* senis. This is one of the very few agricultural metaphors in Terence (see also s.v. *obserere*). The image of diverting water by an irrigation channel is used in *Truc.* 563–4 by a slave justifying the diversion of his master's funds: nam hoc adsimilest quasi *de fluvio qui aquam derivat* sibi:/nisi *derivetur, tamen ea aqua omnis abeat in mare.* Compare also Cic. *Att.* 2.16.1, nam omnis expectatio largitionis agrariae in agrum Campanum videtur esse *derivata* (surely word-play is intended here?), and 4.3.2, poterat infitiari, poterat in alios *derivare* (sc. crimen). Here, as in Terence, the object is an evil to be averted.

Devincire. An. 561   consuetudine et/coniugio liberali *devinctum*; *Hau.* 208, ubi animus semel se cupiditate *devinxit* mala; *Hau.* 394, hoc beneficio ... *devinctum.* This is a standard figurative use of the verb; cf. Pl. *As.* 285, nostro *devinxit* beneficio, 850, istoc me facto tibi *devinxti* ... Terence uses the image of binding both for friendship or obligation, and at *Hau.* 208 in the erotic sense of, e.g., *Bac.* 181, ita me vadatum amore *vinctumque* attines. For the bonds of friendship, cf. Cic. *Att.* 6.2.1, me vel plurima *vincla* tecum summae coniunctionis optare, etsi sunt amoris *artissima*; tantum abest ut ego ex eo quo *astricti* sumus *laxari* aliquid velim. *Devincire*, however, is the most conventional form; cf. *Fam.* 1.7.3; 1.9.21; 3.13.2; 6.10.2; 6.11.1, etc.

Dilapidare. Ph. 897   priu' quam *dilapidet* nostras triginta minas. Cf. Ribbeck, *Com. Inc.* fr. 38, cur te dedecoras, famam cur maculas tuam/cur rem *dilapidas*, quam miser *exstruxit* labor? Thus the metaphor seems to be architectural.

Discruciare. See s.v. *crux.*

Dissignare. Ad. 87   modo quid *dissignavit.* (The reading of Nonius p. 96 and some Terence Mss.) Scholars, whether they read *dissignare* here or *designare* with Bembinus and E, agree that this passage is related to *Mos.* 413, quae *dissignata* sunt et facta nequiter, and Hor. *Ep.* 1.5.16, quid non *dissignavit* ebrietas. Dziatzko-Kauer, *Terentius Adelphoe²* (Vienna 1903), p. 150, relate v87 to the *dissignatores*, the Roman ushers of theatre and funeral. They assume that *dissignare* was used figuratively to describe a "nasty piece of work"; thus

Ad. 87 would be equivalent to "What is his latest piece of dirty work?" This is perhaps more convincing than any other attempt to explain *dissignare/designare* in these passages. If so, here, as at *Hec.* 180, neque *lites* inter eas, *postulatio* numquam, and 414, aliquo mihist hinc *ablegandus*, we may have instances of Roman legal and official terms used in imagery, but it should be noted that this category of metaphor in Terence is usually confined to the most obvious concepts.

Effundere. Ad. 991 *effundite*, emite, facite quod vobis lubet, cf. *ibid.*, 133, *profundat*, perdat, pereat. In both cases the choice of prefix is motivated by the desire for alliteration. Neither verb is used by Plautus of squandering spendthrifts, but compare the same root in *Mer.* Prol. 56–8; ea quae ipsus optuma/omnis labores invenisset perferens/amoris vi *diffunditari* ac didier. The image is conventional by the time of Cicero; cf. *S. Rosc.* 5, per luxuriam *effundere* et consumere; *Fam.* 2.16.1, gratiam effundere; 5.5.3, profundere ac perdere.

Effuttire. See s.v. *rima*.

Emungere. Ph. 862 *emunxi* argento senes. This is a traditional comic metaphor; cf. Pl. *Bac.* 701, 1101, miserum me esse auro *emunctum*; *Epid.* 494, qui me *emunxti mucidum* minumi preti, *Mos.* 1109–10, probe/med *emunxti*. : : vide sis, satine recte: num *mucci fluont*? In Lucil. 881M, quovis posse me *emungi bolo*, the metaphor is incongruously combined with *bolus* (q.v.). McGlynn, 1, p. 162 quotes Men. fr. 427K, γέρων ἀ[πε]μέμυκτ' ἄθλιος, λέμφος, and Pollux 2.78 on ἀπομύττειν in Greek comedy. *Emungere* is absent from Cicero's letters, and in Horace *Ars.* 238 is intended as a reminiscence of comic language.

Evolvere. Eu. 723, *Ph.* 824 me *evolvere* ex his turbis. With this compare the standard phrase, *se ex turba expedire*, in *Ad.* 614. This use of *evolvere* is not found in Plautus, who uses the verb (*a*) of killing, *Men.* 903, quem … vita *evolvam* sua, and (*b*) of unearthing money, *Ps.* 317, *evolvam* id argentum tibi. Terence employs *revolvere* in a related image in *Hec.* 691; in eandem vitam te *revolutum* denuo. The metaphor almost certainly has its origin in hunting and snaring; thus in Xenophon, *Cynegetica*, 8.8, ἐκκυλίνδειν is used of animals escaping from the *nets*; its opposite, ἐγκυλίνδειν, provides a metaphor for the young man ensnared in love affairs at *Mem.* 1.2.22, ἐγκυλίνδειν εἰς ἔρωτας. Xenophon elsewhere uses ἐμπίπτειν in analogies drawn between love and the chase; cf. *Mem.* 2.1.4, τοῖς θηράτροις ἐμπίπτουσιν and 3.11.10, δίκτυα ἱστᾶσιν εἰς τοὺς ἀτραπούς …

ἵνα ἐμπίπτοντες συμποδιζῶνται. In Menander[1] εἰς ἔρωτα ἐμπίπτειν is the normal phrase; cf. *Heros* 5, *Epitr.* 6. The Latin equivalents, *incidere* and its opposite *se expedire*, are so common that where they are not developed by any other word with snaring associations (e.g. *Hec.* 288, *Ad.* 614) the original meaning of the metaphor is probably forgotten. Compare however with the above use of *se evolvere, se expedire* in *Ph.* 823 and Pl. *Per.* 458, lenonem ita *intricatum* dabo/ut ipsus sese qua *se expediat* nesciat; or Cicero *Verr.* 2.2.101, videte *in quot se laqueos induerit, quorum ex nullo se umquam expediet*.[2]

Evomere. Hec. 515, *Ad.* 312, 510   Terence uses this image of expressing anger or indignation, with the notion of obtaining relief from distress; cf. *Hec.* 515, hoc omne quod mihi aegrest *evomam*. It is not found in Plautus or Cicero's letters, belonging rather to the vehement exaggeration of invective: Cic. *Mil.* 78, ne ... odio inflammatus ... haec in illum *evomere* videar; *Phil.* 5.20. However it occurs with a different connotation, that of carefree "blurting out" in Ennius' description of Servilius Geminus' relationship with his confidant, 240–41V, et cuncta malaque et bona dictu/*evomeret*. The affinity of this passage with Ter. *Eun.* 401–7 has been noticed by Otto Skutsch, *Studia Enniana* (London 1968), p. 93. In Terence, at 406 corresponding to Enn. 240–1V, there is the exceptional verb *exspuere*; quasi ubi illam *exspueret* miseriam ex animo. It is probable that Menander in this section of the *Kolax* was parodying the themes of Ennius' source, and that in both the metaphor occurred. Skutsch posits ἐξερυγγάνω[3] as the verb of the originals, since it is used by Callimachus in a similar context fr. 714.4 Pf. (cf. *Aitia* 75.7 Pf.). From New Comedy we may compare *Diphilus* KII, p. 554, fr. 43[21], λαλῶν τὰ ναῦλα κὰι δάνει' ἐρυγγάνων (here close to Ennius' mild sense of *evomere*). But why did Terence here choose *exspuere* instead of his usual verb *evomere*? He may have been adapting his language to Gnatho's coarse nature. (The only contemporary use of *exspuere* is vulgar and facetious: *Ps.* 76, non queo lacrimam exorare (sc. oculos) ut *exspuant* unam modo.) On the other hand, *exspuere*

---

1 On the use of metaphors from hunting and snaring in Greek Comedy and prose of the fifth–fourth centuries B.C., see C.J. Classen, *Untersuchung zu Platons Jagdbildern* (Berlin 1960), pp. 20–5. See also above pp. 39–41 and notes 27, 29.

2 He returns to the same metaphor: *Verr.* 2.5.151, si ex *his te laqueis exueris* ac te aliqua via ac ratione *explicaris, in illas tibi maiores plagas incidendum est*. For Cicero's use of snare-imagery, see chap. 5 *Beyond Sermo Familiaris*, p. 116 and note 3; 132.

3 The literal equivalent in Latin, *eructare*, is metrically inconvenient, but even in prose it is not used in this sense except at Cic. *Cat.* 2.10, Catilinarii ... *eructant* sermonibus suis caedem, where the context shows that literal belching was intended.

used figuratively as in Terence occurs several times in Senecan tragedy (*Tro.* 1169, *Thy.* 245, *Phoen.* 44) which might suggest that, like the more abstract synonym *expectorare* (Enn. *Sc.* 23v, Accius, *Tr.* 301, 595), it was part of the vocabulary of early tragedy, and was here parodied[4] by Terence. Whatever the stylistic tone of *exspuere*, as distinct from *evomere*, it does convey deliberate, rather than involuntary, vomiting; it is perhaps this psychological aspect of the verb which has motivated Terence's preference in *Eu.* 406.

Excidere. An. 423 Erus uxore *excidit*. On this Donatus comments, quod Graeci dicunt ἀπέτυχεν. The fact is that both ἀποτυγχάνειν and ἐκπίπτειν are used of missing or being deprived of a desirable thing, but the latter at any rate would not have a personal object. The imagery of *An.* 423 is related to *Hau.* 250, 851a, quanta de spe *decidi* – the wife too is a kind of prospect – and the exceptional use of the personal noun, without any preposition, is probably intended to reflect Davus' earthly realism; the (unwanted) wife is treated as a thing. By contrast, Pl. *Men.* 667, ex hac familia me plane *excidisse* intelligo, can be taken as a physical image, "I realize I have been thrown out of this household." *Excidere* acts as the passive of *eicere*, as ἐκπίπτειν does for ἐκβάλλειν.

Excruciare. See s.v. *crux.*

Excutere. Hau. 167 Lacrimas *excussit* mihi. Cf. Pl. *Capt.* 419. ut lacrimas *excutiunt* mihi. This idiom is common to both authors, but Terence avoids extravagances like Pl. *Aul.* 151–2: quia mihi misero *cerebrum excutiunt/tua* dicta, soror; *Mer.* 576, utine adveniens *vomitum excutias* mulieri. The verb is typical of comedy's tendency to give energy to language by the suggestion of violence.

Exedere. See s.v. *comedere.*

Exornare. See s.v. *depectere.*

Exsculpere. Eu. 712 Possumne ego hodie ex te *exsculpere*/verum? cf. Pl. *Cist.* 541; vix *exsculpsi* ut diceret. The same verb, (used literally of gouging out an eye in *Ph.* 189) occurs in Lucil. fr. 70, nomen patriamque rogando ... *exsculpo* and 286M. Both instances in comedy occur in plays adapted from

---

4 There is a parody of Ennian tragedy at *Eu.* 590, according to Donatus *ad loc.* Skutsch, *op. cit.*, pp. 177 f. argues that *Eu.* 590 quotes the opening of Ennius' *Alcumena* prologue.

Menander, but I have found no similar image in Menander or New Comedy
which could have suggested this figurative use. In subsequent Latin authors
the word has only its literal meaning.

Exsercire. Hau. 143   sumptum *exsercirent* suom. This correction of Mss
exercerent, based on a scholiasts' gloss, is a ἅπαξ λεγόμενον, but compare the
more common *sarcire*, applied to making good losses, in Cic. *Fam.* 1.9.5
(*sarcire damna*); 3.1.1. (*sarcire usuram temporis*), and 13.62 used absolutely.
Pl. *Trin.* 317: *sarta tecta tua habui praecepta*, is a different image, based on the
common use of *sarta tecta* for the maintenance of property; so *sarcire* occurs
literally in *Mos.* 115, 147, of patching a house.

Exspuere. See s.v. *evomere.*

Exsulare. Eu. 610   domo *exsulo* nunc. metuo fratrem, is a comic exaggeration
of the conventional *exclusus sum*. The finite verb *exsulare* occurs only once in
Plautus: *Per.* 555, perfidia et peculatus ex urbe ... si *exsulant*, again figuratively,
and here in tragic style. The common phrase *exsulatum abire*, is itself often a
metaphor for disappearing or perishing; cf. *Mer.* 43, res *exsulatum* ad illam
clam abibat patris; 593, *exsulatum* abiit salus. It is also applied to the absconding
business-man in *Cur.* 559 and *Rud.* 325. Since Gk. φεύγειν covers both volun-
tary flight and formal exile, the Latin texts may offer a humorous formalization
of what was neutral in Greek.

Fenestra. Hau. 481   quantam *fenestram* ad nequitiam *patefeceris*. This seems to
be an entirely original metaphor in Terence. I have found no precedents in
Greek, and in Latin, the first figurative use of *fenestra* for an opening admitting
trouble is Suetonius' citation from Tiberius (*Tib.* 28), si hanc *fenestram*
aperueritis, nihil aliud agi sinetis. But *ianua* is used similarly by Cic. *Red.*
Sen. 14: non *ianua* receptis, sed *pseudothyro* intromissis voluptatibus. For a favourable application of the image, cf. *de Orat.* 1.204, vos ad ea quae cupitis perven-
turos, ab hoc *aditu ianuaque patefacta.*

Flos. Eu. 318   Anni? : : Anni sedecim. : : *flos* ipse. Flos, unqualified, in the
sense of *flos aetatis*, occurs in Catullus, 17.14, *viridissimo ...flore* puella, but elsewhere it is usually qualified by a genitive. Ἄνθος with or without ἥβης, is more
common in all periods of Greek, particularly in erotic literature; cf. Theogn.
994, παῖς καλὸν ἄνθος ἔχων; Plato, *Symp.* 183e and passim; *Resp.* 601b, ὅταν

αὐτὰ τὸ ἄνθος προλίπῃ. From Menander compare the description of a pretty serving girl in *Dysk*. 950–1, προσώπου/ἄνθος κατεσκιασμένη.

Foro uti. Ph. 79   Scisti *uti foro*. "You knew how to handle your market." Donatus' comment shows that this is a commercial, not a forensic allusion. The Greek equivalent ἀγορᾷ χρῆσθαι occurs literally in Men. *Sicyonius* (Kassel) v7.[5] Pl. *Mos.* 1051, *venire in meo foro* is probably to be interpreted on the same lines as *Bac.* 814–15, stulte, stulte, nescis nunc *venire* te/atque in eopse astas lapide ut praeco praedicat; the person betrayed is described as sold into slavery – and in his own territory.

Fugitivus. Hau. 677–8   Retraham hercle opinor ad me/idem ego illuc hodie *fugitivum* argentum tamen. The use of *retrahere* for recovering runaway slaves and deserters is technical: cf. Caes. *B.G.* 5.7; Sall. *Cat.* 39.5; 47.4 ex fuga retractus; Livy 25.7.14, comprensos ... retraxerunt. The personification of the money is more characteristic of Plautine verbal humour than of Terence. Such "*Belebung des Unbelebtes*"[6] is a special talent of Plautus. Things are often treated as slaves; cf. *As.* 386, *Cur.* 40, and (closer to *Hau.* 677–8) *St.* 312, nimis vellem hae *fores erum fugissent*, ea caussa ut haberent ma ⟨lum mag⟩ num, and *ibid.*, 751, vapulat peculium, actum est : : *fugit libertas hoc caput.* At *Cist.* 731, cistellula hinc mi ... *evolavit*, and *Epid.* 34, arma ... *travolaverunt* ad hostes, the objects are depicted as taking flight like a bird, and deserting, respectively. On these passages, Fraenkel, *El. Pl.*, p. 78 n.1 argues that they are purely Plautine fantasy, not derived from the Greek. Personification of things, as opposed to abstractions, is extremely rare in New Comedy. However, it should be noted that the image of the runaway slave is applied by Plato not only to men (Alcibiades of his own flight from Socrates, *Symp.* 216b), but also to the works of Daedalus, and to true opinions as contrasted with permanent knowledge; *Meno* 98a, πολὺν δὲ χρόνον οὐκ ἐθέλουσι παραμένειν, ἀλλὰ δραπετεύουσιν ἐκ τῆς ψυχῆς τοῦ ἀνθρώπου ... ἕως ἄν τις αὐτὰς δήσῃ. The same metaphor is used by Baton, κιιι, 328, fr. 5[14–15], τὸν φρόνιμον ζητοῦντες ἐν τοῖς περιπάτοις/καὶ ταῖς διατριβαῖς ὥσπερ ἀποδεδρακότα. In quoting v.14, Athenaeus at 8.278 reads τὸ φρόνιμον; with this reading we have a personification of the abstract similar

5 In Anaxandrides κιι, p. 137, fr. 3, it is a political allusion, symbolizing the winning of citizenship, and hence attendance in the Assembly.

6 Cf. Fraenkel, *Plautinisches im Plautus*, chap. ιν; the German *Belebung* here is superior to the Italian translation *Personificazione*, because Plautus gives inanimate objects life and movement.

to *Meno* 98a; with the reading of Athenaeus 3.103, τὸν φρόνιμον, a person to person comparison as in *Symp.* 216b. Thus it is possible that in Menander's Ἑαυτὸν Τιμωρούμενος, Terence may have found the imagery in the more casual form of a simile such as has survived in Baton.

Gannire. Ad. 556   quid ille *gannit*? (cf. *Ph.* 1030, habet haec ei quod ... usque ad aurem *ogganiat*). The verb is applied in both passages to grumbling or complaining: Pl. *As.* 422 (the only instance in Plautus), "quin centiens eadem imperem atque *ogganiam*, itaque iam hercle/clamore ac stomacho non queo labori suppeditare," suggests a louder form of nagging, yet Donatus on *Ad.* 556 "veluti ploratus vapulantium," implies something nearer to a howl. Whatever noise is involved, *gannire*, like *latrare* and possibly *ringi*, transfers the behaviour of a dog to humans. With the picture of the nagging wife in *Ph.* 1030, compare *Mil.* 681, in which a wife is seen as an *oblatratrix*, and the allusion to Hecuba, *Men.* 716–8. So also Men. fr. 592κ: τὸ δ᾽ ἐπιδιώκειν, εἴς τε τὴν ὁδὸν τρέχειν/ἔτι λοιδορουμένην, κυνός ἐστ᾽ ἔργον, Ῥόδη.

Gestare. Eu. 402   rex ergo *te in oculis* : : scilicet : : *gestare. Ad.* 709, hicin non *gestandus in sinust*? The phrase *in sinu gestare* is naturally used of cherishing; cf. *Ad.* 563, *in manibus gestare*, of holding a little child, and the metaphor of *Ad.* 709, although without parallel, is unambiguous. But *Eu.* 402 is different, one more example of Gnatho's idiosyncratic vocabulary (cf. s.v. *exspuo, uro, iugulo*), conflating *in oculis habere* with *in sinu gestare*. Plautus uses *gestare* of carrying in the mind at *Bac.* 375; egon ut haec conclusa *gestem* clanculum, but has no usage similar to *Ad.* 709.

Grex. Hau. 245, *Eu.* 1084   ut me in vostrum *gregem* recipiati'; *Ad.* 362, hic de *grege* illost. *Eu.* 1084 shows that *grex*, though familiar, need not be contemptuous in tone. It is more commonly contemptuous in Cicero, but cf. *Att.* 6.1.10, ac vellem te in *tuum veterem gregem rettulisses* – a good parallel for *Eu.* 1084. The intimate use of the word is also shown in the *sermones* of Horace: *Sat.* 2.3.44, and *Ep.* 1.4.16 and 9.13.

Haerere. See s.v. *lutum.*

Impingere. Ph. 439   dicam tibi *impingam* grandem. Plautine instances of this verb show that its normal context is physical violence; cf. *pugna* (pugnum) *impingere*, *Bac.* 800, *Rud.* 710; compedes *impingere*, *Cap.* 734, *Per.* 269. So also

Pompey, in Caelius' letter, *Fam.* 8.8.9, quid si filius meus *fustem* mihi *impingere* volet? Similar to *Ph.* 439 is Cic. *Att.* 6.1.6: *impingit* mihi epistulam Scaptius Bruti (here the letter is a weapon in the dispute); so also Seneca, *Prov.* 6.8; *Ben.* 1.1.7.

Terence reinforces the physical effect of *impingere* by his use of *grandis*, a word properly applied to things, instead of the more general *magnus*.

Ingerere. An. 640   *ingeram* mala multa. On this, Donatus comments *quasi tela.* Cf. Pl. *Bac.* 875, ut tibi mala multa *ingeram*; *Men.* 717, omnia mala *ingerebat* ... ; *Ps.* 359, *ingere* mala multa (which introduces the *flagitatio* scene). This was probably no longer felt as a metaphor in Terence's time. See Usener, *Kleine Schriften*, vol. 4, p. 378 on the association of *ingerere* and *onerare* (q.v. p. 62) with abuse in the *flagitatio* procedure.

Labascere. Eu. 178   *Labascit* victus uno verbo quam cito; *Ad.* 239, *Labascit*, unum hoc habeo. Donatus derives the metaphor from a tree falling under the axe. Plautus uses the same imagery: *Rud.* 1394, salvos sum, leno *labascit*, libertas portenditur, and, more fully, *St.* 521-2:

si res firma, ⟨item⟩ firmi amici sunt, sin res laxe *labat*
itidem amici *conlabascunt.*

Compare also the active form: *Mer.* 403, *labefacto* paullatim, "I'm gradually weakening him."

Lapis. Hau. 831, 917   ni essem *lapis*; *Hec.* 214, me omnino *lapidem* non hominem putas. Donatus quotes Apollodorus' original version of *Hec.* 214, σύ με παντάπασιν ἤγησαι λίθον. The image is common in Plautus as a term of abuse, *Cur.* 197 and *Mer.* 632. *Saxum* in *Eu.* 1085, satis diu *hoc* iam *saxum vorso*, probably carries the same connotation, as well as the allusion to Sisyphus' punishment; cf. Pl. *Mil.* 1024, nullumst hoc stolidius *saxum*. See Otto, *Sprichworter*, p. 185.

Leges. Hau. 998   tam facillime patri' *pacem* in leges *conficiet suas*. The terms of the victor after reconciliation in comedy are seen as clauses of a treaty; cf. *Mer* 1015-16, immo dicamus senibus *legem* censeo/... qua se *lege* teneant contentique sint ...; 1024, haec adeo uti ex hac nocte primum *lex* teneat senes. A similar metaphor expresses the role of the mediator in the final scene: *Mos.* 1126, ego ... solus sum orator datus/qui a patre eius *conciliarem pacem*; Ter.

Hau. 1046, exeo ergo ut *pacem conciliem.* This imagery is developed in Propertius 4.8, of the guilty lover's surrender: supplicibus palmis tum demum ad foedera veni (71) ... : :accipe quae *nostri formula legis* erit (74) ... *indixit leges*: respondi ego *"legibus utar"* (81).

Linea. Eu. 640 certe *extrema linea*/amare haud nihil est. This metaphor has not yet been explained satisfactorily. Otto, p. 194, seems to favour Donatus' second explanation "longis lineis quid fieri," and relates it to the furthest section of spectators in the amphitheatre. The apparently similar phrases in Greek: Eur. *Ant.* fr. 169N, ἐπ' ἀκρὰν ἥκομεν γραμμὴν κακῶν, and Diod. Sic. 17.118, ἡ ἐσχάτη τοῦ βίου γραμμή (cf. Hor. *Ep.* 1.16.79; mors *ultima linea* rerumst) belong to the language of racing, of the line that marks the beginning and end of the track, a context which is familiar in Terence (cf. *Ad.* 860, s.v. *spatium*), and New Comedy, but irrelevant here.

Lucrum. Ph. 246, 251 omne id deputabo esse in *lucro.* Both here (251 parodies 246) and in *Ad.* 816, where *de lucro* is naturally applied to material gain, the phrase is introduced by *praeter spem evenire. Lucrum* is also applied to time gained beyond expectation; cf. *Hec.* 287, omne quod est interea tempu' priu' quam id rescitumst *lucrost* (here Donatus provides the words of Apollodorus [cf. KIII, p. 284, fr. 10], οἱ γὰρ ἀτυχοῦντες τὸν χρόνον κερδαίνομεν, showing that the metaphor was Greek). Plautus, *Mer.* 553–4, id iam *lucrumst*/quod vivis; Cic. *Fam.* 9.17.1, *de lucro* prope iam quadriennium vivimus. In *Fam.* 7.24.1, id ego *in lucris* pono, non ferre hominem pestilentiorem patria sua, the meaning is rather "to count among the profits." *Deputare* in *Ph.* 246, 251 contributes to the metaphor (compare *putare* in the sense of "reckon up" at *Ad.* 208 in a context of literal accounting; and at *Ph.* 718 and *Ad.* 796, rem ipsam *putemus*, used figuratively. This metaphor is more explicit at *Ad.* 855 (see s.v. *subducere*).

Ludere, ludus. Eu. 373 adsis, tangas, *ludas*, propter dormias; 586–7, quia consimilem/*luserat* olim ille *ludum.* In 586–7 Chaerea uses *ludere* and *ludus* of Jupiter's seduction of Danae. The erotic sense of *ludere* is perhaps not yet established in the time of Roman Comedy.[7] In Plautus the only clear examples of this sense of *ludere, ludus,* occur in *Rud.* 426, tum tibi operam *ludo* et deliciae

---

7 Cf. Keith Preston, *op. cit.*, pp. 31–2. On *Eu.* 373, he comments, "We seem to have a sequence in which the verbs increase in boldness, and *ludo* is not so definite here as in later Latin."

dabo, and 468, commodule *ludis*.[8] The use of *ludere* here may be the result of euphemism rather than conscious metaphor. The predominant significance of the root in both Plautus and Terence is trickery and deception (cf. *Ph.* 347, postilla iam ut lubet *ludas* licet). No similarly erotic use of παίζειν and παιγνία occurs in Menander, and Preston, *op. cit.* can give only one example from New Comedy: Ephippus ΚΙΙ, p. 254, fr. 7, a *hetaera* speaks of τοῖς ἡμετέροισι παιγνίοις, again perhaps euphemism or irony. By contrast both παίζειν and παιγνία are common in the erotic epigrams of the Anthology. (For *Ludus, ludere*, etc. in Roman Lyric and Elegy, see Appendix.)

Lupus. Eu. 832   ovem *lupo* commisisti; *Ph.* 506, auribu' teneo *lupum*; *Ad.* 537, *lupus* in fabula. On these proverbial phrases, which have equivalents in Greek, see McGlynn, vol. I, p. 339; Otto, p. 199.

Lutum. Ph. 780   in eodem *luto* haesitas: vorsuram solves. Cf. Pl. *Per.* 535, *tali ut in luto haeream*; *Ps.* 984, nunc *homo in medio lutost*, and the climax of the ox and ass parable of *Aulularia*, act 2, sc. 5, 230, iaceam ego asinus *in luto*. Otto, p. 201, argues that the Terentian passage, obviously the parent of Lactantius 2.8, *in eodem luto haesitans, versura solvis*, is also the source of all later instances. This metaphor probably underlies Demea's comment in *Ad.* 403, metui ne *haereret* hic, since he views Micio's household as a source of folly and corruption. *Haerere* and *caenum* are used of the lover held fast to his place of corruption in Plautus, *Epid.* 191, nam eum audivi *haerere* in amore apud nescio quam fidicinam, and *Bac.* 384, ut eum *ex lutulento caeno* propere hinc eliciat foras. Horace, *Sat.* 2.3.260, *haeret*/invisis foribus, of Phaedria in Terence's *Eunuchus*, could be literal, with the lover clinging to his mistress' door, but is better taken as a metaphor. In 2.7.26, *haeres*/nequiquam *caeno cupiens evellere plantam*, *caenum* is the symbol of self-indulgence that prevents man from following the path of virtue.

Macerare. An. 685   modo tu, anime mi, noli te *macerare*; *ibid.*, 886, quor me excrucio? quor me *macero*? *Eu.* 187, rus ibo; ibi hoc me *macerabo* biduom. This is one of the regular images for anguish, especially lovers' torment; so also Plautus, *Trin.* 225, egomet me coquo[9] et *macero* et defetigo. In *Capt.* 133–4,

---

8 This is, however, a conjecture of Fleckeisen for the Mss *melius*, which Lindsay retains, reading *commodule meliust*.

9 On the culinary associations of *macerare* in imagery apparent in *Trin.* 225, see

ego qui tuo maerore *maceror*/macesco et consenesco et *tabesco* miser (one of several passages in Plautus where *macero* is not in an erotic context), it is combined with the near-synonym *tabesco* (cf. *Cor ... guttatim contabescit, Mer.* 205, and *Ps.* 21, me miseria et cura *contabefacit,* both of lovers' sufferings). *Tabescere* is found only once in Terence, of a girl "quae dolore et miseria/*tabescit*," *Ad.* 602–3. (It is predominantly applied to females in Elegy; see Appendix.) With *tabescere*, Preston, *op. cit.*, p. 48, compares τήκομαι in the erotic epigrams, *A.P.*5, 210, 259. There is one instance in New Comedy: Euboulus, κΙΙ, p. 200, fr. 104, ἔρωτι κατατετηκώς.

Macula. Ad. 954 Hanc *maculam* nos decet/effugere. For *macula* of moral stain or guilt, cf. Pl. *Poen.* 198–9, inest amoris *macula* huic homini in pectore/ sine damno magno quae elui ne utiquam potest. (In *Capt.* 841, iam ego ex corpore exigam omnes *maculas* maerorum tibi, there is no notion of moral blame; the image is suggested by the idea of Hegio's mourning – *squalor*, and the alliterative effect to be obtained.) *Macula* is twice associated with public censure in Lucilius: 896M, deliciis *maculam atque ignominiam* imponere, and 1033M, *maculas notasque*; compare the verb *maculare* in an unknown Palliatawriter, Ribbeck, Com. Inc. 38, famam cur *maculas* tuam? Compare also Catullus 57.3–5, *maculae* pares utrisque ... *impressae resident nec eluentur.* For the use of *macula* as an abusive epithet in Cicero, see p. 133 and n. 36.

On *Ph.* 973, venias *lautum peccatum tuom,* Donatus comments *ut labem vel maculam* (compare *lavere* here with *eluere,* the vox propria with *macula, Poen.* 199, Cat. 57.5, above). However, the use of *lavere* here has a secondary function of anticipating the use of *lacrimis exstillare* in 975; for *lacrimis lavere,* cf. Pl. *Ps.* 21.

Mordere. Eu. 411 omnes ... *mordere clanculum*; 445, par pro pari referto quod eam *mordeat; Ad.* 807, si id te *mordet,* sumptum filii quem faciunt. Only *Eu.* 411 refers to actual abuse or back-biting.[10] *Eu.* 445 and *Ad.* 807, with their emphasis on the victim's distress, are close to the Ciceronian usage; cf. *Fam.* 3.12.2, neque non me tamen *mordet* aliquid; *Att.* 6.2.8, *morderi* te interdum quod non simul sis; 13.12.1, valde me *momorderunt* epistulae tuae. In the solemn vein of

---

D. West, *Reading Horace,* pp. 65–68, discussing Horace *Carm.* 1.13.8, *quam lentis macerer ignibus.* The parallel use of *coquere* in *Trin.* 225 is absent from Terence, but cf. Enn. *Ann.* 335–6 V curam .../quae nunc te coquit et versat in pectore fixa, and West's comments (*loc. cit.*).

10 This usage is classical; cf. Hor. *Carm.* 4.3.16, iam dente minus *mordeor* invido; Ovid, *Trist.* 4.10.123–4, nec ... livor iniquo/ullum de nostris dente *momordit* opus.

Att. 12.18.1, he speaks of *recordationes ... quae quasi morsu quodam dolorem efficiunt.* The idiom was common in all genres, and *Att.* 13.20.4, where Cicero substitutes the Greek δεδῆχθαι for *morderi*, shows that he was aware of the identity of the metaphor in both languages. A similar use of *remordere* occurs in *Lucr.* 3.827; 4.1135, and Verg. *Aen.* 1.261, *quando haec te cura remordet,* whereas in these authors *mordere* is always literal. The metaphor is absent from Plautus. In Menander the equivalent δάκνειν is common in the sense of *Eu.* 411; cf. *Sam.* 141K, δακὼν δ'ἀνασχοῦ, and 169, 172, but compare with *Ad.* 807, *Kith.* fr. 2K, τὸ κουφότατον σε τῶν κακῶν πάντων δάκνει/πενία.

Obsaturare. Hau. 968 ne tu propediem/... istius *obsaturabere.* McGlynn compares Pl. *St.* 18, *haec res vitae me, soror, saturant.* Both occur in plays derived from Menander, and it is remarkable that there are no other instances in Roman comedy, unless we compare the erotic use of *satietas* in Pl. *Am.* 472, *Mos.* 196, Ter. *Ph.* 834, *quo pacto satietatem amoris ait se velle absumere?* There is no comparable use of κορέννυμι or κόρος in Menander.

Obserere. Hau. 294 anus ... *pannis obsita*; *Eu.* 236, eum sentum squalidum aegrum, pannis arnisque obsitum, "Overgrown and beset with rags and age." In Men. fr. 130K compared by McGlynn, there is no counterpart to *obserere.* Donatus identifies *Eu.* 236 as *metaphora ex agro*, and the verb is, of course, agricultural. But when Plautus uses *obserere* in *Trin.* 530-1 "frumenti quom alibi messis maxumast/tribus tantis ille minu' reddit quam *obseveris* ... /em istic oportet *obseri* mores malos," the hostile force of the prefix is absent, whereas *Men.* 756, *consitus sum senectute* presents the same image as *Eu.* 236. *Obserere*, however, reappears in this usage at Verg. *Aen.* 7.790, *Io saetis obsita*, and 8.307, *rex obsitus aevo.* Norden on *Aen.* 6.462, starting from *loca senta situ*, the only other instance of *sentus* besides *Eu.* 236, deduced for both *sentus* and this use of *obsitus* in Terence and Virgil an origin in early tragedy. If *sentus* is, in fact, related to *sentis* (bramble – cf. the gloss ἀκανθώδης), it extends the image implied by *obsitus* in the *Eunuchus* passage.

Obtundere. Hau. 879 ohe iam desine, uxor, deos gratulando *obtundere*; cf. *An.* 348, *Eu.* 554, *Ph.* 515, *Ad.* 113, and *tundere, Hec.* 123, *tundendo* atque odio denique effecit. Although Donatus on *An.* 348 identifies this as *translatio a fabris, qui saepe repetunt aliquid malleo et idem obtundunt atque hebetant*, the idiom is fixed in Plautus; cf. *Cist.* 118, aures graviter *obtundo* tuas, and *Po.* 434, pergin auris *tundere*, and is so common in Terence that it had probably ceased to be a living and felt metaphor. Compare from Cicero's intimate letters, Lucceius *Fam.* 5.14.3, cupio ... non *obtundere* te; *Att.* 8.1.4, tam longis te epistulis non *obtunderem*. The *Cistellaria* reference might suggest a common basis in Menander, but the equivalents in Menander are rather ἀποκναίειν, *Mis.* fr. 9κ, *Flor.* 83κ (with which cf. *conterere* in, e.g., Pl. *Epid.* 609, *conteris* tu/tua me oratione, mulier) or κατακόπτειν, *Sam.* 70, ἱκανὸς γὰρ εἰ/λαλῶν κατακόψαι πάντα; ibid. 77, κατακόπτεις γέ με/εἰ λανθάνει σε, φ[ί]λταθ' εἰς περικόμματα.

Occludere. An. 557   dumque eius lubido *occlusast* contumeliis. This is close to Plautus' use of the verb in the phrase *linguam occludere, Mil.* 605, *Trin.* 188 (cf. *Trin.* 222, *occlusiorem* habent *stultiloquentiam*). Thus *occludere* is a more vivid synonym for *comprimere, continere, cohibere*. The idiom seems to be confined to Comedy, and I have found no similar expression in the Greek material.

Olfacere. Ad. 396–7   aut non sex totis mensibus/prius *olfecissem* quam ille quicquam coeperet. Unlike *subolere (Hau.* 899, *Ph.* 474, cf. Pl. *Trin.* 615, 698, etc.), *olfacere* is not used figuratively elsewhere in Comedy. It seems likely that Terence has deliberately chosen the coarser form of the metaphor to characterize Demea's ἀγροικία. ὀσφραίνομαι is only used literally in New Comedy.

Onerare. An. 827   *onerare* iniuriis; *Ph.* 841–3, quantis commoditatibus/quam subito meo ero Antiphoni ope vostra hunc *onerastis* diem/ ... nosque ... *exonerastis* metu. The first instance is conventional; cf. Pl. *Cist.* 556, *Mer.* 978, *Ps.* 357, *onera* hunc maledictis, and the note on *ingerere* above. This is the only figurative use of *onerare* in Cicero's correspondence; cf. *onerare contumelius; Fam.* 5.3.1; *malis* (= abuse) *Fam.* 9.20.1, *mendaciis, Fam.* 3.10.7. In the Phormio passage, Terence seems to combine two Plautine uses of the image; for the *onerare/exonerare* word-play and the personal object laden with good fortune, cf. *St.* 531–2, hodien *exoneremus* navem frater? : : clementer volo./nos potius *oneremus* nosmet vicissim voluptatibus (also *Capt.* 827, *Mil.* 677, *St.* 276). The quasi-personification of *dies* as object in 842 is a reversal of the more drastic idiom in Pl. *Capt.* 464, 774, ita me amoenitate amoena amoenus *oneravit* dies.[11]

11 For the Plautine personification of *dies* see Fraenkel, *El.Pl.* pp. 101–4.

Onus. Ph. 93–4 numquam aeque ... ac modo/paupertas mihi *onu'* visumst. This is surely Greek. Men. *Kith.* fr. 2 called poverty κουφότατον/τῶν κακῶν πάντων – the opposite of what is claimed here, but for the burden of poverty, cf. *Monost.* 450, πενίας βαρύτερον οὐδέν ἐστι φορτίον. In New Comedy old age (Anaxandr. κιι, p. 159, fr. 53), fortune (Apollodorus κιιι, p. 294, fr. 17), and wives (Antiphanes κιι, p. 134, fr. 329) are similarly treated as burdens upon a man.

Os. Eu. 806 eam esse dico liberam : : hem : : civem Atticam : : hui : : meam sororem : : *os durum*! (cf. *Ad.* 864: clemens placidu', nulli laedere *os*, adridere omnibus.) *Eunuchus* 806 is not very far from the modern idiom "the cheek of it." As Donatus points out, this is merely a stronger version of *os impudens*, literal and visible at *Eu.* 597, 838, and hardly metaphorical in comparison with the use of *os* unqualified in Pl. *Mil.* 189, *os habet*, linguam, perfidiam, or the colloquial language of Vatinius, Cic. *Fam.* 5.10a.2, si mehercules Appi *os haberem*. However it would be mistaken to see this usage as a vulgarism. Cicero uses *os* not only in letters (*Fam.* 9.8.1. nosti profecto *os* illius adulescentioris Academiae) but in the urbane conversation of *de Oratore*: 1.175; 2.29, quoniam ... studium dicendi, nisi accessit *os*, nullum potest esse, docebo vos, discipuli, id quod ipse non didici. Here there is probably a pun: the figurative sense of "effrontery" is primary; the rhetorical sense of "style" or "delivery" (as in *de Or.* 3.221, *in ore sunt omnia*) is latent.

Palaestra. Ph. 484 eccum ab sua *palaestra* exit foras. Just as the pimp's establishment is Phaedria's daily exercise ground, so in Pl. *Bac.* 66 ff., Pistoclerus calls the house of the *hetaerae*, huiusmodi ... *palaestram*/ubi damnis desudascitur ... and extends the comparison to the equipment of the brothel and that of the wrestling ground.[12] Elsewhere in Plautus, *Aul.* 410, me iste habuit senex *gymnasium*, and *As.* 297, *gymnasium flagri*, the beaten slave is the exercise

12 For metaphors based on the *palaestra* and *gymnasium* in amatory contexts, see Preston, *op. cit.*, pp. 51–3; he establishes that these were current in Greek erotic literature, and that the analogy of *Bac.* 66 ff. almost certainly had a similar form in the Menandrian original. He quotes as parallels for *palaestra* in *Ph.* 484, *A.P.* 5.259, Theocr. 7.125, and from New Comedy, Antiphanes, κιι, p. 135, fr. 332, γερόντειαι παλαίστραι, but acknowledges that "in all these cases the word is apparently somewhat more drastic than the Phormio passage." In fact, neither in *Ph.* 484 nor *Bac.* 66 ff. is there any emphasis on physical sexual activity, but merely an intended contrast between the *palaestra* as the proper place for a young man to spend his time, and its improper substitute – a point illustrated by Philolaches' regrets in *Mos.* 149–55.

ground of the lash or the lasher. Terence's image is found also in Cicero, *Att.* 5.13.1, *utemur ea palaestra quam a te didicimus*, but in the more abstract sense of training, which *palaestra* often represents in the philosophical works; e.g. *de Orat.* 1.73, *didicerintne palaestram an nesciant.*

Pascere. Ph. 85   restabat aliud nil nisi oculos *pascere. Pascere* is not metaphorical in Plautus: for oculos *pascere*, cf. Cic. *Verr.* 2.5.65, eius cruciatu atque supplicio *pascere oculos; Phil.* 11.8, ut in eius corpore lacerando ... oculos *paverit* suos. The use of *pascere* is striking, with a more vivid physical impact than the comparable oculos *explere, Verr.* 2.4.47, or *satiare, Mil.* 58.

Perreptare. Ad. 715   *perreptavi* usque omne oppidum. While the verb graphically expresses Demea's elderly gait, it also follows the Plautine use of the same image in *Am.* 1011, omnis plateas *perreptavi* (with an enumeration of places searched) and *Rud.* 233, omnia iam circumcursavi atque omnibu' latebris *perreptavi*/quaerere conservam. One may perhaps compare the use of καθέρπειν in Aristophanes, *Ran.* 129, 485, but it should be noted that the only use of ἕρπειν (καθέρπειν is not found) in Menander, fr. 679κ, νῦν δ'ἕρπε ἀπ'οἴκων τῶνδε, is a simple equivalent of ἰέναι, parodying tragic diction.

Praesens deus. Ph. 345   ea qui praebet, non tu hunc habeas *praesentem deum?* In presenting the parasite's patron as a θεὸς ἐπιφανής Terence goes further than anything in Plautus, who limits himself to *Men.* 138, teneo dextera *genium meum*, or the conventional *meus rex* of *As.* 919, *Capt.* 92, *St.* 455. The Greek θεὸς ἐν ἀνθρώποις, applied in all seriousness by Aristotle (*Pol.* 3.8.1) to the ideally good and wise man, seems to have become a cliché of eulogy in New Comedy, and is freely bestowed by Antiphanes (fr. 209κ) on the successful poet. This is probably the reason for the surprising frequency of such claims in Terence (see Appendix, p. 90 for its occurrence in amatory contexts). *Men.* fr. 1κ, τὸ γὰρ τρέφον με τοῦτ' ἐγὼ κρίνω θεόν, quoted by McGlynn, refers to the speaker's native land, and is not really comparable.

In proclivi esse. An. 701   id faciam, *in proclivi* quod est. The same force ot *proclivis* in the sense of sloping downhill, and hence easy, is found in Pl. *Capt.* 336 (cf. Lindsay, *ed. maior, ad loc.*), "tam hoc quidem tibi in *proclivi* quam imber est quando pluit," whereas in *Mil.* 1018, *Rud.* 1132, ex *proclivi planam* facere,[13] Plautus contrasts the easy level ground with the difficult

13 The declension of the adjective appears to be still indeterminate in Plautus; at *Mil.*

uphill slope. The latter sense of the adjective is not attested in Cicero. For *proclive* "easy" cf. *Off.* 2.69, *dictu quidem est proclive*, and *Fam.* 6.10.6, in a context of prolonged metaphor of falling and sloping:

> et ipse ... cotidie *delabi* ad aequitatem, et ipsa causa ea est ut iam simul cum re publica quae in perpetuum *iacere* non potest necessario reviviscat ... quae quoniam in temporum *inclinationibus* saepe parvis posita sunt, omnia *momenta* observabimus neque ullum praetermittemus tui iuvandi et *levandi* locum. itaque illud alterum, quod dixi, litterarum genus cotidie mihi ut spero fiet *proclivius*.

Profundere. Ad. 133; see s.v. *effundere*.

Protelare. Ph. 213   ne te iratus suis saevidicis dictis *protelet*. Dziatzko-Hauler, *ad loc.*, see the whole phrase as a parody of tragic style. On their interpretation *protelare* here as at Turpilius 90R, indignissime patria *protelatum* esse saevitia patris, implies driving out; cf. Festus, p. 267L., *protelare: longe propellere*. Although the verb, like the adverb *protelo*, probably derived from the *protelum* (ἔξαμπρον), a rope to which oxen were harnessed one behind the other, Walde-Hofmann,[3] II. 376, believe Terence's use here assumes an original derivation from *telum*. If so, the underlying metaphor is military, not agricultural.

Provincia. Ht. 516   idcirco huic nostro traditast *provincia*; *Ph.* 72, O Geta, *provinciam*/cepisti duram. These examples merely continue the Plautine tradition by which *provincia* was applied in grandiose language to any task, particularly that of a slave. Compare Pl. *Ps.* 158, te cum securi caudicali praeficio *provinciae*; *St.* 698, cape *provinciam*/ : : quid istuc est *provinciae*? : : utrum Fontine an Libero/*imperium* te inhibere mavis; *Trin.* 189–90, nunc ego te quaeso ut me opera et consilio iuves,/communicesque *hanc* mecum *meam provinciam* (here addressed to a free citizen by another citizen). The related and equally common use of *imperium* in Plautus is confined to serious use (especially of the *patria potestas*) in Terence.

Rabies. Eu. 301   ludum iocumque dices fuisse illum alterum/praeut huius *rabies* quae dabit. *Rabies* is not used elsewhere in Plautus or Terence for the

---

1018 the second declension form *proclivo* is attested; in *Rud.* 1132 the text is damaged and the form due to a supplement.

frenzy of love. (In Plautus *rabies, rabiosus*, denote real madness, or are associated with dogs as a symbol of savage anger; cf. *Men.* 936.) The coarse word here is probably chosen to fit the speaker's character; he is the rascally slave Parmeno. The use of *rabies* for sexual passion in Lucretius, 4.1083, 1117, is not intended as a metaphor, but as a true description, but cf. Hor. *Epod.* 12.9 (perhaps the most savagely coarse of the *iambi*), dum pene soluto/indomitam properat *rabiem* sedare. (See Appendix, for the use of words denoting madness to describe love and the lover in Elegy and Lyric.)

Reflectere. Ad. 306–7   quem neque fides neque iusiurandum ... /repressit neque *reflexit*. Although *flectere* may occur once in Plautus (if Ussing's conjecture *flexi ingenium meum* is retained at *Mer.* 668 for the meaningless *feci* of the Mss) with a personal subject and the mind as object, Terence's use of abstract subject and personal object here makes the image original. For the conventional usage cf. Cicero, *ad Brut.* 24.11, si *flexerit* adversus alios iudicium suum; *Att.* 11.18.2, ut eam (sc. iram Antoni) *flectas* te rogo. The metaphor, derived from chariot racing, is common at least in Plato of bending the will, persuading to relent, etc., cf. *Prot.* 320, *Resp.* 494e, *Menex.* 244e, ἀλλ' ἐκάμφθη κὰι ἐβοήθησε, *Laches* 192e, εἴ τις ... μὴ κάμπτοιτο ἀλλὰ καρτεροῖ.[14]

Retrahere. See s.v. *fugitivus.*

Retundere. Hau. 945   ut eius animum qui nunc luxuria et lascivia/diffluit *retundam* redigam ... One thing is clear about this, the only use of *retundere* in Terence: the imagery of beating or blunting (as in *obtundere, q.v.*) is incompatible with the liquid implications of *diffluere*. Since the speaker is the pompous Chremes, the absurdity is no doubt intentional. A similar use of *retundere* occurs in Cic. *Fam.* 12.14.3 (from Lentulus Spinther), quorum improbitatem aliquando *retundere* utile est rei publicae; cf. also Caelius, *Fam.* 8.6.1, Appius *rettudit* sermones.

Revolvere. See s.v. *evolvere.*

Rima. Eu. 105   plenus *rimarum* sum, hac atque illac *perfluo*, developing the imagery suggested by *contineo* in 103. The metaphor is completed in 121, utrumque hoc falsumst, *effluet*. McGlynn compares Hor. *Sat.* 2.6.46, *rimosa* ...

14 For a different metaphorical use of *flectere* implying deviation from the right course, compare Ennius, vv202–3v, quo vobis mentes, rectae quae stare solebant/antehac dementes sese *flexere* viai.

aure.[15] The leaky vessel in Plautus is merely a symbol of wasted labour: *Ps.* 369, in *pertussum* ingerimus dicta *dolium*, a proverbial form which recurs in Lucr. 3.936, *pertusum* congesta quasi in vas/*perfluxere.* Only in Terence and Horace is the image associated with indiscretion. Since Horace in *Sat.* 2.3.259 f., gives a vivid paraphrase of this scene from *Eunuchus*, we may perhaps assume that 2.6.46, is a reminiscence of *Eu.* 105, and not an independent usage.

Ringi. Ph. 341 dum tibi fit quod placeat, ille *ringitur*; tu rideas. On this Donatus interprets *stomachari tacitum*; est enim *translatio a canibus* latratoriis. The verb is rare but classical; cf. Cic. *Att.* 4.5.2, et ii *subringentur* qui villam me moleste ferunt habere; Hor. *Ep.* 2.2.128, sapere et *ringi* – to suffer and grit the teeth. See Dziatzko-Hauler, *Phormio, ad loc.*, p. 311, and s.v. *gannire* above.

Saxum. See s.v. *lapis.*

Sepelire. Ph. 943 *sepultus sum*: "I'm as good as dead"; "I'm ruined." So also Caecil. fr. 11R, depositus modo sum anima, *vita sepultus.* This is interesting chiefly because the image is carried through into the final scene, where in 1015, *verba fiunt mortuo*, Phormio sees in Demipho's attempts to excuse his father the funeral *laudatio*, and in 1026, *exsequias Chremeti quibus est commodum ire*, em tempus est, proclaims the funeral procession; in itself, *sepultus sum* is merely a more drastic equivalent of the clichés *perii, interii.* The different allusions of the imagery occur in an absurd, reverse order – burial – *laudatio* – announcement of procession. In the final scene of *Asinaria* the parasite indulges in the same joke; 910, *ecquis currit pollinctorem accersere*, explained by 911, *mortuos est Demaenetus.* The dramatic situation is identical, as he announces the ruin of the faithless husband whom he has exposed. This is probably a traditional motif older than Apollodorus or Demophilus.

Somnium. Ph. 494, 874 (as an exclamation "nonsense"), *Ad.* 394–5 tu quantu' quantu's, nil nisi sapientia es/ill' *somnium.* Micio's alleged folly and Demea's good sense are dramatized by the identification. The phrase *vigilantiam tuam*

---

15 According to Donatus on *An.* 609, servon fortunas meas me commississe *futtili*, and *Ph.* 745–6, ne vos forte imprudentes foris/*effuttiretis*, the same image of a leaky container underlies the adjective *futtilis*, and the verb *effuttire*: translatio est a vase futili nomine, quod patulo ore, fundo acuto instabile nihil per se contineat, unde et futilis dicitur eiusmodi homo, qui nihil intra se contineat et semper inanis sit. (Wessner II p. 472, on *Ph.* 746). The verb is applied by Horace, *Ars.* 231, *effuttire* leves indigna tragoedia versus, to suggest the stylistic incongruity of colloquial diction which he is rejecting.

tu mihi narras in 397, immediately following, suggests that *somnium* stands here for blind indifference to what is taking place, rather than as so often in Plautus, crazy delusions (for the latter compare the verb *somniare*, *Cist.* 291, "utrum deliras quaeso an astans *somnias*," and the oxymoron *vigilans somniare*, *Am.* 697, *Capt.* 848.) A similar metaphor is used by Aeschinus (*expergisci*, *Ad.* 631, *q.v.*) and Micio (*dormire*, 693) to describe Aeschinus' thoughtless folly.

The metaphor may derive from Menander, but there is no parallel from a nearer source than Plato, *Symp.* 175e, ἡ μὲν γὰρ ἔμη (sc. σοφία) φαύλη τις ἂν εἴη καὶ ἀμφισβητήσιμος, ὥσπερ ὄναρ οὖσα. Here we have the contrast implied between true σοφία and ὄναρ which may have been adopted from philosophical language by New Comedy. The only instance of ὄναρ in New Comedy is Alexis κπ, p. 306, fr. 25, ἀρεταὶ δὲ πρεσβεῖαί τε καὶ στρατηγίαι/κόμποι κενοὶ ψοφοῦσιν ἀντ'ὀνειράτων, again with the force of nonsense.

Spatium. *Ad.* 859–60 vitam duram quam vixi adhuc/iam *decurso aetatis spatio* omitto (Donatus, metaphora a cursoribus). This Greek metaphor is found in Plato; cf. *Leg.* 802a, ἅπαντά τις τὸν βίον διαδραμὼν τέλος ἐπιστήσηται καλόν, and *Resp.*613b, of old men, ἐπὶ τέλους τοῦ δρόμου. So also in a similar context to *Ad.* 859–60, Alexis κπ, p. 383, fr. 235, τὸν γὰρ ὕστατον/τρέχων δίαυλον τοῦ βίου ζῆν βούλομαι, and in Plautus' versions of Menander, at *St.* 81, *decurso aetatis spatio*, and Philemon, *Mer.* 547, breve iam reliquom *vitae spatiumst*. It was also a commonplace in Latin authors influenced by Greek philosophy; cf. Cic. *Sen.* 83, quasi *decurso spatio*, and Lucr. 2.78–9, inque brevi *spatio* mutantur saecla animantum/et quasi *cursores* vitai lampada tradunt. References to the art of the runner also occur in *Cist.* 379 and *Trin.* 1015–6. However, the word-play in the former, and the identification in the latter are Plautine in type, so that we cannot assume without doubt that anything similar stood in the original of either passage.

Speculum. *Ad.* 415 inspicere *tamquam in speculum in vitas omnium.* With this compare Plautus, *Epid.* 383–6, non oris caussa modo homines aequom fuit/ sibi habere *speculum* os ubi contemplarent suom/sed *qui perspicere possent* [cor sapientiae/igitur perspicere ut possint] *cordis copiam*, and for the form of *Ad.* 415, Cic. *Pis.* 71, versibus in quibus si qui velit, possit *tamquam in speculo vitam intueri*. Literature as a mirror of life goes back to Alcidamas' praise of the Odyssey as βίου κάτοπτρον, in Latin *speculum consuetudinis* (Cicero, ap. Don. de Comoedia 5; cf. Fraenkel, *El.Pl.* 368n2). But Terence makes life itself the mirror of the soul, as in Plato *Phaedr.* 255d; *Leg.* 905b from which the image passed to New Comedy, and was directly adopted by Cicero in *Rep.* 2.69 *ut sese splendore animi ... sicut speculum praebeat civibus.* The established nature of the simile in Greek, together with the characterization of the sententious Demea and Syrus' sly mockery in 428 (the brass cooking pots are compared in an echo of the phrase to the bronze mirror), suggests that *Ad.* 415 was intended by Terence (and Menander) as a philosophical cliché.

Subducere. Ad. 855 Numquam its quisquam bene *subducta ratione* ad vitam fuit. *Subducere ratiunculam* is used by Plautus twice, *Capt.* 192, *Cur.* 371, of actual accounting; cf. *rationes subducere,* Lucil. 887M; *summam subducere, ibid.,* 886M, Cic. *Att.* 5.21.11. Cicero, like Terence, uses the idiom figuratively, *Fam.* 1.9.10, *rationibusque subductis summam feci cogitationum mearum omnium.* Financial imagery is particularly appropriate to Demea's materialistic values; cf. 870, hoc fructi ... fero (these are my dividends); 891–2, hominem maxumi preti. So also in 796, *rem ipsam putemus,* Demea sees the whole educational issue before him in terms of accounting. The use of λογίζεσθαι, λογισμός is so common in Greek that they need not imply any financial imagery, but from Menander, cf. *Sam.* 274–5, ὡς δὲ μᾶλλ[ο]ν ἔννο[υς γί]νομαι/καὶ λαμβάνω λογισμόν (λογισμὸν λαμβάνειν, to hold an audit; cf. *rationem subducere*), and *Perik.* 173, καὶ τὸ κεφάλαιον οὐδέπω λογίζομαι (τὸ κεφάλαιονλ; cf. *summam subducere*), both used of "summing up" the situation.

Sudare. Ph. 628 *sudabis* satis, si cum illo inceptas homine. Neither *sudare* nor *sudascere* are used figuratively in Plautus. For *sudare* = *laborare,* cf. Cic. *Fam.* 3.12.3, vides *sudare* me iamdiu laborantem quomodo ... te non offendam, and Horace, *Ep.* 2.1.168–9, creditur (sc. comoedia) ex medio quia res accersit, habere/*sudoris* minimum; and *Ars* 241, *sudet* multum frustraque laboret. So also *Sat.* 1.10.28, cum Pedius causas *exsudet.*

Suere. Ph. 491 metuo lenonem ne quid ... : : suo *suat* capiti. The meaning of the reply here is uncertain, but the use of *suere,* for devising or plotting is borne out by the Plautine *consutis dolis, Ps.* 540, and *Am.* 367 (where it is used to lead into a pun on *consutis tunicis*). Festus, p. 406L gives *sutelae* as "dolosae astutiae a similitudine suentium." Compare the use of ῥάπτειν in Greek of all periods, and especially Alexis κιι, p. 329, fr. 98, ῥάπτουσι δε/πᾶσιν ἐπιβουλάς.

Tabescere. See s.v. *macerare.*

Tesserae. Ad. 739   ita vitast hominum quasi quom ludas *tesseris,*
si illud quod maxume opus est iactu non cadit,
illud quod cecidit forte id arte ut corrigas.

For Greek antecedents, see McGlynn, II, p. 233, especially Alexis

κII, p. 310   τοιοῦτο τὸ ζῆν ἐστιν ὥσπερ οἱ κύβοι,
fr. 34   οὐ ταῦτ' ἀεὶ πίπτουσιν ...

The comparison was already established in Plato, *Resp.* 604c, ὥσπερ ἐν
πτώσει κύβων πρὸς τὰ πεπτωκότα τίθεσθαι τὰ αὑτοῦ πράγματα, recommending
"quod cecidit forte id arte ut corrigas." For the form of this, the only extended
analogy in Terence, compare Men. fr. 416[8] ff., πανήγυριν νόμισόν τιν' εἶναι
τόν χρόνον (derived from Alexis κII, p. 377, fr. 219[10–17]?) and the following
lines on the nature of life and art of living. Such deliberate comparisons are
frequent in New Comedy and often recognizable in Plautus; see Fraenkel,
El. Pl., pp. 162 ff., for illustrations of εἰκάζειν in Greek authors and in Plautus.
He sees reflected in *Ad.* 739–41 Menander's elegant improvement of the
commonplace found in Alexis, by compressing the analogy into one statement
(vv 740–41) applicable to both elements compared.

Via. An. 190   ut redeat iam *in viam; Eu.* 245, *tota erras via; Eu.* 247, hanc
primus inveni *viam; Ph.* 326, iam *pedum* visast *via.* The idea of wandering from
the road of virtue, implied in *An.* 190 and *Ad.* 829, quovis illos tu die/*redducas,*
is common in all languages. To the references quoted by McGlynn, II, p. 274,
add these Plautine metaphors: *Cas.* 369, tandem *redii* vix *veram in viam;* 469,
in rectam redii semitam; Ps. 668, *redduxit* me *usque ex errore in viam; Trin.* Prol.
45; ne quis *erret,* paucis *in viam deducam. Eu.* 247, hic novomst aucupium. ego
adeo hanc primus *inveni viam,* relates *via* to a way of life, and is the more
striking since there is no explanatory clause or phrase; it follows very closely
on 245 above, which serves perhaps to introduce the metaphor, but in the
absence of a dependent clause, it differs significantly from Verg. *Aen.* 4.478,
inveni germana *viam,* quoted by Ruhnken. For ὁδός as the proper way of life,
cf. Plato, *Leg.* 803e, ὁδοὶ τετμήνται καθ' ἃς ἴτεον; *Ep.* 7, 330d, ὀρθῇ πορευομένης
ὁδῷ τῆς πολιτείας; *Resp.* 600a, ὁδόν τινα ... βίου Ὁμηρικήν; *Axioch.* 367a, τίνα
τὴν τοῦ βίου ὁδὸν ἐνστήσονται. In general this image is more frequently
expressed by the use of πορεύεσθαι or a similar work. In Menander the metaphor
of the road of life is presupposed by the figurative use of ἐφόδιον, fr. 416[12]; cf.

ἐφόδιον βίῳ (βίου) in frr. 407², 550, For ὁδός as method, approach, cf. *Epitr.* 383, τὴν ἑτέραν/πορεύεται ὁδόν.

Vorsuram solvere (see also s.v. *lutum*) *Ph.* 780   *vorsuram solves, Geta; praesens quod fuerit malum in diem abiit; plagae crescunt.* This phrase has been the subject of conjecture since Guyet and Bentley, because the normal usage of *versura*, is in the idiom *versuram facere*, to raise a secondary loan, or *versura solvere*, to pay by means of a second loan; cf. Cic. *Att.* 5.1.2; *quae* quidem ... vel *versura facta solvi volo*; 5.15.2; vereor ne *illud* quod tecum permutavi *versura mihi solvendum sit.* Accordingly Bentley proposed *vorsura solvis* (the present tense read by the correctors of D and L, and in Lactantius 2.8.24). This would offer excellent sense here; "you are paying your debts by a further loan, Geta." But the traditional reading offers a sense equally appropriate to Geta's dramatic situation: he has already avoided immediate disaster by duping the old men into a payment; it is this payment, seen as a secondary loan, which he will have to raise in the future; meanwhile his beatings are accumulating like compound interest. Metaphors based on interest are common in Greek and Latin. Compare Men. fr. 198.8–9, οἱ δ'εἰς τὸ γῆρας ἀναβολὰς ποιούμενοι/οὗτοι προσαποτίνουσι τοῦ χρόνου τόκους, where the image is applied to the tribute owed to the god of love, and the use of *faenerato* "with interest to pay" in Pl. *As.* 902, *Men.* 604. The Menandrian image becomes a commonplace of Hellenistic erotic literature; cf. Prop. 1.7.26, saepe venit *magno faenore* tardus amor.

3

A comparison of imagery in
Plautus and Terence

In the introduction to this analysis I gave reasons for choosing Terence rather than Plautus as a source for the study of imagery in the *sermo familiaris* of early second-century Rome. In the preceding discussion of themes and allusions I have concentrated on the resemblances and coincidences in the two dramatists; at this point it seems desirable to focus on the significant differences between them in their choice and treatment of imagery. To obtain a fair sample of Plautine usage for statistical comparison I have balanced against the six thousand (6064) lines of Terence, six plays of Plautus amounting to 5808 lines; *Aulularia, Bacchides Cistellaria*, and *Stichus* based on Menandrian originals, and the *Mercator* and *Trinummus* derived from Philemon.

It may seem foolish to attempt any statistical comparison; the total number of figurative uses in a literary work is bound to be arbitrary, depending on the critic's classifications; was the figurative sense of a particular phrase still alive in the minds of audience and author? Should a repeated image be counted twice? Should proverbial phrases containing a metaphor be included in the count?[1] At the same time the total arrived at gives no indication of the proportion of original or distinctive metaphors and of merely conventional figurative language. However, the use of statistics does reveal a relative pattern: the number of figurative uses in Terence varies from approximately fifteen in *Hecyra*, to about thirty each in *Andria* and *Heauton Timoroumenos*, and more than forty-five each in *Eunuchus, Phormio*, and *Adelphoe*. While the small total for *Hecyra* is related to its brevity (880 lines) there is a real correspondence between the sparser imagery of the more static,[2] early plays, and the greater abundance in the *"motoriae," Eunuchus, Phormio*, and *Adelphoe*.

---

1 I have preferred to be inclusive in the complete list on which my statistics are based, while being more selective (e.g. excluding proverbs) in the separate discussions.

2 Donatus classifies *Andria* as *maiore ex parte motoria* (Praef. *Andr.* I.2) but its language is

A statistical count of imagery in the six Plautine plays gives approximately 30 examples each in *Aulularia* (two of them extended analogies, 229-35, 595-8) and *Cistellaria* (three extended passages 71-4, 203 ff., 728-30), 50 in *Bacchides* (many at length, especially 66 ff., 709-12, and act 4, sc. 9, the slave as general and conqueror of Troy, 1121 ff.), nearly 40 in *Stichus*, 50 in *Mercator* (extended metaphors, 292 ff., 875 ff.), and over 70 in *Trinummus* (extended analogies, 28-33, 169-72, 305-12, 313-17, 363 f., 468 f., 675-9). But not only does Plautus display more imagery and figurative language, the actual images are more visualized, more detailed, more explicit. Many take the form of a comparison between man and animal, stage character and social or professional type; most are developed with ornamental detail, quite a few as full analogies. In all of Terence there are only two extended comparisons: the leaky vessel of Parmeno's ears, *Eu.* 103-5, and 121, and the formal comparison of life to a game of dice in *Ad.* 739-41.

I have suggested a relationship between the proportion of imagery and the "mobile" or "static" quality of the individual plays of Terence. We may also raise the question of the individual roles; how far is the quantity and range of imagery related to either the type – in terms of social status, age, and sex – or the individuality of the speaker?

Character differentiation by means of language and style, careful and subtle in Menander,[3] is often blurred by both Plautus and Terence. In Plautus concern for the humour of wisecrack and insult approximates the refinement of an old man such as Daemones in *Rudens*, or Periplectomenos in *Miles Gloriosus*, downwards to the more colourful idiom of a young man, while young men, in turn, utter scurrilous jokes more appropriate to slaves. Yet some distinctions are preserved such as those which enabled Fraenkel in *Museum Helveticum* 25, 1968, 231 f., to restore the long speech of *Mil.* 215-28, with its grandiose metaphorical allegory of the slave as general, to the slave Palaestrio, where the Mss tradition had given it to the old man. Old men, even allies, may praise slaves, but the military imagery is peculiar to the slaves themselves.

In Terence, concern for elegance and purity of diction approximates

generally more sedate than that of its successors, except *Hecyra. Heauton Timoroumenos* is a *stataria* (cf. Prol. v36); *Hecyra* is *mixta motoriis actibus et statariis* (Praef. *Hec.* 1.2); *Eunuchus ex magna parte motoria* (Praef. *Eu.* 1.2); *Phormio prope tota motoria* (Praef. *Ph.* 1.2) *Adelphoe, maiore ex parte motoria* (Praef. *Ad.* 1.2).

3 See the studies of Sergio Zini, *Il linguaggio dei Personaggi nelle comedie di Menandro* (Florence 1938) and Juliane Straus, *Terenz und Menander, Beitrag zu einer Stilvergleichung* (Zürich 1955).

upwards; his language is *Kunstsprache*, even more than that of Plautus,[4] and his lower orders, like those in Plautus, do not express their class by means of dialect or syntactical vulgarisms.[5] Although Terence generally avoids the abusive epithets and sadistic elaborations on corporal punishment which colour the language of Plautus' slaves (and alas! gentlemen), he achieves some class and role differentiation through the use of emotive language, and through imagery. I have commented (p. 8) on the apparent vulgarism of transitive *ardere*, spoken by Geta, *Ph.* 82. At a different level, one of aesthetics, Gnatho is characterized by his crude metaphors (I have commented on *exspuere*. *Eu.* 406, p. 52. We might add *urere*, 274, 438, used by no other speaker, and absent from Cicero's letters, *iugulare* 417; Demea's ἀγροικία may be reflected in his use of *olfacere* (*Ad.* 397, see p. 62), *evomere* (510, see p. 52), and *iugulare* (930). More generally slave metaphors are less inhibited, and slaves share with parasites the exploitation of paramilitary language; cf. Syrus, *Hau.* 668 f.;

4 See H. Haffter, *Untersuchungen zur Altlateinischen Dichtersprache*, Problemata 10, 1934, and Happ, "Die Lateinische Umgangssprache und die Kunstsprache des Plautus." *Glotta* 45, pp. 60–104. However, the criterion of distinction between levels of language in dialogue *senarii* and long-verse evolved by Haffter, and used by Happ in his study of "archaisms," has not proved relevant to the statistics of imagery in Terence. Imagery, as a figure of thought rather than diction, does not require a setting of high style. Neither the quantity nor the development of metaphor in Terence is significantly related to the type of metre used. Thus the relative frequency of imagery in long-verse as opposed to senarii varies from *Eunuchus* (approximately one image in 25 lines of either category) and *Hecyra* (one in 50 lines of each category) through *Heauton Timorumenos* (one in 30 for long-verse, one in 40 for *senarii*) and *Phormio* (one in 21 for long-verse, one in 25 for *senarii*) to the extreme of *Andria* (one in 25 for long-verse, one in 45 for *senarii*) and *Adelphoe* (one in 15, one in 30). The great variation shows that Terence did not use imagery primarily as ornament for emotional or stylistic purposes, but for psychological clarification, which can be as desirable in sedate *senarii* as in excited long-verse or *canticum*.

5 Cf. P. Wahrmann, "Vulgar-Lateinische bei Terenz," *W. St.* 30, 1908, pp. 75 ff. He distinguishes (pp. 7–8) between the Aristotelian characterization of status, age, and sex (ἠθικόν), using language to achieve psychological authenticity, and class-distinction through dialect or solecism. Linguistic elements which have been singled out as vulgar in Terence, because of their appearance in a vulgar context in later sources, or because of their absence from the higher genres of later literature, were, he shows, not felt as vulgar in Terence's days, as their even distribution among the different types of role confirms. In the Aristotelian category might come examples of legitimate slave colouring such as the use of diminutives and frequentatives for emotional effect, or imagery such as Syrus' *argentum fugitivom* (*Hau.* 678), where the metaphor is derived from slave experience. His conclusion is (p. 103) "Er (Terence) handhabt dieselbe Sprache, mag er nun einen Sklaven auftreten lassen, oder in den Prologen sich mit seinen literarischen Gegnern auseinandersetzen."

Ph. 230, 346. As an illustration, consider the role of Syrus in *Heauton Timorou-menos*; he is the only slave, which limits his verbal freedom to some extent, but he has the unparalleled phrase *sermones caedimus*, 242; *pannis obsita* 294 (echoes by Gnatho, *Eu.* 236); the verb *concaluit*, 349; the elliptical *duras dabit*, 402, *intendere fallaciam*, 513 (so also Davus, *An.* 733); colloquial *deperire*, 525, a rich load of imagery in his soliloquy (act 4, sc. 2), *palmam dare*, 709 (the nearest equivalent is *palmarium*, Parmeno, *Eu.* 930); and *argentum cudere* 740. This imagery is vigorous and drastic; it could have been employed by a rake like Clitipho, but not by his father, and the parallels I have quoted derived from low class roles.

The question of imagery as a feature of characterization in Terence has recently been discussed with much insight by W. G. Arnott, "Phormio Parasitus," *G. and R.* 17, 1970, 32–57 (esp. pp. 35–7, 46–8). He shows (p. 35) how imagery has been concentrated in the speeches of Phormio to build up his importance; indeed Terence has heightened this effect by toning down the language of Phormio's interlocutors, and muting the passage immediately preceding his grand entry. The type of imagery given to Phormio, abundant and many-hued, also features a high proportion of parasitical eating-metaphors; so Donatus on 318, *apta parasito quia de cibo est*; but then he adds on 327, παρασιτικῶς *totum translationibus loquitur*; *huiusmodi est enim umbraticorum hominum scurrilis oratio*. In a later section on linguistic characterization in general (pp. 52–5) Arnott emphasizes the greater restriction on metaphor and other expressive language in the free-born, bourgeois roles. He singles out Chaerea as an exception, "his speech is more loaded with metaphor than that of any other lover in Terence ... and this raciness is the outward expression of an adolescent exuberance." But he is careful to point out that this raciness varies with the respect due or felt towards Chaerea's interlocutors. It is appropriate to recall that Aristotle (*Rhet.* 3.11.16) described hyperbole and hyperbolic metaphors as μειρακιώδεις· σφοδρότητα γὰρ δηλοῦσιν ... πρεσβυτέρῳ λέγειν ἀπρεπές. Chaerea is the most σφοδρός of Terence's young men, and his imagery expresses his temperament. It is not surprising that the nearest approach to his idiom is to be found in the letters of M. Caelius Rufus.

Yet it is types such as the vulgar Gnatho, or Geta and Phormio, who contribute the greater share of figurative language in Terence. If we count only slaves and parasites, Parmeno, Pythias, Dorias, and Gnatho are responsible for about three-fifths of the metaphors in *Eunuchus*: Geta, Davus, and Phormio for nearly two-thirds of the examples in *Phormio*. Most of these instances are noticeably Plautine in type, military allusions, or descriptions of violence – some boastful, some insulting, certainly not intended to reflect the *purus sermo* of the educated man.

By contrast I believe that Terence, especially in the *Andria*, was adhering closely to the imagery of his original: there is only one Roman allusion (*auspicato*, 807); the most frequent metaphors are nautical (480, 562, 845, perhaps 193, and 446), or medical (193, 468, 559, 831, 944). Other references – to inflamed passion (308), to teacher and pupil (192, 477), to wandering from the road of virtue (190), to driving into the snare of marriage (602, 620, 667) – all find parallels in Greek. The same is largely true of the *Hecyra*, which is conventionally accepted as the second play actually written by Terence.[6]

In the *Hecyra* only the reference to *postulatio* (180–1) transferring legal terminology to private life, does not have a precedent in New Comedy. *Postulatio* may have been intended and felt as a Roman procedure, but the imagery of the rest of the play is in Greek. Thus the war of love waged by the meretrices in Act 1, sc. 1 recalls Alexis κII, fr. 98, 1–3, τὸ συλᾶν τοὺς πέλας/... ῥάπτουσι δὲ/πᾶσιν ἐπιβουλάς. The other images all find precedents either in New Comedy itself or the language of the philosophical tradition which so strongly influenced New Comedy. *Heauton Timoroumenos*, although a "static" play, as is reflected in the low proportion of imagery, has much more that is independent of known Greek metaphor and related to established Plautine language. Compare the *provincia* allusion in 516, the triumph and other military terms in 669, 672–3, the use of *obsitus* in 294 (see s.v. *obserere*), and the violence disguised by euphemism of 950–1 (on the lips of a *senex*). The imagery is altogether nearer to that of Plautus in its colouring; indeed, there is no metaphor in the play which is obviously Attic in origin. In this one respect it is further from New Comedy than either those that precede or follow it. Even in *Eunuchus* and Apollodorus' *Phormio*, with their abundance of slave idiom and imagery, there is more that is identifiably Greek than in the *pura oratio* of *Heauton Timoroumenos*.

In Plautus the actual range of imagery is far wider than in Terence. All the main categories found in Terence and discussed in chap. 1, I–VII occur in the six plays of Plautus chosen for comparison. But metaphors from nature, alluding to both tame and wild animals, plants and agriculture, are more common. I have found only two agricultural metaphors in Terence, the use of *obsitus* (possibly also *sentus*, at *Hau*. 294; *Eu*. 236) and of *derivare*, *Ph*. 323.

6 Cf. Beare, *Roman Stage*, p. 94; Duckworth, *Nature of Roman Comedy*, p. 60; H. Haffter, "Terenz und seine kunstlerische Eigenart," *Museum Helveticum* 10, 1953, 10–11.

Animals are limited to sheep and wolves (these in proverbial phrases, *Eu.* 832; *Ph.* 506; *Ad.* 534) and the shrewmouse of *Eu.* 1024, also apparently proverbial. Contrast with this the following menagerie in the six plays of Plautus:

Aulularia: 198, the polypus; 229, the ox and ass in harness;[7] 628, the earthworm; *Bacchides*: 38, the nightingale; 51, dove; 274, hawk; 372, leeches; 792, the thrush; 889, the shrewmouse, 1121 ff., sheep and lambs; *Cistellaria*: 307, the old hack and the young filly; 728, the caterpillar; *Mercator*: 361, the housefly; 761, the snake; *Stichus*: 139, hounds; 605, the wolf; 724, the snake; *Trinummus*: 101, the vulture; 169, the wolf and sheepdogs; 835, hounds.

For references to plants and agriculture, natural features, cf. *Aul.*: 45, *seges*; *Bac.*: 85, the swift river; 283, the mushroom; so also 821; *St.*: 724, a snake? 773, the mushroom; *Trin.*: 29–33, crops and weeds; 531, the sowing of bad habits; 851, the mushroom again. Metaphors based on *arare*, *serere* and compounds, *messis* and *metere* are common in Plautus.[8] Of country pursuits, only snaring, hunting, and fishing are equally represented in both authors. See chap 1, VII above.

References to Roman institutions are, perhaps surprisingly, not much less frequent in Terence than in Plautus; compare from Terence *An.* 807, *auspicato*; *Hau.* 516, *Ph.* 73, *provincia*; *Hau.* 672, *Eu.* 394, *Ph.* 543, the triumph; *Hau.* 709 *palmam dare*; *Eu.* 348, the *conclamatio* over the dead; *Eu.* 770, 887, *patronus* and *patrona*; *Ph.* 230, the reserve *centuria*; 964, gladiators: probably *Hec.* 180, *postulatio* and *Ad.* 87, *dissignare*. *Vorsuram solvere*, *Ph.* 780, and *plebs*, *Ad.* 898, though technically Roman, have close Greek equivalents, and might not strike the audience as specifically Roman allusions.

With these compare Plautus *Aul.* 576, *colonia*, 601, the *censio*; *Bac.* 92, *emancupare*, 181, *vadare*, 814–5, the praetor and the public auction, 972 and 1073 the triumph, 1205, judgment debtors (*addicti*), *Cist.* 460, the *foedus* (context uncertain), *Mer.* 996, the client, *St.* 688, *polluctura*, the public banquet, 689–9, *provincia*, *imperium*, *Trin.* 190, *provincia*, 300–4, *imperium*, 484, *sine sacris hereditas*, 706, *palma*, 822 *potestas*; 1002, *concenturiare*, the military muster.

---

7 Probably based on Aesop: cf. Aesop, fable 104 (Halm) on the yoked ox and ass (with a different version of the consequences), or 177[b] on the ass and mule in harness, with the ass's subsequent collapse.

8 *Arare*: *As.* 874, *Truc.* 148–50, both in sexual allusion; *serere*; *Epid.* 265, *Men.* 1012 (*sementem facere*) *Mos.* 1100; *messis*: *Epid.* 718, *Rud.* 637, 763; *metere*: *Epid.* 265, 718, *Mos.* 799, *Trin.* 32. At least some of these may represent the imagery of the Greek originals; cf. Men. *Perik.* 282–3, πολλῶν γεγονότων ἀθλίων κατὰ τὸν χρόνον/τὸν νῦν – φορὰ γὰρ γέγονε τούτου νῦν καλή, with, e.g. *Rud.* 637, *uberem ... messem mali*; *Ep.* 718, *quom ... mali messim metas*.

Cist. 188–9, *nomen expungi*, like *vorsuram solvere* above, though a technical term of Roman accounting, may represent an exact equivalent in Greek.

However, general references to social and professional habits are far more common in Plautus, usually in the form of allusions to the person, or actual personifications: cf. *Aul.* 59 (*discipula*), 73 (*sutor*), 401 (*ludius*), 408 (*Bacchae*), 410 (the gymnasium), 595 (the swimming lesson and the "life belt"), 626 (dancing); *Bac.* 66 (the palaestra), 349 (weaving; the loom), *Cist.* 379–80 (running), 450 (the *insula* and *aedes*), 503 (the *tessera hospitalis*), 769 (deposited money); *Mer.* 303–4 (the elementary school), 845, 869, friends and travelling companions, *St.* 81 (the foot-race), 105 (pupil and teacher), 348–9 (weaving and the loom), *Trin.* 81 (the steward – *promus*), 226 (the mind as trainer), 132 and 318, 323, building and roofing-over, 363–5 (the *fictor* – image maker[9]), 467 (the public dinner, rich man, and clients), 512 (the wet-nurse – *nutrix*), 673 (the inn), 1016 (runner and trainer), 1038 (the laws as parents). A large proportion of these are recognizably Greek in inspiration. However, similar allusions and imagery are absent from Terence's plays:[10] the only professional and social imagery is that based on medicine, navigation, teaching, hunting, warfare, and the drama.

In these and other limitations imposed by Terence on metaphor, the avoidance of the specifically Roman (or Greek), the suppression of images drawn from familiar crafts and social activities, even the distaste for personified abstractions in gnomic statements, the same tendency is at work which Haffter repeatedly underlines in *Terenz und Seine Kunstlerische Eigenart*: all elements that distract from the purely human aspects of the drama are played down, in imagery as in the general text of the plays. Haffter has documented the elimination of Greek references (p. 82), of "milieu" in favour of "das Allgemein-Menschliche" (pp. 83–4), the absorption of generalized gnomic utterance into personal comment (pp. 85–6), and illustrated the evolution of this tendency through Terence's career.

---

9 Cf. Philemon xii, fr. 72; *fictor*, cf. ἀνδριαντοποιός.

10 This raises the unanswerable question: how much imagery was there in Terence's originals comparable to, e.g., *Ad.* 739 ff., but which Terence deliberately omitted? The fragments of Menander (and Philemon) suggest a greater richness of imagery in New Comedy than Terence transmitted, but a study of *Epitrepontes* or *Dyskolos* yields only a small number of brief allusions. There are just over 20 in *Epitrepontes*, of which half depend on verbs: only 735 f. extends beyond a single word. In *Dyskolos*, which has fewer figurative uses, over half consist only of a verb whose meaning has been transferred from a different sphere. Two instances (209–11 on poverty as a lodger, and 535 ff. which compares the man digging to a swing-beam on a well, thus anticipating an important crisis in the play) extend beyond the single-word imagery that seems characteristic of both Terence and Menander.

Imagery too must not be more vivid than the behaviour it is designed to illuminate, or distract the audience by material details from the psychological concerns of the action. It is for this reason that Terence generally avoids noun-images and expresses the metaphor through a verb, comparing the psychological activity of his character to some other social activity, not person to person,[11] and avoiding references to the accessories or setting of the social activity he compares. Many of these allusions in Plautus are to purely physical resemblances or describe physical phenomena, e.g. *Aul.* 59, *discipulam* cruci; 401, glabriorem quam volsus *ludiust*, 410, iste me habuit senex *gymnasium*. They have no psychological significance.

Reliance on verbs is perhaps the most conspicuous characteristic of Terentian metaphor – a characteristic that, as we have seen, echoes Menander's usage. In any given play, over half the images are implied by and concentrated in the verb alone: most often the figurative use is of the simplest type, where a physical verb is applied to a psychological activity.[12] Compare from the *Andria* 181, *interoscitare*, 260, *trahere*, 308, *incendere*, 423, *excidere*, 557, *occludere*, 561, *devincire*, 562, *emergere*, 573, *claudere*, 602, *conicere* (also 620, 667), 640, *ingerere*, 650, *conflare*, 685, *macerare*, (cf. 886), 913 *conglutinare*, 944, *medicari*. The proportion is not much less in the more verbally exuberant *Phormio* 40, *conradere*, 47, *ferire*, 82, *ardere*, 85, *pascere*, 108, *exstinguere*, 186, *incendere*, 318, *adcingi*, 321, *instruere*, 323, *derivare*, 341, *ringi*, 382, *expiscari*, 439, *impingere*, 491, *suere*, 682, *emungere*; 822, *mederi*, 842–3, *onerare*, *exonerare*, 856, *delibuere*, 973, *lavare*, 974–5, *incendere*, *exstinguere*, 1030, *ogganire*.

In *Bacchides* or *Trinummus* only about one third of the examples are of this type, concentrated in the verb without further development. Compare *Bacchides* 92, *emancupare*; 181, *vadare*, *vincire*; 213, *sauciare*; 239, *extexere*; 251, *findere*; 349, *onerare*; 375, *concludere*; *gestare*; 493, *cruciare*; 693, *conglutinare*; 869, *exsorbere* (cf. 372, 472, expanded); 1091, *urere*; 1092, *eradicare*; 1094, *lacerare*, *spoliare*; 1095, *attondere*; 1199, *terebrare* (18 out of 50). *Trinummus* 132, *exaedificare*; 155, *permanascere*; 188, *occludere*; 216, *prosilire*; 265, *praecipitare* (but this is explained by 266); 287, *excruciare*; 292, *lutitare*; 299, *considere*; 323, *pertegere*, *perpluere*; 336, *confringere*; 615, *subolere*; 639, *migrare*; 649, *obtegere*; 667, *opscurare*; 693, *conlutulentare*; 699, *astringere*; 755, *indagare*; 797, *texere*; 839, *deluctare*; 1002, *concenturiare*; 1092, *animam agere* (22 out of 70).

Finally the variety of imagery in Plautus is greatly enlarged if we consider under this heading the various types of metaphor-substitute employed.

11 The only personal nouns used figuratively in Terence are *discipulus*, *An.* 477; *magister*, *An.* 192; and *magistra*, *Hec.* 204; *paedagogus*, *Ph.* 144 (cf. p. 36 above).
12 Cf. Donatus on *Ph.* 856, *ad animum transtulit quod est corporis.*

1   The comparative phrase: cf. *Aul.* 297, pumex non aeque est ardus atque hic est senex, 402, glabriorem reddes quam volsus ludiust, 421, fustibus sum mollior magis quam ullus cinaedus, 600, citis quadrigis citius ... persequi, *Bac.* 767, tam frictum ego illum reddam quam frictum est cicer, 821, tantist quantist fungus putidus. This has the same effect as a simile, and is very rare in Terence. I can compare only *Ad.* 534, tam placidum quam ovem (a traditional phrase) and *ibid.*, 849, tam excoctam ... atque atram quam carbost.

2   The comic adjective. Compare *Aul.* 607, *censione bubula* (the scrutiny of the ox-thong); *Cist.* 62, *ut facias stultitiam sepelibilem*; *Trin.* 1011, *bubuli cottabi* (shots of the ox-thong); cf. *Trin.* 851, hicquidem *fungino generest*: capite se totum tegit.

Perhaps the only instances of this technique of imagery in Terence are *Eu.* 316, reddunt (sc. virgines) curatura *iunceas*[13] (cf. tam graciles quam iunci), *Ph.* 964, *gladiatorio animo* ad me adfectant viam (cf. tamquam gladiatores).

3   The identification technique (cf. Fraenkel, *El. Pl.* chap. II, "Identificazioni e Trasformazioni"). Add to *Trin.* 851 above, *Bac.* 85, *rapidus fluvius* est hic, non hac temere transiri potest, *Mer.* 361, *muscast meus pater*; nil potest clam illum haberi; *Trin.* 1016, huic ... /*gurguliost exercitor*; is huic homini cursuram docet. In these the metaphor of identification usually precedes the explanation, but compare, in reverse order, *Mer.* 125, perii, *animam nequeo vortere, nimi' nihili tibicen siem*. The only example in Terence: *Eu.* 426, lepus tute es: pulpamentum quaeris?, is significant. Terence's character is quoting an outmoded jest (vetus credidi, 428) which derives from Livius Andronicus. The form then was traditional in Roman comedy before Terence, and is singled out by him as appropriate to a fatuous speaker: the example confirms his rejection of the device.

4   The mythological image or identification. Cf. *Bac.* 155-6, "fiam, ut ego opinor, *Hercules*, tu autem *Linus* ... pol metuo magis ne *Phoenix* tuis factis fiam"; 810, "aha *Bellerophontem* tuus me fecit filius"; and the whole Troy-Priam allegory of act 4, sc. 9. The only image with any mythological content in Terence seems to be *Hec.* 852, "qui ab Orco mortuom me redducem facis," which would more properly be called religious. Mythological parallels are humorously rejected in *An.* 194, "Davo' sum, non Oedipus," *Hau.* 1035, "non si ex capite sis meo/natus, item ut aiunt *Minervam esse ex Iove*," and

---

13 The adjective occurs already in Plautus in a different image: *St.* 639, *potione iuncea* onerabo gulam.

suggested for deliberate absurdity in *Eu.* 1027, "qui minu' quam *Hercules* servivit *Omphalae*?"

Each of these techniques is in varying degrees a type of imagery since it evokes a comparison between the thing or person described and one derived from another field of activity. In all of them, however, there is a strong element of the facetious, a humorous abuse of language or reality which explains their almost complete absence from Terence. The figurative language and metaphor which Terence admits is more restricted, both by his fidelity to the imagery of the original, which has been confirmed in many of the instances discussed by coincidence with Greek imagery in philosophical writings and New Comedy, and by his concern for neatness and restraint. It is no doubt this feeling for neatness of expression which explains his avoidance of the simile. In all of Terence's works there is only one simile, *Ad.* 415 (subsequently parodied at 428) and one analogy expressed as a simile, *Ad.* 739–41, both Greek in theme and function. He aimed to achieve what Leo[14] has called "eine neue römische Urbanität," the speech of the "urbani, parcentis viribus atque/ extenuantis eas consulto," characterized by *pura oratio* (*Hau.* Prol. 46) and the freedom from exaggeration or buffoonery of true gentlemanly humour.[15] The new standards which he set in the control of language were not surpassed or outmoded in the ensuing century and are recognizable in the artistic *sermo familiaris* of Cicero and his most talented friends. Their language and their imagery, conservative as it was, may have derived in part from the same Greek literary background that Terence reflects; it may have represented a continuous tradition of imagery from Terence's generation to their own; it may even at times have been a direct and conscious echo of Terence's original phrase. Whatever the relationship, the range and application of figurative language is the same in the educated speech of the high classical period as it was in the pre-classical comedies of Terence.

14 *Geschichte der Römischen Literatur*, p. 293.
15 See G.C. Fiske, *Horace and Lucilius* (Madison, Wisconsin 1920), chap. 2 for an idealized presentation of the literary principles of Terence's patrons and the "Scipionic circle." The appraisal of A.E. Astin, *Scipio Aemilianus* (Oxford 1967), Appendix vi, pp. 294–306, is more sceptical. "It *may be* that particular *litterati* associated with Scipio exercised exceptional influence upon later generations, and that *in this respect* the term 'Scipionic circle' *defined with suitable caution, may have* a valuable application." His concern, however, is to warn against assuming common political and philosophical ideals among Scipio's associates or their exclusive patronage of such ideals. For their acknowledged influence in matters of linguistic purity and propriety, *elegantia sermonis*, compare Cicero *Brutus* 111–13, and 258–60, and see Dihle, "Analogie und Attizismus," *Hermes* 85, 170–205, esp. 179 f. In both verbal style and social tone Terence offered to the wider public of the theatre what Scipio and Laelius, or their friend Lucilius writing for reading or recitation, could confer only on a limited audience of senators and *nobiles*.

APPENDIX I

The imagery of love in Terence and *sermo amatorius*

In the preceding discussion figurative language has been presented largely in terms of the field of metaphor, in an attempt to show from which fields imagery was drawn, and what restrictions Terence imposed on its form and application. But it is useful and desirable to adopt the reverse approach; thus I want now to examine Terence's figurative language in terms of one category of experience – love, and the lover's condition – and the variety of images by which it is expressed. At the same time it seems useful to compare the imagery of love developed in the later Roman poetry of Elegy and Lyric, not because I wish to argue for any direct dependence of the Roman love-poets on Roman Comedy. Since Leo's discussion in *Plautinische Forschungen*[2] (pp. 140–57) scholars have agreed that the affinities of subject matter and treatment between, say, the Elegists and Plautus and Terence can only derive from the Greek sources – from the treatment of lover and love affairs in Greek New Comedy and Hellenistic Epic, Epigram, and Bucolic, if not from the subjective love elegies postulated by Leo and rejected by Jacoby, *Rh. Mus.* 60, 1905, 38–105.

But independence of treatment and subject matter does not preclude affinities of language; the imagery of the love-poets develops in many ways the pattern established by Terence, and I believe that his range of erotic, or rather, sentimental vocabulary, more restricted and urbane than that of Plautus, embodied a norm which survives as the basis of the usage in the Elegists. Coincidence is such as to suggest the continuity of his influence in this respect. This may be considered as indirect, but some support for the direct influence of Terence's *sermo amatorius* is lent by the almost verbatim adaptation into hexameters of *Eunuchus* act I, sc. I, 46–64 in Horace's portrayal of the lover, *Sat.* 2.3.259–71.

This body of material, then, may help readers to estimate for themselves the degree of kinship between the imagery of Terence and that of late love-poetry, and whether similarities should be considered as the outcome of a continuing literary and spoken tradition, or of a direct debt, based on familiarity with Terentian comedy.

For Roman Comedy, *sermo amatorius* has been fully discussed by Keith Preston, *Studies in the Diction of the Sermo Amatorius of Roman Comedy* (Chicago 1916), and its imagery in particular is treated on pp. 48–57. But because the language is so varied and inventive in the plays of Plautus, Preston takes few of his examples from Terence, and gives no picture of the imagery of love as it appears in his plays. This imagery is more muted than that of Greek erotic poetry, partly because Terence (and Menander) see the lover from the outside, from the position of a writer of High Comedy to whom the lover is at least partly absurd. At the same time the florid conceits of the Greek Anthology would hardly be at home in the naturalistic genre of comedy; the imagery of Terence is normally *sermoni propiora*, nearer to that of prose than poetry. Yet this sobriety of metaphor found in Terence is more characteristic of the Roman love-poets than the elaborations of Hellenistic epic and epigram; both elegy and lyric concentrate on the basic themes – love as fire, sickness, madness, and torment, or, in the rare happy moments, love as a blessed state akin to immortality or divinity – which are already to be found in Terence. Only Ovid, in mockery of literature, life, and himself, distorts the old metaphors into a new artificiality, parodying the rules of the game in imagery as in morality.

From the individual metaphors already discussed it is possible to outline a portrait of the Terentian lover similar to the famous description of the Elegiac lover in Kirby Flower Smith's *Tibullus* (pp. 27–9). To this, *Andria* and *Adelphoe* contribute a picture of the loyal but tormented lover, *Eunuchus* the finest picture of the sufferings of jealousy (Act 1, sc. 1 and 2) and the ecstasy of first union (Act 3, sc. 5). *Hecyra* presents briefly in act 1, sc. 1. the other, female, side of the war of the sexes.

Love itself is a kind of single combat (*Eu.* 53–5); it involves *inimicitae, indutiae,/bellum, pax rursum* (*Eu.* 60–1), as opposed to rational behaviour as insanity itself (*Eu.* 61–4). For the woman, that is, the hetaera-meretrix, it is an opportunity to pillage and plunder whatever adversary one can find (*Hec.* 65); to plot treacherous attacks (*insidiari, Hec.* 70), to be avenged on the enemy, and trap them by their own deceits – *ulcisci advorsarios*, aut qua via te *captent*, eadem ipsos *capi* (*Hec.* 72–3).

The lover, especially the jealous one, is on fire with passion (*Eu.* 72, *Ph.* 82, *ardere*), his desire inflamed (*An.* 308, *Hau.* 367, *incendi*); the thought of his rival burns him (*Eu.* 438, *urere*). His beloved herself is the fire that kindles him (*Eu.* 85, but this is a facetious use of the image). He is ruined, or will die of love (*perire, Eu.* 73; *perdite amare, ardere, Hau.* 97, *Ph.* 82; *deperire, Hau.* 525; *emori, Eu.* 888). At the least his mind is sick (*aegrotus: An.* 192, 559; *Hau.* 100) and needs healing (*An.* 831, 944, *medicari; Ph.* 822, *mederi*). The lovesick girl even wastes away (*tabescere, Ad.* 603). Naturally our lover is tormented (*discruciare, Ad.* 610; *excruciare, Hau.* 177; *macerare, An.* 685, *Eu.* 187). The *meretrices* are instruments of torture (*cruces, Eu.* 383). If they are cruel, they have but to weep and accuse and the lover will offer himself for any punishment (*Eu.* 69–70). But, if his love is required after suffering, he is as one brought back from the dead (*Hec.* 852), immortal (*An.* 963), even a god in his happiness (*Hau.* 693, *Hec.* 843, *deus sum, si hoc ita est*).

Despite the fragmentary nature of the surviving works of Menander, most of these Terentian metaphors can be attested either directly from Menander, or from the surviving Menander-based plays of Plautus (especially *Cistellaria* and *Bacchides*). The most conspicuous omission from Menander himself is that of fire-imagery (there is no single example in erotic contexts: nor are there any in *Cistellaria* and *Bacchides*).[1] Examples of this are relatively rare in other Greek erotic material (absent for instance from the *Symposium*), and the metaphor may be more at home in Latin. But madness, sickness, torment, and the warfare of love are all represented, if not in the relatively complete plays of Menander, in the fragments, and in the Plautine adaptations. From *Cistellaria* compare: 59, torture, *excruciare, macerare*; 71–5, sickness, *morbus-medicus-medicina*; 203–8: torture again, cf. especially *vorsor in amoris rota*; 221 shipwreck at the hands of the Love-God; 250, self-punishment to please a mistress; 298, the poison (arrow-poison?) of love; 300, war with the Love-God. From *Bacchides*, with the traditional greedy *meretrices*, metaphors from bird-snaring, 50–1, 1158, *viscus*; fishing, 101; bloodsucking leeches, 372. The lover himself is physically and legally bound, 181, *ita me vadatum amore vinctumque attines*.[2]

It is interesting that, although every play of, or derived from, Menander has a love element in the plot, only in certain plays (and in certain scenes of those plays) is love imagery found. Thus there is little or nothing comparable in *Aulularia, Heauton Timoroumenos* (and Apollodorus' *Phormio*), and the few erotic metaphors in Menander himself occur in the fragments, rather than the relatively complete plays. Relevant here are *Perikeiromene* 466/7 – the

1 Preston, p. 48, n. 73, quotes parallels from *A.P.* 5.5; 6; 10; and 50 (καίω, καταφλέγω, πῦρ) from Alciphron 1.13, and one example from Aristophanes, Lys. 221, ἐπιτύφομαι.
2 On all these metaphors see *Preston, op. cit.,* pp. 47–56. His Greek parallels are almost entirely from the *Anthology*, and other sources later than New Comedy. I have added the material from New Comedy which is quoted below.

soldier in love taken by storm like a city,[3] fr. 79, ἀλλ᾽ ὅταν ἐρῶντα νοῦν ἔχειν
τις ἀξιοῖ/παρὰ τίνι τ᾽ἀνόητον οὗτος ὄψεται – closely related to *Eu.* 61–3; fr. 80 –
from the Ἀφροδίσιος: hence the νόσος is presumably love sickness; fr. 198,
penalties to the love-god for intransigence; fr. 200, caustic surgery for love the
disease; fr. 258, Sappho goaded into madness by love; fr. 568, the sickness and
the wound of love; fr. 570, the lover captured; fr. 571, virtue as a love philtre
enabling woman to conquer her man; and fr. 656, in which the comparison
of love to a whirlwind or shipwreck is rejected, because the speaker is
ἅπαξ/ἀψάμενος ... καὶ φιλήσας ἐν βυθῷ – drowned instantly.

Of the imagery found in both Menander and Plautus' Menander-plays,
shipwreck (Men. fr. 656 and *Cist.* 221) is absent from Terence; so also are
references to Ἔρως as equivalent to Amor (Men. fr. 198; Pl. *Cist.* 203 ff.,
300; cf. Philemon's *Trinummus* 236–41), and to the wounds caused by his
arrows (Men. fr. 568, ὁ πληγεὶς δ᾽ εἴσεθ᾽ ᾗ τιτρώσκεται; perhaps *Cist.* 298;[4]
cf. also Plautus, *Persa* 24–5, *saucius* factus sum in Veneris *proelio,/sagitta
Cupido cor meum transfixit*; *Trin.* 242, saviis *sagittatis perculsus*).

I shall consider the imagery illustrated on pp. 83–4, and outline for each
instance, in order of mention, its subsequent history in Roman love poetry
with some additional comment.

Love as single combat: *Eu.* 54–5, actumst, ilicet/peristi: *eludet* ubi te *victum*
sensent. Compare with this use of *eludere*, Prop. 4.1.139–40, nam tibi *victrices*
quascumque labore parasti/*eludet palmas* una puella tuas. Here both *eludere*
and *palmae* derive from the gladiatorial combat.

War and peace in love: *Eu.* 53.61–2; *Pax*: Prop. 2.2.2, at me composita *pace*
fefellit Amor; 2.13.15, si forte bonas *ad pacem* verterit auris; 3.8.34, in te *pax*
mihi nulla placet; 4.5.32, post modo *mercata pace* premendus erit; Ovid *Am.*
1.2.21, nil opus est *bello, veniam pacemque* rogamus. For *Bellum* add to Ovid
Am. 1.2.21, above, Tib. 1.10.53, sed Veneris tum *bella* calent (but this is actual
sexual combat). Propertius prefers *proelia* in this context (2.1.45; 3.5.2: cf.
also Tib. 1.3.64, adsidue *proelia* miscet Amor; Hor. *Carm.* 1.6.17–18, *proelia*

---

3 The military vocabulary of the siege scene – *Perik.* 198–234 is not really imagery,
although Polemon is conducting a lover's siege. To him the military aspect of his
attack on the house is reality and not a form of extraneous comparison.
4 Latin dictionaries take *toxicum* here of poison, but the use of *tangere* in the phrase
tactum toxico argues for a wound: this can be solved by taking *toxicum* as Greek τοξικὸν
φάρμακον, arrow poison; cf. Caecil. fr. 50R, ut hominem ... *toxico* transegerit, referred
by Festus p. 468L to arrow poison.

virginum/sectis in iuvenes unguibus) or *arma*: 3.20.20, dulcia ... nobis concitet
arma Venus; 4.8.88, toto solvimus *arma* toro. The image was further developed
and elaborated, together with that of the lover's *militia*, in Propertius and
Ovid (cf. especially *Amores* 1.9).

Insanity: cf. *An.* 469, adeone est *demens*?; 692, si hic non *insanit* satis sua sponte
instiga. The equation of *amare* with *insanire* in *Eu.* 61–3 is similar to Menander
fr. 79K. *Rabies* in *Eu.* 301 is the coarse expression of a slave – one not used elsewhere of love except in fiery contempt by Lucretius (4.1083, 1117, see s.v.).
But the mad folly of love is a source of pride to Catullus (7.10, *vesano* ...
Catullo; cf. *vesana* flamma, 100.7), Tibullus (1.2.11, *dementia* nostra; cf.
2.6.17–18, tu me .../cogis et *insana* mente nefanda loqui; *ibid.*, 51, *mens* mihi
perdita fingit) and Propertius (1.1.26, *non sani* pectoris; so love itself is insane;
2.14.18, *insano* ... in amore; 2.15.29, *vesani* ... amoris; 3.17.3, *insanae* Veneris ...
fastus, and the lover raves; 2.34b.25, seros *insanit* amores.) It features in Virgil's
Eclogues: 2.69, Corydon, quae te *dementia* cepit?, and the Gallus eclogue,
perhaps echoing Gallus himself, 10.22, Galle, quid *insanis*? *Furor* and *furere*
do not belong to the vocabulary of comedy, but compare Cat. 15.14, *mala*
mens furorque vecors; 64.54, 94, and 197, *amenti* caeca *furore*; 68.129, tu horum
magnos vicisti sola *furores*; Verg. *Ecl.* 10.60, tamquam haec sit nostri medicina
furoris; Propertius, 1.1.7; 4.11; 5.3; 13.20 (*demens* ... *furor*), 18.15;[5] Ovid *Am.*
1.2.35, etc. Often *furor* is applied specifically to lovers' anger; thus Tib. 1.6.74
(the only instance of *furor* in Tibullus), Ovid *Am.* 1.7.2–3 (echoing the
Tibullus passage?). Compare Propertius' use of *insanus* and *furibundus* in
3.8.2–3, 4.8.52 and 60.

In *Hec.* 70 and 73 the verbs *insidiari* and *capere* describe the treachery of
lovers. This is less characteristic of elegy, but cf. Cat. 15.16 (to a rival), ut
nostrum *insidiis* caput lacessas; Tib. 1.6.4, *insidias* homini composuisse deum;
Prop. 2.32.19–20, *insidias* in me componis inanes/*tendis* iners docto retia nota
mihi; 3.25.6, semper ab *insidiis*, Cynthia, flere soles; Ovid *Am.* 1.8.69–70,
parcius exigito pretium dum *retia tendis*/ne fugiant; *captos* legibus ure tuis;
2.4.12, uror et *insidiae* sunt pudor ille meae. The use of *capere* is too common
to illustrate, from the opening of Propertius' *Monobiblos* to Ovid *Am.* 1.8.70
above.

The imagery of fire in Terence is limited to the use of *incendere*, which is
virtually absent from Elegy, *ardere*, and the personified, if not serious, use of
ignis for the beloved (*Eu.* 82).

5 *Furor* is here applied to the source of maddened love; cf. Propertius' use of *ardor* in
1.20.6, discussed below.

Ardere and *ardor*, metaphors of general non-erotic application and common in prose, have a special role in erotic poetry. For *ardere* cf. Cat. 45.16; 64.197 (cf. *exardesco*, 64.93), 68.53 (Lucretius uses *ardescere* similarly in 4.1090); Verg. *Ecl.* 2.1, formosum pastor Corydon *ardebat* Alexim; Hor. *Epod.*14.9–10, non aliter Samio dicunt *arsisse* Bathyllo/Anacreonta Teium; Ovid, *Am.* 1.9.33; 2.8.11 (both of Achilles). The verb is absent from Tibullus except with reference to Love's torches in 2.1.82. In Propertius it is only literal, except in 3.13.21, *ardent* victrices *et flammae pectora praebent*, which is certainly literal, but may intend erotic imagery in a kind of grisly word-play. Thus *ardere* seems to have been avoided in Elegy, although Ovid can use it in a heroic context.

The noun *ardor*, absent from Terence, seems to have had a wider use than the verb in Elegy.[6] Compare Prop. 1.3.13; 7.24; 10.10; 13.28 (20.6 uses *ardor* like *ignis* of the beloved himself as an object of burning desire), and Ovid, *Am.* 2.9b.3; 2.16.11–12, at *meus ignis* abest. verbo peccavimus uno! – quae movet *ardores* est procul; *ardor* adest, a witty comment on the application of *ignis* to the beloved; see below.

Ignis is used of the fire in the lover's heart by Lucretius, 4.1138 (probably literal in intention, see note on his use of *ardor*); by Catullus (25.15; 45.16 – its seat is the *medullae*); by Propertius, 1.9.17; 3.6.39, me quoque consimili impositum torquerier *igni*; by Ovid, *Am.* 1.2.9, an subitum *luctando accendimus ignem*? etc. But Elegy extends the use. The plural becomes a synonym for the lover's passion: Prop. 1.6.7; 11.7; 2.34b.44; 3.17.9; Ovid, *Am.* 2.19.15, tepidosque refoverat *ignis*; *Trist.* 4.10.45, saepe suos recitare solitus Propertius *ignis*; cf. Verg. *Ecl.* 5.10, Phyllidis *ignes*; Hor. *Carm.* 1.27.15–16, non erubescendis adurit/*ignibus*. The singular describes the beloved: Verg. *Ecl.* 3.66, *meus ignis*, Amyntas, Hor. *Epod.* 14.13, *ureris* ipse miser: quod si non pulchrior *ignis*/accendit obsessam Ilion; and the convention is mocked by Ovid in *Am.* 2.16.11–12 above.[7]

The verb *uro* is used by Terence only of the pain of jealousy (in *Eu.* 274, not necessarily erotic; in 438, erotic). In Plautus, e.g. *Bac.* 1091, *Per.* 801b, it is used similarly of resentment, and has no connection with love. But in later poetry in which the image of the fire of love becomes so common, *uro* is perhaps the most frequent vehicle for the metaphors; cf. Cat. 61.170, pectore *uritur* intimo *flamma*; 72.5, 83.6. The instance at 77.3 is rather different: the rival is called a *pestis* ... intestina *perurens*. Tibullus makes Venus or Cupid the

---

6 In Lucretius, 4.1077, 1086–7, 1098, 1116, the literal sense of *ardor* as physical heat is probably predominant. Catullus has it once in hendecasyllables: 2.9, credo, ut tum gravis acquiescat *ardor*.

7 Tibullus does not use *ignis* as an erotic metaphor.

subject of the verb: 1.2.98, quid *messes uris*, acerba, *tuas* – a double image; 1.8.7, 2.4.5–6, 2.6.5. In Verg. *Ecl.* 2.68, love or the Love-God burns the lover, me tamen *urit* amor (Amor?). From Horace, cf. *Epod.* 14.13 above, *Carm.* 1.6.19; 13.9; 19.5.7, and 27.15–16 above. The most frequent form is the passive (*uror*, etc.) This is found in Prop. 2.24.8, in the usual sense – *urerer*, et quamvis non bene, verba darem (I would be consumed by jealousy), but at 2.3.44 and 3.9.45, Cynthia and his poetry respectively inflame with *desire* and *emulation*. Ovid's use follows the convention of Horace and Tibullus – first person passive: *Am.* 1.1.26; 2.4.12; the Love-God as subject, *Am.* 1.2.43; 2.9a.5; 17.3; more general *Am.* 1.8.70; 19.3.

Catullan love poetry and the Elegists greatly enlarged the vocabulary of love's fire beyond this range. Catullus 64.91–3 is an example of Epic colouring:

> non prius ex illo *flagrantia* declinavit
> lumina, quam cuncto *concepit* corpore *flammam*
> funditus, atque imis *exarsit* tota medullis.

Thus *flamma*, Cat. 64.92 is a symbol in 61.171; 100.7; Ovid, *Am.* 2.1.10. It is used of lover or beloved in Propertius 2.34b.86, Horace. *Carm.* 1.27.20, digne puer meliore *flamma*. *Flagrare*, Cat. 64.91, occurs also in 68.73; Prop. 1.13.23, 2.3.33, 3.19.13; *faces* (the torches of the Love-God) occur principally in allegory involving the god: Tib. 2.1.82; 2.4.6; 2.6.16; Prop. 2.29.95; Ovid. *Am.* 2.9a.5; more sophisticated images appear in Prop. 1.13.26; 2.13.14; 2.7.8 (faces = amorem), 4.3.50; 4.4.70, Vesta ... culpam alit, et plures condit in ossa *faces*. *Torrere*: cf. Cat. 68.52; 100.7, cum vesana meas *torreret* flamma medullas; Prop. 3.24.13, correptus saeva Veneris *torrebar* aeno; Hor. *Carm.* 1.33.5–6, insignem tenui fronte Lycordia/Cyri *torret* amor. All these are expressions too "poetic" or "heroic" for the naturalistic language of Terentian comedy.

The common verbs for dying of love, on the other hand, *perire*, *deperire*, etc. are widely found: cf. Cat. 45.3–5, ni te perdite amo ... quantum qui pote plurimum *perire* (the tone and structure of ordinary speech), 35.12, illum *deperit* impotente amore, 100.2; Verg. *Ecl.* 8.41, ut vidi, *ut perii*, ut me malus abstulit error; 10.10, indigno cum Gallus amore *peribat*; Hor. *Carm.* 1.27.11–12, quo beatus/volnere, qua *pereat* sagitta; Prop. 1.4.12; 14.14; 15.41; 2.15.13, ipse Paris nuda fertur *periisse* Lacaena. Love-sickness in its most desperate sincerity occurs in Cat. 76.25: ipse valere opto, et taetrum *hunc* deponere *morbum*; cf. Tib. 2.5.109–10, iaceo cum saucius annum/et faveo *morbo*, cum iuvat ipse dolor; Prop. 2.1.58, omnis humanos sanat *medicina* dolores/solus amor *morbi* non amat artificem. For *remedium* in Terence, *medicina* is metrically a necessary substitute; cf. Verg. *Ecl.* 10.60, tamquam haec sit nostri *medicina* furoris; Prop. 1.5.28, cum mihi nulla mei sit *medicina* mali (cf. Ter. *An.* 468); 1.10.18; 2.1.57-8; 2.14.16; 3.17.4; *tabescere*, to waste away, is used by Lucretius, 4.1121, incerti *tabescunt* vulnere caeco, Cat. 68.55, assiduo *tabescere* lumina fletu. Propertius, like Terence, applies it to women: 1.15.20 (Hypsipyle); 3.6.23 (Cynthia); 3.12.9 (Galla). Ovid limits the image to heroic contexts: cf. *Met.* 4.259, *tabuit* ex illo dementer amoribus usa. (But add *Trist.* 5.1.77, animum *tabescere* curis, applied to himself). *Macerare*, which is close in meaning to *tabescere* but also related to the imagery of torment, is avoided by Elegy, on stylistic grounds.[8]

The lover's torture or self-torture (in Terence *excruciare*, *discruciare*) is still an important image in Catullus: cf. 66.76, afore me a dominae vertice *discrucior* (the lock speaks in the language of a lover: *discruciare* is probably preferred over *excruciare* for metrical convenience); 76.10, cur te amplius *excrucies*?; 85.2, 99.11-12, omnique *excruciare* modo, cf. *ibid.*, 4, *suffixum in summa* me memini esse *cruce*. *Cruciare* seems to be the verb of Prop. 2.25.40, quantus sic *cruciat* lumina vestra dolor (Barber, alii alia), but this root is avoided by Tibullus and Ovid, who prefer *torquere*; cf. Tib.: 1.4.81, lento me *torquet* amore; 1.5.5, ure ferum et *torque*; 1.8.49; 2.6.17; Ov. *Am.* 1.4.46; 2.5.53; 2.19.34; *Ep.* 9.36, etc. So too Prop. 3.6.39, me quoque consimili impositum *torquerier* igni; 3.17.11, vacuos nox sobria *torquet* amantis.

So far we have dealt with the sufferings of love. On the happier side occurs the frivolous use of *ludus* and *ludere* in *Eu.* 373 and 586, quia consimilem *luserat*/iam olim ille *ludum*: we compared with this Pl. *Rud.* 426 and 468,[9] the only clearly erotic uses of *ludus/ludere* in Plautus;[10] This use occurs in Cat. 61.203-5, vestri .../multa milia *ludi*./*ludite* ut lubet, et brevi liberos date; cf.

---

8 Except Ovid, *Ep.* 19.125. On the different vocabulary of the "paired" *Epistulae Heroidum*, see Axelson, *Unpoetische Wörter*, p. 144, n. 21.

For the humorous effect of *macerare* intended in Horace *Epod.* 14.15-6, *Carm.* 1.13.8, see the discussion on *macerare*, above, p. 59, n. 9.

9 The reading of Leo, following Fleckeisen.

10 Preston, pp. 31-3, compares the use of *iocu' ludus* in *Ps.* 64-5, nostri amores mores consuetudines/iocu' ludus sermo suavisaviatio; *Ps.* 65 is almost certainly interpolated into the list of 64-8 which is exclusively plural, from its occurrence in a list of singular deities at *Bac.* 116. The pairing of *ludus* with *iocus* seems to exclude any specifically erotic meaning. Elsewhere in Plautus, *Capt.* 770, *Mer.* 846, *Truc.* 107, and in Terence, *Eu.* 300, the phrase occurs sometimes in an amorous context, but as often simply denotes amusement and festivity.

68.156, in qua *lusimus* et domina (99.1?); Prop. 2.15.21, necdum inclinatae prohibent te *ludere* mammae; 2.32.29, sin autem ... nox ... *lusu*/consumpta est; Tib. 1.3.64, at iuvenum series teneris inmixta puellis/*ludit*, et adsidue proelia miscet Amor; 2.1.87; Ovid., *Am.* 2.3.13, est etiam facies, sunt apti *lusibus* anni, etc.

Finally the consummation of love, or the prospect of true reconciliation brings the hyperbole of restoration from the dead, immortality, even deification. For the first, *Hec.* 852, there is no real parallel in Greek or later Latin authors: the spirit of Prop. 2.27.15–16, si modo clamantis revocaverit aura puellae/concessum nulla lege redibit iter, is quite different. The death is real, the restoration to this world an ἀδύνατον; in *Hec.* 852 the image seems rather to imply a possibility of suicide now happily rejected. *Immortality* is the theme of Pl. *Poen.* 275–6, di immortales ... quid habetis qui mage inmortalis vos credam esse quam ego siem,/qui haec tanta bona oculis concipio? The allusion of *An.* 960 ff., mi. immortalitas partast, si nulla aegritudo huic gaudio intercesserit, is, we are told by Donatus, derived from Menander's *Eunuchus*, and its natural place would be in *Eu.* act 3, sc. 5, the scene of Chaerea's exultation at his passionate conquest.[11] Comparison with the gods seems to have been made lightly in New Comedy; cf. Philemon ΧΙΙ, fr. 79²⁴⁻⁶: the cook claims: ἅπαντες οἱ φαγόντες ἐγένοντ' ἂν θεοί/ἀθανασίαν εὕρηκα. τοὺς ἤδη νεκροὺς/ὅταν ὀσφρανθῶσι, ποιῶ ζῆν πάλιν. Here we have all three hyperboles associated by Terence with the consummation of love. For immortality conferred by success in love, cf. Prop. 2.14.10, immortalis ero si altera (sc. nox) talis erit; 2.15.39, si dabit haec multas (noctes) fiam immortalis in illis/nocte una quivis vel deus esse potest. This is absent from Tibullus, and I know of no examples from Ovid or other Latin erotic poetry. Equality with the gods, implied in *An.* 959, *Hau.* 693 (cf. Pl. *Cur.* 168) and declared outright in *Hec.* 843, *deus sum si hoc ita est*, reappears, with a notable modification (ille *si fas est superare* divos) in Catullus' Sappho poem, 51.1–2, and Prop. 2.15.40, above. But such comparison is made freely in Terence, as in New Comedy, in other more trivial contexts: see s.v. *praesens deus* above.

Thus, in the imagery of love employed by Terence, despite its simplicity, we have the nucleus of the more baroque imagery of lyric and elegy. Of the traditional figurative language of the *sermo amatorius* over a century after Terence, the imagery of *servitium* to the mistress, of the *foedus* as a sanctified

11 Cf. Fraenkel, *El. Pl.* pp. 208–9 and n. 2. Korte, vol II, p. 68, accepts this derivation; cf. in this connection *Eu.* 551–2, nunc est profecto interfici quom perpeti me mavelim/ne hoc gaudium contaminet vita aegritudine aliqua with *An.* 961.

equivalent of marriage, and of the *furtum* are alien to the situation and values of Terence's characters: the arrows of the love-god and his wounds must have featured in New Comedy, as they do in Plautus, in Elegy, and in early Horatian lyric, but seem to have been rejected by Terence. Similarly the lover's shipwreck on the seas of passion, found only once in Plautus (*Cist.* 221), is absent from Terence, although developed elaborately in Elegy. The concept of the *militia amoris*, on the other hand, is merely a development of allusions to the warfare of love found more fully in Terence than in Plautus; all the other dominant imagery, of madness, sickness, inflammation, torture, ruin, and the rare exaltation to immortality, are already to be found in the language of Terence's lovers and those who have to grapple with their follies.

PART II Artistic deviation and development

4

Plautus and the imagery of fantasy

Comparison of the imagery found in Terence with similar passages in Plautus has shown a central core of metaphor common to both playwrights, largely derivable from the Greek originals of these Roman comedies, but no less at home in subsequent "familiar" Latin prose. However, by far the greater quantity of imagery in Plautus is quite different in tone – comic or fantastic, designed to amuse and delight rather than to convey a real or plausible psychological insight. Choice of image, choice of syntactical form, even the multiplicity of near-imagery achieved by comparisons, identifications, personifications, all go far beyond what would be natural to educated *sermo familiaris*. Indeed, one might take Cicero's careful limitations of *translatio* (metaphor and allied forms) in *de Oratore* 3.162–4 and use what he excludes from the range of tasteful metaphor as an index to some of the methods adopted by Plautus to give his imagery vitality.

Quo in genere *primum est fugienda dissimilitudo*: "caeli ingentes fornices." quamvis sphaeram in scaenam, ut dicitur, attulerit Ennius, tamen in sphaera fornicis similitudo inesse non potest ... deinde videndum est *ne longe simile sit ductum*: "Syrtim" patrimoni, "scopulum" libentius dixerim: "Charybdim" bonorum "voraginem" potius; facilius enim ad ea, quae visa, quam ad illa, quae audita sunt, mentis oculi feruntur; et quoniam haec vel summa laus est in verbis transferendis, ut sensum feriat id, quod translatum sit, *fugienda est omnis turpitudo earum rerum*, ad quas eorum animos qui audient, trahet similitudo. Nolo dici morte Africani "castratam" esse rem publicam, nolo "stercus curiae" dici Glauciam; quamvis sit simile, tamen est in utroque deformis cogitatio similitudinis; *nolo esse aut maius quam res postulet*; "tempestas comissationis" *aut minus*: "comissatio tempestatis:" *nolo esse verbum angustius id, quod translatum sit, quam fuisset illud proprium et suum ... atque etiam si vereare, ne paulo durior translatio esse videatur, mollienda est praeposito saepe verbo ... etenim verecunda debet esse translatio, ut deducta esse in alienum locum, non inrupisse, atque ut precario, non vi, venisse videatur.*

It is these very categories, either described or illustrated by Cicero, which contribute most to the kaleidoscopic brilliance of Plautine language. But whereas many of these extravagances (such as personification of parts of the body) find parallels in Greek Old Comedy,[1] this element of fantasy is totally alien to New Comedy. Indeed, in discussing such personification in Plautus, Fraenkel has shown for countless examples that, on purely dramatic grounds, they must occur in passages of Plautine expansion, and cannot represent the imagery of the Greek original. With his licence of fantasy in both conception and vocabulary, Plautus is capable of infinite and almost indefinable variation on any type of image; however I hope by concentrating on a few favourite categories to show something of the range and development of the purely comic image in his plays.

I DESCRIPTIONS OF VIOLENCE

The violence of slave-beating and torture which is a frequent source of verbal fantasy in Plautus is generally accepted as his own contribution to the comedies (cf. Fraenkel, *op. cit.* p. 17). In describing such punishments, Plautus may use the relatively unimpressive verb-based metaphor, usually made more appealing by alliteration or assonance; a simple example is *pugnis pectere* (*Men.* 1017, *Poen.* 358, *Rud.* 661; non-alliterative *fusti pectere* only once, *Capt.* 896). Compare:

Aul.

414   me atque hos *onustos* fustibus

Epid.

93   virgis dorsum *despoliet* meum

Epid.

121   quem quidem ego hominem *inrigatum* plagis pistori dabo;

In the last example the image of the slave's back as a hill-side scarred by the weals of irrigation channels is strongly (and sadistically) visual.

---

1 See Fraenkel, *Elementi Plautini* (Florence 1960), pp. 95–7. His book is a prerequisite for any attempt to discuss Plautine imagery, and this chapter relies throughout on his arguments for distinguishing what is original in Plautus' handling of metaphor and related forms.

Capt.

650-2   vae illis virgis miseris quae hodie in tergo *morientur* meo

... quid cessatis compedes

currere ad me atque *amplecti* crura, ut vos *custodiam*?

The humour here lies in the reversal of the normal relationship, with the blows and shackles personified and made pathetic. A less effective use of the same technique is *Rud.* 816; extemplo *amplectitote* crura fustibus where the verb is inappropriate to *fustes*, motivated by alliteration with *extemplo* rather than by sense. Verbal and substantival imagery are combined in, e.g. *Aul.* 454, *implevisti* fusti *fissorum* caput, or *Rud.* 732, *quasi myrteta iunci*, item ego vos virgis *circum vinciam.* (Here, however, a damaged text leaves the intention of the image obscure.)

Metaphor conveyed through nouns is more extravagant, often through deliberate incongruity. The victim of the goad is variously described as *stimulorum seges* (*Aul.* 45), *stimulorum loculi* (*Cas.* 447) a "case" for the goads or, by a similar twist to that of *Capt.* 650, *stimulorum tritor* (*Per.* 795) "you goad-breaker." There can be play on coincidence of function, with personification of the instrument of torture: *Aul.* 59, te dedam *discipulam* cruci; *Mil.* 184, omnis crucibus *contubernales* dare; similar is *Epid.* 140, ut meum tergum tuae stultitiae subdas *succidaneum* (a substitute sacrifice). Plautus also delights in presenting his metaphors as identifications; cf. *Rud.* 721-2

te follem pugilatorium
faciam et pendentem incursabo pugnis ...

explaining the enigma of the identification by the clause which follows. The blows themselves are seen as a sowing; *Men.* 1012, hisce ego iam *sementem* in ore faciam, pugnosque *obseram*; or as a herd of sheep, *Ps.* 333, duo *greges* virgarum ... ulmearum *adegero* (provoked by an allusion to real sheep in the preceding line); or as contributions to a feast, *Epid.* 125, paratae iam sunt scapulis *symbolae.* The Greek institution of the *symbola* need not imply a Greek origin for the image. More fantastic is 311 of the same play; metuo/... *ne ulmos parasitos faciat quae usque attondeant*, because two separate metaphors are involved – parasites metaphorically fleece their victims (see below, p. 103); blows metaphorically fleece the back; therefore, blows are turned into parasites.

This type of imagery through nouns is often expressed by Plautus through the use of a coined adjective.[2] Thus in *Ps.* 545, *stilis* me totum usque *ulmeis conscribito*, the verb *conscribere* is reinforced by the noun *stilus*, and this is identified with the elm-rods through the adjective *ulmeus*. This adjective alone suffices to indicate a beating in *Epid.* 625–6 (see below) and *Rud.* 636, ut tibi *ulmeam* uberem speres esse *virgidemiam*, "a rich vintage of elm-rods"; *virgidemia* is an *ad hoc* coinage by analogy with *vindemia*. The adjective *pugneus* (a coinage, of course) fulfils the same function in *Rud.* 763, iam hercle tibi *messis* in ore fiet *mergis pugneis*, changing the sowing metaphor of the similar *Men.* 1012 into a "harvest of fist-forks."

Finally the imagery can develop into full-scale fantasy analogies. The simple (and alliterative) idea of the slave marked by weals, *varius virgis Mil.* 216, takes on rich aesthetic associations:

Epid.

625–6   e tuis verbis meum futurum corium *pulchrum* praedicas
           quem Apelles et Zeuxis[3] duo *pingent pigmentis ulmeis*

Poen.

1289–91   iam pol ego illam pugnis totam faciam ut sit *merulea*
           ita replebo atritate, atritior multo ut siet
           quam Aegyptini qui cortinam ludis per circum ferunt.

---

2 Coined, or comically misused adjectives are a favourite device in Plautus to convey imagery through identification, since the adjectives are used as definition. Compare from *Pseudolus* alone: 47–8, pro *lignean* salute vis *argenteam*/remittere illi? "Do you want to be sent her welfare in silver, in return for a mere wooden fare-well?" (the wooden letter tablets bore her greeting *salutem impertit*, 41); 75, *pumiceos* oculos habeo (my eyes are made of pumice-stone); 100, lacrumis *argenteis* (tears made of cash); 105, auxilium *argentarium*; 158, *caudicali* provinciae (the province of log-chopping?); 300, inopia *argentaria* (here an objective genitive, not making an identification); 312, *argentata* ... querimonia (a protest in terms of cash); 347, amicam tuam esse factam *argenteam*, here a transformation, not an identification: "your girl has been converted into cash." 545 above, stilis *ulmeis*; 766, oppidum *lenonium*; 911, *verberaum* statuam (the slave is compared to a statue made of blows; cf. *Capt.* 951) and 1064, arce *Ballionea*. One of the most complex and compressed examples is *St.* 639, *potione iuncea onerabo* gulam. Images accumulate here: I will load my throat; the throat suggests drink; the rope then becomes a drink, but it is a drink made of reed fibre. This technique is very rare in Terence, but cf. *Eun.* 316, reddunt curatura *iunceas*: "they make them reed-slim by dieting," and 586, imbrem *aureum*, the golden shower with which Jupiter seduced Danaë.

3 On *Epid.* 625–6, *Poen.* 1271, cf. Fraenkel, *op. cit.*, 17: "ed e innegabile che in questo campo egli agisce con assoluta indipendenza degli originali ..."; p. 18: "nell' originale dell 'Epidicus, una menzione dei due pittori e impensabile ... l'impiego die celebri nomi in entrambi i passi fa pensare ad un autore che non aveva nessuna idea precisa ne del grande artista del secolo v, ne del contemporaneo di Alessandro Magno, un autore per il quale Zeusi e Apelle non erano in fondo nient'altro che i nomi dei due piu famose pittori."

Ps.

145-7   ita ego vostra latera loris faciam ut valide *varia* sint
         ut ne peristromata quidem aeque *picta* sint Campanica
         neque Alexandrina beluata tonsilia tappetia;

All of these examples are based on visual appeal, and in all of them the object
compared with the beaten victim has been given a life and interest of its own.

Although not itself an image, the comic comparison inevitably involves
an element of imagery, even outright visualization; an example in this
category is *Rud.* 753-4,

ni offerumentas habebis pluris in tergo tuo
quam ulla navis longa clavos.

Such comparisons occur frequently alongside metaphor, to achieve variety,
and are even preferred to plain metaphor or identification because of the
superlative value they confer on the comic hero or his experience.

II VIOLENT DESCRIPTION OF THE NON-VIOLENT

It is a natural feature of lively or emotional speech in any genre to substitute
violent[4] physical words for milder physical or psychological equivalents.
Thus *auris ... obtundo tuas* (*Cist.* 118) or *conteris*/tu tua me oratione (*Cist.* 609)
use strong verbs to express their vehemence. Such idioms are found in
Terence also (*obtundere*, *An.* 348, *Hau.* 879, etc.; *conterere* [in a different

---

4 On this category of imagery in Plautus, see P.B. Corbett, "Vis Comica," *Eranos*, vol. 62,
1964, 52-69. He provides a full list of verbs expressive of violence used figuratively in
Plautus and Terence, and comments briefly on the difference between the usage of the
two playwrights. Unfortunately, he is not interested in the handling and application of
these verbs by either author, nor does he distinguish between conventional and unconventional, fresh and dying metaphor. Nevertheless, his final comment is worth quoting
here: "the words we have listed for our survey suggest, albeit for comic effect, killing
and destruction, striking, beating, tearing, and other forms of violence. They do so
because they are part and parcel of the *sermo cottidianus* of the still young, vigorous
and aggressive nation to which both poets belonged." I differ from Corbett primarily in
treating separately the milder usages common to both Plautus and Terence and found in
subsequent *sermo familiaris* (listed individually in chap. 2 above). Under the present
heading I have selected some of the deliberately unconventional and fantastic usages
which I believe are peculiar to the language of popular comedy. (Because of the loss of
Naevius and lesser comic authors, this is now represented for us almost exclusively by
Plautus.) This section includes imagery of violence in *any* syntactical category, but only
such examples as are neither to be found in Terence, nor in Greek New Comedy, and
can be regarded as Plautus' own contribution to his figurative language.

metaphor], *Ph.* 209, *Hec.* 815, etc.) and in Cicero's letters, and their equivalents occur in the paler vocabulary of New Comedy. But with, e.g. *Aul.* 151,

> quia mi misero cerebrum excutiunt
> tua dicta, soror, *lapides loqueris*

the same general conception has become fantastic, ending in an impossible
identification. Fraenkel, *op. cit.,* p. 98, gives many similar examples of Plautine
surrealism with the now dead metaphors of winged voices, sounds beating
on ears, and the like. Thus the idea found in Greek[5] that a harsh word is a
goad or sting to the hearer is developed in all directions by Plautus. The simple
form is *cor stimulo foditur* (*Bac.* 1158; cf. *ibid.* 214, cor odio *sauciat*). Yet even the
plain verb *fodere* is too strong to be found metaphorically in Terence.[6] A
typical variant, with identification, occurs in *Cas.* 360–1, *stimulus ego nunc sum
tibi; fodico corculum.* The same image is fuller and more concrete in:

> *Trin.*
> 1000   iamdudum meum ille pectus *pungit aculeus,*
> *Truc.*
> 853   ne ista *stimulum longum habet* quae usque illinc *cor pungit meum*

(here the image is made more visual by *longum* – the Meretrix is operating at
long-distance).

> *Bac.*
> 63   eadem in usu atque ubi periclum facias *aculeata* sunt;
>   animum *fodicant*, bona *destimulant*, facta et famam *sauciant*

(the imagery becomes progressively more far-fetched as the tricolon develops).

Again, it is traditional in Greek and Latin erotic vocabulary that the lover
should describe his emotions in terms of torture and torment; thus *macero,
excrucio* (see p. 84) are commonplaces of all erotic poetry. But Plautus seeks
more intense effects:

---

5 Cf. the use of κέντρον in *Eupolis* 94.7; *Phaedo* 91c, quoted below, p. 157 n. 19. The
nearest equivalent in Menander is δάκνειν, see s.v. *mordere* in the alphabetical list of
Terentian imagery, p. 60.

6 In Terence *stimulus, aculeus* are not found in metaphor; *stimulare* only in *Hau.* 223,
magis me amicae dicta *stimulant. Ph.* 78, advorsus *stimulum* calces, represents the Greek
proverb: πρὸς κέντρα λακτίζειν, not itself found in Greek comedy. See Otto,
Sprichwörter, pp. 331–2.

Epid.

320   expectando *exedor* miser atque *exenteror* ...

322   nimis diu maceror.

Cist.

203   credo ego Amorem primum apud homines *carnificinam*
       commentum

205   ... qui omnes homines supero, antideo *cruciabilitatibus* animi
           iactor, crucior, agitor,
               stimulor, vorsor
           in amoris rota, miser exanimor
           feror, differor, distrahor, diripior ...

This second example is, of course, the highly stylized rhythmic language of anapaestic canticum, but the same colouring is apparent in *Mer.* 469–70:

Pentheum *diripuisse* aiunt Bacchas; nugas maximas
fuisse credo, praeut quo pacto ego *divorsus distrahor.*

The lover sees himself as physically torn apart with suffering, not merely like, but surpassing, that of a heroic mythological figure. A more humorous instance of such language is *Trin.* 242, quom extemplo saviis *sagittatis* perculsust (the Greek cliché of love's arrows made more lively by the Plautine adjective *sagittatus* coined for the occasion), or 247, ibi illa *pendentem ferit*; the mistress' cruelty is like blows administered to a slave hanging on the *crux* or *furca* (cf. the use of *pendere* in *Am.* 280; *As.* 301; *Cas.* 390, etc.).

The trickery of the Meretrix is several times depicted as blood-sucking, a concept probably derived from Hellenistic erotic literature. Thus the simple form of the image occurs at *Bac.* 372: apage istas a me sorores quae *hominum sorbent sanguinem*, and *Cur.* 152: quae mihi misero amanti *ebibit sanguinem*. But when Plautus converts the image to apply it to his slave hero Epidicus, he makes it more striking by substituting a full transformation[7] (cf. Fraenkel,

---

7 The transformation theme is a special feature of Roman comic invention; examples are innumerable in Plautus, in Terence, very rare. It is this which enables Fraenkel, in *Gnomon* 35, 1964, 779, to vindicate the originality of Terence in *Eu.* 584–9: Iovem/quo pacto Danaen misisse aiunt quondam in gremium *imbrem aureum.*/egomet quoque id spectare coepi, et quia consimilem luserat/iam olim ille ludum, impendio magis animu' gaudebat mihi/deum sese *in hominem convortisse* atque in alienas tegulas/venisse clanculum fucum factum mulieri. The Danaë story, used as a parallel in *Men. Sam.* 252, has taken on the Roman colouring of the transformation, and even the Plautine device of the comic adjective – imbrem *aureum* (see above, n. 3).

op. cit., p. 35), *me convortam in hirudinem* atque eorum *exsugebo sanguinem* (*Epid*. 188); similarly in *Bac*. 869, iam illorum ego *animam* amborum *exsorbebo* oppido, the soldier's threat, probably suggested to Plautus by 372 above, is physically incomprehensible.

The personification of inanimates is often used as an excuse for violent language. To return to *cor*, compare two versions of one theme:

Cas.

414–5   cor lienosum opinor habeo, iam dudum *salit*
          de labore *pectus tundit* ...

Ps.

1045–6   mihi cor *retunsumst oppugnando pectore*.

This at least can be explained in physical terms, but Plautus' personification of *dies* goes beyond this into fantasy; *St*. 435–6, hunc tibi dedo diem: meam culpam habeto, nisi probe *excruciavero*, and 453, ego hunc *lacero* diem, use only the dying metaphors of *excruciare* and *lacerare*. But compare

Capt.

464   nam hercle ego huic diei, si liceat, *oculos ecfodiam* lubens,

Men.

152, 154   clam uxorem ubi sepulchrum habeamus atque hunc *comburamus*
           diem
           ... dies quidem iam *ad umbilicum est dimidiatus mortuos*,

Here the day is not merely personified but conceived as a physical human body. However, opportunity for violence of expression is only one aspect of Plautus' love for personifying the inanimate. Most of the examples discussed by Fraenkel in chap. IV of *Elementi Plautini* under this heading are vehicles of imagery, and the immense range of this comic weapon can best be appreciated by turning to his account.

III DECEIT AND INTRIGUE

Trickery and intrigue dominate many of Plautus' plays, whereas in Terence they occupy a relatively subordinate position. The vocabulary of trickery derives largely from the spoken slang of low life, and thus has a place in the *sermo* of Petronius' many shady characters, if not at the social level of Cicero's letters. Thus we have some check on the extent to which Plautus goes beyond the normal prosaic imagery of deceit. At the literary level, deceit is strongly associated with certain types of metaphor: those of hunting, fishing, and fowling feature in Plato, Xenophon, New Comedy, and in Terence and Cicero's letters as well as Plautus; also represented are the metaphors of military attack, in ambush or by frontal assault. We saw, however (p. 40), that Terence's usage is so discreet that in the case of, for example, *intendere*, *An*. 753: repudio quod consilium primum *intenderam*, and *Hau*. 513: *intendenda* in senemst fallacia, no visual image is evoked, and we cannot even decide with certainty whether the verb implies a hunting image of setting a snare, or the military one of the *telum* or *ballista*. Perhaps the only other deception metaphor common to Plautus and Terence is *emungere* (in Terence only *Ph*. 682), an idiom which is paralleled in the language of Menander, but whose use does not really suggest a living metaphor.[8]

The image of shearing (fleecing) is a particularly fertile source of invention for Plautus. Thus, in *Mer*. 524–5, the pretence that the Meretrix is to be bought for wool-working is combined with the metaphorical use of (*at-*)*tondere*, to present the foolish old man who is to be her dupe as a sheep (note the absurdity of the age given):

ovem tibi eccillam dabo, natam annos sexaginta,
peculiarem
eam si curabis, perbonast, *tondetur nimium scite*

This is exploited at greater length in *Bacchides*, a play in which *attondere* virtually provides a leit-motif. The first occasion is 241; Chrysalus' threat of deception is presented in the form of a mythological identification, an enigma only explained by the phrase which follows,

quem quidem ego hodie faciam hic arietem
Phrixi, itaque tondebo auro usque ad vivam cutem.

Fleeced of his gold, Nicoboulus will become the golden ram of Phrixus and Helle. This is recalled by a casual allusion in 1095; *is me scelus auro usque attondit dolis doctis indoctum ut lubitumst*; but the final appearance of the idiom, in the last scene, 1125: *attonsae hae quiden ambae usque sunt*, has been used by Plautus as the basis for a whole canticum for four performers; vv

---

8 Plautus leaves *emungere* undeveloped: verb alone, *Bac*. 701, 1101; slightly fuller, *Epid*. 494, homo es, qui med *emunxti mucidum* minimi preti. For ἀπομύττειν, in Menander and Aristophanes, see s.v. *emungere* in the alphabetical list of metaphors in Terence. Plautus is similarly indifferent to the potential of *os oblinere/sublinere*: *Cur*. 589, *Epid*. 429, 491, *Ps*. 719, etc.; it is slightly amplified in *Capt*. 656, os sublevere *offuciis*.

1120–48. Fraenkel has shown in *El. Pl.* 68–70 how Plautus has combined the ideas of *Mer.* 524–5 and *Bac.* 242 to generate a passage for which there need have been no equivalent in the Δὶς Ἐξαπατῶν, just as by a similar grafting of images from *Bac.* 711 and *Ps.* 1063, 1244, Plautus created the great Iliad canticum of *Bacchides* act 4, sc. 9 (see below). From 1121a–40 the Bacchides sisters comment in antiphony. To introduce the *attondere* theme the old men are described as *oves*; the shepherd must be asleep to let them wander bleating from the flock, 1122–3; but they are glossy and in good condition; the fleecing motif in 1125 is applied to the twice-deceived Nicoboulus: pol hodie altera *iam bis detonsa certo est*; inconsistently the same sister who in 1124 called them *hau sordidae* now mocks them as *vetulae*. But Plautus has to recall the main action; hence Philoxenus is allowed an aside, and, within the sheep metaphor, the sisters move towards inviting the old men in; *cogantur* quidem intro. 1130–9 shifts from sheep 1134, to humans – *exsolvere quanti fuere*, and back, omnis *fructus* iam illis *decidit*, by introducing a third element; the "dead" metaphor *fructus* creates a moment of ambiguity. Like 1129, 1138a contradicts what has already been said (*ne balant quidem*, opposed to 1123, *eunt a pecu balitantes*), and there are signs of flagging invention; 1140 provokes Nicoboulus into speech; his acceptance of the identification, *hae oves volunt vos*, provides an obviously Italian jest, *prodigium hoc quidemst*, based on the standard portent, "*pecudesque locutae*." Finally the real issue of the confrontation, the rescue of the sons, is presented by a multiple identification: 1145–6, the sons are the *agni conclusi*, Chrysalus the *mordax canis* (but this is inconsistent; the dog should protect the lambs, not lead them into danger); finally (1148) the *oves* will undergo a Plautine transformation and change sex to become butting rams. It is unlikely that there was anything comparable in Menander, beyond a possible reference to making the old men as meek as sheep (cf. Ter. *Ad.* 534, tam placidum quam ovem reddam). The whole song has been created by reviving the power of an existing hackneyed metaphor.

But Plautus is capable of another, independent development. In *Captivi*, the image is transferred to the barber's shop; *Capt.* 266–9

> nunc senex est in tonstrina, nunc iam cultros adtinet,
> ne id quidem, involucre inicere, voluit, vestem ut ne inquinet
> sed utrum strictimne *attonsurum* dicam an per pectinem
> nescio; verum si frugist, *usque admutilabit probe*.

The point of the vignette is deliberately delayed by the two lines of irrelevant (but doubtless well-mimed) detail. *Admutilare*, the climax of this description, is used for *attondere* in *Per.* 829: qui me usque *admutilasti* ad cutem, and *Mil.* 768: inveni lepidam sycophantiam/qui *admutiletur* miles usque *caesariatus* (where *caesariatus* has suggested the literal application of the shearing-theme). This coinage is typical of Plautus' search to give fresh vigour to imagery by substituting a new word, or one with violent physical associations for the traditional idiom.

An equally sadistic effect is conveyed by the Plautine word *exenterare* (cf. Gk. ἐξεντερίζειν, to disembowel).[9] Fraenkel, *El. Pl.* 100, n[4] suggests that this was probably current slang in Greek Italy. Plautus uses the word only in the *Epidicus*, once of lover's torment (320 above); in three parallel cases of slave deceit: 511, meum *exenteravit* Epidicus *marsuppium*; 672, ut illic autem *exenteravit* mihi *opes argentarias*; and 185, acutum cultrum habeo, senis qui *exenterem marsuppium*. The added detail of the *culter* in the first instance in the play at 185 may serve to revive the literal meaning of a metaphor that was becoming fossilized. Gronovius derived the word from gutting fish: perhaps the idea of filleting explains how *exenterare* could become cutpurse's slang; this interpretation is borne out by Plautus' use of *exossare*, literally of physical violence; *Am.* 319 (cf. 318, 320, 342), me quasi murenam exossare cogitat, "he's planning to fillet me like an eel," and figuratively, *Ps.* 382, exossabo ego illum simulter itidem ut murenam coquos. *Vorsare* supplies another culinary image for trickery in

Bac.
766   vorsabo ego illunc hodie si vivo, probe
       tam *frictum* ego illum reddam quam frictumst *cicer.*

but elsewhere the use of *vorsare* is left undeveloped.

We should probably assume a Greek[10] origin for the "web of deceitful invention" theme found in

9 The search for violence in imagery explains in part the prevalence of *ex*-compounds coined or reapplied by Plautus. To *exentero* here add: *eradicare, Aul.* 299, *Bac.* 1092, *Epid.* 434, etc.; *exballistare, Ps.* 585; *excisare, Cist.* 383; *excutere, Aul.* 152, *Capt.* 419 (cf. Ter. *Hau.* 167), *Mer.* 576; *exossare, Ps.* 383; *expalpare, Poen.* 357, *Vid.* fr. XVI; *expilare, As.* 826; *exsculpere, Cist.* 541 (also in Terence; *Eu.* 712); *exsorbere, Bac.* 869; *exsugere, Epid.* 188, *Poen.* 614; *exterebrare, Per.* 237; *extexere, Bac.* 239; *extundere, Mos.* 221; *exurere, Bac.* 940. These are all metaphorical uses of the verbs. Another motive for the compounding with *ex* lies in the use of several of these words for wheedling money or favours *out of* a person.
10 The appearance of this image in Cicero's speeches and rhetorical works, e.g. *de Orat.* 2.226, *ea tela texitur,* and the no longer metaphorical *exordiri,* seem to guarantee that its origin is Greek, and literary. See 159 n. 21.

Bac.

350   *exorsa haec tela* non male omnino mihist,

Ps.

399–400   neque *exordiri* primum unde occipias habes

neque ad *detexundam telam certos terminos,*

but it is noteworthy that there is nothing comparable in Terence. *Bac.* 239, *extexam* illum pulchre iam, si di volunt, although based on weaving, is unrelated to these passages, and probably best taken as synonymous with *attondere* – "I'll unravel him." Incompatible images are accumulated in successive lines: *Bac.* 350 above is preceded by a totally different metaphor – the old dupe as a pack-mule; 349, ille est *oneratus* probe et *plus iusto vehit*; with this compare the fuller treatment in *Mos.* 778–82:

vehit hic clitellas, venit hic autem alter senex,
novicium mihi quaestum institui non malum
nam muliones mulos clitellarios
habent, at ego habeo *homines clitellarios*
magni sunt oneris; quicquid imponas vehunt.

An obvious image is that of aiming a weapon at the proposed dupe; we have seen that in Terence the plain verb *intendere*[11] (e.g. *Hau.* 513) may be used with this implication, but the verb is also associated with nets and snares (cf. *Bac.* 792–3) and it is therefore impossible to determine what traditional image underlies Terence's use of the verb. There are many simple examples of this motif in Plautus:

Epid.

690   *tragulam in te inicere* adornat; nescio quam fabricam facit:

Ps.

407   et volui *inicere tragulam* in nostrum senem;

Poen.

201–2   quoi iam infortuni *intentast ballista* probe

quam ego haud multo post *mittam e ballistario;*

Mos.

570   continuo adveniens *pilum iniecisti* mihi.

11 See Fraenkel, *op. cit.*, 59, and especially n. 3, on the Ciceronian use of *telum conicere.* Thus *tela conicere* in *Har.* 2, *ea tela quae coniecerit,* is followed by "si quod in me *telum intenderit,* statim me esse arrepturum arma," *ibid.,* 7. For other uses of *intendere* to denote hostile "intent," cf. *Sest.* 15, *intentus est arcus in me unum;* 42, *intenta signa* legionum ... *cervicibus ac bonis vestris; Mil.* 37, haec (sica) *intenta est nobis;* 67, *illa omnia in hunc unum constituta, parata, intenta sunt.*

From the very nature of the intrigue, Plautine slaves usually depict their plots with the imagery of aggressive combat, and I shall return to two of the most famous examples later. *Mil.* 218–28, however, presents the slave in a defensive situation – his intrigues have been detected – and the metaphors with which he urges himself on [12] are based on the requirements of a general under attack:

> viden *hostis tibi adesse*, tuoque tergo *obsidium?* consule,
> arripe opem auxiliumque ad hanc rem; propere hoc, non placide decet.
> *anteveni aliqua, aliquo saltu circumduce exercitum,*
> *coge in obsidium perduellis, nostris praesidium para;*
> *interclude inimicis commeatum, tibi muni viam*
> *qua cibatus commeatusque ad te et legiones tuas*
> *tuto possit pervenire;* hanc rem age; subitaria est.
> reperi, comminiscere, cedo calidum consilium cito
> : : magnam illic homo rem incipissit, *magna munit moenia,*
> : : tute unus si recipere ad te hoc dicis, confidentiast
> *nos inimicos profligare posse.*

The details of this narrative metaphor are exceptional in Plautus, and seem to relate quite closely to the dramatic situation. The enemy, the slave Sceledrus, has seen Palaestrio's former master Pleusicles kissing the soldier's concubine inside the next-door house, to which Palaestrio and Pleusicles have engineered a passage. He is naturally going to tell the soldier unless Palaestrio can circumvent him, and the method hit upon involves (v. 182) transferring the girl back to her own house, while continuing to conceal from the enemy that there is an access (*commeatus*) between the houses. The fact that this plan is subsequently changed (237 ff.) need not affect the general associations which have dictated the imagery here. Palaestrio must anticipate the enemy; lead his army round by some defile; drive the foe into a blockade, and obtain protection for his own forces; he is to cut off access or supplies from the enemy (223) and lay a road by which food and supplies can safely reach himself and his legions ... on which Periplectomenus comments, 228: "that fellow's starting on a great enterprise; he is constructing mighty defences." Following Fraenkel's allocation of speakers, Palaestrio turns to him, "only if you take on this undertaking,

---

12 I follow Fraenkel in *Museum Helveticum* 25, 1968, 1231–4, attributing *Mil.* 215, *age si quid agis* ... to 227, *facta ut facta ne sient*, to the slave Palaestrio; his arguments are decisive for identifying 215 onwards as "Selbstanrede." It seems equally certain that 228, magnam illic homo rem incipissit, *magna munit moenia*, must be the words of a new speaker, describing the ambitious schemes of the planner in 220–7, and parallel in function to the admiring comment of 201 f.

is there confidence that we can rout the enemy." This does not give a consistent picture of the slave general's strategy (in particular *magna munit moenia*, 228, while alliteratively satisfying, seems to imply a much more passive form of defence than Palaestrio has outlined). Plautus seems to have been inspired by the physical assumptions of the plot, and the *commeatus*-theme, to create a sequence of manoeuvres which then get out of hand, and take on their own life. Palaestrio is not without other military language in the course of the play, but the only instance which appears specially related to the dramatic circumstances is 266–7.

> si invenio qui vidit, *ad eum vineam pluteosque agam*;
> res paratast, *vi pugnandoque hominem caperest* certa res.

Now Palaestrio, with the change of plot after 237 ff., has become aggressive, and sees himself in the traditional role of the general laying siege to the enemy.

This role is given its richest development in Plautus' two greatest plays of intrigue, *Bacchides* and *Pseudolus*. Both Pseudolus and Chrysalus in soliloquies portray themselves as commanders laying siege to a city. The form and presentation of this image is simpler in *Pseudolus*, and in view of this, and the pun, *Ballionem exballistabo* lepide (*Ps.* 584) arising from the name of Pseudolus' chief victim, it may be legitimate to suggest that Plautus evolved this image first in *Pseudolus*, and then recalled his own inspiration when he came to elaborate upon it in *Bacchides*.

The first appearance of the motif in *Pseudolus* is 384, hoc ego oppidum *admoenire* ut hodie capiatur volo, a metaphor apparently provoked by nothing more than the verb *imperare* in the previous line "ecquid imperas?" and dropped as soon as uttered. But when Pseudolus in his two great soliloquies act 1, sc. 5 and act 2, sc. 1 returns to the theme, this line occurs again in the Mss within the enlarged context, and was rightly rejected by Ritschl. In act 1, sc. 5, the only hint of the siege theme is 572, *dum concenturio in corde sycophantias* – the general is mustering his army of tricks; when Pseudolus returns in the next scene he resumes his narrative of the siege starting from the same theme of tricks acting as an army:

> *nam ego in meo pectore prius ita paravi copias*
> duplices triplices dolos perfidias, ut ubiquomque hostibu' congrediar
> ... facile ut vincam, facile ut spoliem, meos perduellis meis perfidiis
> nunc inimicum ego hunc communem meum atque vostrorum omnium
> *Ballionem exballistabo lepide*; date operam modo.

[hoc ego oppidum admoenire ut hodie capiatur volo.] 585a
   atque hoc meas legiones adducam; si *hoc expugno*
   facilem hanc rem meis civibu' faciam
post *ad oppidum hoc vetus continuo* meum exercitum protinus obducam,
ind' me et simul participes omnes meos praeda onerabo atque opplebo.

Omitting 585a, Ballio is represented as the first object of the siege – but not necessarily as a city; then in 587 the old man Simo, Pseudolus' subsidiary victim, is the town to be besieged. But consistency is unimportant, and in the next allusion at 766, *iam ego hoc ipsum oppidum expugnatum faxo erit lenonium*, the pimp is now under the town under assault.

In *Bacchides*, Chrysalus has only one victim in mind, but more than one trick to his credit; the siege-theme is first introduced by the *Ballista* motif:[13] 709 ff.

de ducentis nummis primum *intendam ballistam in senem*
ea ballista si pervortam turrim et propugnacula
recta porta invadam extemplo in oppidum antiquom et vetus
si id capso, geritote amicis vostris aurum corbibus.

When the theme returns in act 4, sc. 9, the great triumph canticum of Chrysalus, it is given new mythological dress:

925 Atridae duo fratres cluent fecisse facinus maximum,
     quom Priami patriam Pergamum divina moenitum manu
     armis, equis, exercitu atque eximiis bellatoribus
     milli cum numero navium decumo post anno subegerunt.
929 non pedibus termento fuit *praeut ego erum expugnabo meum*
     sine classe sineque exercitu et tanto numero militum
     cepi, expugnavi amanti erili filio aurum ab suo patre ...
933 O Troia, O patria, O Pergamum, O Priame periisti senex,
     qui misere male mulcabere quadrigentis Philippis aureis.

In this great paean of self-praise, Chrysalus (and Plautus) is not content with one identification, or one set of analogies, as he works out the parallels between his deceits and those by which the Greek heroes captured Troy; even in the first few lines quoted Chrysalus has set siege to two objects – the old man

---

13 On the Plautine origin of the *ballista*-image, see Fraenkel, *El. Pl.*, 59. My discussion of the *Pseudolus* and *Bacchides* passages depends on Fraenkel's analysis.

(929, as in 711, and *Ps.* 587) and the gold (931). He himself is comparable to the Atridae in 925–9 and Agamemnon in 946 (since Menelaus is now the Miles of the play), but in the intervening passage 936–44 he is Ulysses[14] (940). The old man is the city in 929 and 945, "nostro seni huic stolido *ei* profecto *nomen facio ego Ilio*," but Priam in 933–4, and again in 973 ff. Mnesilochus, who in 937 plays the role of Sinon, has become Alexander (Paris) in 947 and, by implication, Bacchis who is in 939 compared with the fire-signal to the Greek ships, in 947 plays the part of Helen.[15] Even the gold leads a double life: in 931 the object of the siege (i.e. the city?), the *quadrigenti Philippi aurei* of 934, later (973–4) become by a further flight of fancy, Priam's four-hundred sons.

The fantasy of imagery could hardly go further; within this passage one can also illustrate two opposing aspects of Plautus' comic use of imagery. Comparison of the pedestrian commonplace figure, usually the slave, with the great and noble, a comic figure made more comic by its depiction in terms of tragedy, is balanced by the opposite humour of comparing a dignified or neutral figure with the absurd. Here it is not a character of the play (as is usually the case) who is belittled, but the hero used for the comparison who is dismissed with the contemptuous image of the foot-towel – *pedibus termento fuit* ... 929.

It is in terms of these two comic differences of scale that I would like next to illustrate the humour of Plautine imagery. Many of his metaphors derive their impact from the very qualities which Cicero deprecates: ne *longe* simile sit *ductum* ... nolo esse aut *maius quam res postulet* ... *aut minus*. In all these instances it is the incongruity which would be distasteful in oratory that provides the charm of fantasy in comedy.

IV THE HUMOUR OF THE INCONGRUOUS

Under the first heading, an interesting category is the comparison of persons and personal behaviour with food: simple examples are *St.* 92, ita meae animae *salsura* evenit, *Trin.* 368, sapienti aetas *condimentumst*, sapiens aetati *cibust*. Food in return is given the dignity of military or legal status:

---

14 This identification is presented in connection with Ulysses' theft of the Palladium in *Ps.* 1063: viso quid rerum *meus Ulixes* egerit/iamne habeat signum ex arce Ballionia (= *Ba.* 954: *signum ex arce si periisset*). Compare also *Ps.* 1244: *superavit dolum Troianum atque Ulixem Pseudolus.*

15 But 947–8 may be interpolated. See Fraenkel, *op. cit.*, 62, n. 1. In 939–40, the identification of Bacchis with the fire of the signal, followed by *hunc ipsum exurit*, plays on the "fire of love" metaphor as in Ter. *Eu.* 85 (p. 9, above).

Capt.
153   quia nunc remissus est edendi exercitus
     : : nullumne interea nactu's qui posset tibi
      remissum quem dixti imperare exercitum?
      ... multis et multigeneribus opus est tibi
      militibus; primundum opus est Pistorensibus (etc.)
Men.
107   id quoque iam, cari *qui instruontur deserunt.*
(Even my dear dishes who are arrayed for battle are deserting me.)
Capt.
907–8   nunc ibo ut *pro praefectura mea ius dicam* lardo
      et *quae pendent indemnatae* pernae *is auxilium ut feram.*

A man can cheerfully be compared with a lantern, *Bac.* 446; it magister *quasi lucerna* uncto expressus linteo;[16] a building, *Cist.* 450: *meae issula sua ⟨aede⟩s egent* ("my house needs to cling to your block" – as the young man clutches his girl-friend); to a wheel, *Capt.* 369: pro *rota* me uti licet./vel huc vel illuc *vortor* quo imperabitis (cf. *Epid.* 371: *vorsutior* es quam *rota* figularis;[17]) to a tomb, *Ps.* 412: ex hoc *sepulcro*[18] vetere viginti minas/*ecfodiam* ego hodie (a double point here; Simo is old enough to be fit for the tomb, and the dead metaphor *ecfodere* is brought to life again); to an anvil, *Ps.* 614: haec mihi *incus* est, *procudam* ego hodie hinc multos dolos (again the origin of the metaphor is the special sense of *procudere* – to *forge* great plots). It is more common to find the comparison (often abusive) of man with beast or plant. Such a simile as *St.* 724, suffla ... buccas *quasi proserpens bestia*, is trivial and obvious; so is the simple identification metaphor, *Ps.* 747, *anguillast; elabitur.* More subtle and whimsical is *Cist.* 728–30

imitatur nequam bestiam et damnificam
involvulum, quae in pampini folio *intorta* implicat se
itidem haec exorditur sibi *intortam* orationem ...

Here the point of comparison is slight; the development of the simile is for its own exuberant verbal fun.

16 Cf. *Aul.* 566, of a lamb which is mere skin and bone: nam is pellucet *quasi lanterna punica.*
17 The point here is the connection of *vortere* with *rota*; cf. *Cist.* 215: *vorsor/in amoris rota.*
18 For the old man as a tomb, cf. τυμβόγερων, Ari. fr. 55D, ὦ τύμβε, ibid., *Lysi.* 372. The idea is also found in Euripides (*Heracleidae* 167, *Med.* 1209), so that Plautus is probably translating here, not originating. The originality lies in the apposite use of the double entendre *ecfodere.*

In *Ps.* 1021: ne in re secunda nunc mihi *obvortat cornua*, Simia is compared to a wild bull (or goat?). Earlier, in 812–83, an identification

qui mihi condita *prata* in patinis proferunt
boves qui convivas faciunt, *herbasque oggerunt*

suggests briefly and fantastically the same image, with a flash picture of oxen reclining at table to eat seasoned grass. In the great soliloquy of Ergasilus which opens *Captivi*, parasites are compared within 10 lines (77–87) to mice (for eating other men's food), snails (for ceasing to eat in the hot holiday season and living on their own "fat"), and hunting dogs (presumably for their shameless hunt for food). Only 30 lines later, his master compares, with more dignity, an unbound captive to a wild bird:

116   liber captivos *avi' ferae consimilest*
        semel fugiendi si data est occasio
        satis est; numquam postilla possis prendere.

This may well have stood in the Greek original, but it is taken up by the Lorarius, 123: *avi' me ferae consimilem faciam* ut praedicas, and answered; ita ut dicis; nam si faxis, te in *caveam* dabo/sed sati' verborumst, a slave-threat followed by an abrupt change of theme which suggests Plautine writing-in.

Many of Plautus' images derive their fun from the comparison of the vulgar with the heroic. We have already looked at the slave as general and mythological hero in discussing the metaphors of intrigue. The element of the grandiose may be merely a word or concept more proper to tragedy than comedy, *Bac.* 601: illius sum *integumentum* corporis, "I am the buckler of his body." But more often the slave or low-life character claims association with the noblest Roman institutions. The senate, *Epid.* 159, iam *senatum convocabo* in corde *consiliarium*; the foundation of a colony, *ibid.*, 343, sed ego hinc migrare cesso/ut *importem in coloniam hunc ⟨meo⟩auspicio commeatum* (cf. *Ps.* 1100: quid ego cesso Pseudolum/facere ut *det nomen ad Molas coloniam?*). The power of auspice of a commander is another favourite; *Epid.* 381, virtute atque *auspicio* Epidici cum *praeda* in *castra* redeo (only the commander with *auspicia* could celebrate the triumph), and 183, *liquido exeo foras auspicio, avi sinistera* (for the many parallels, see Duckworth, *ad loc.* 220). Or the slave can preside over a *iudicium publicum* in a capital case, *Ps.* 1233 (cf. *Truc.* 819), Pseudolus mihi *centuriata* habuit *capitis comitia*.

Roman public honours are accumulated with Greek; a final example is *St.* 698 ff.:

cape provinciam.
: : quid istuc est provinciae? : : utrum *fontine an Libero*
imperium te *inhibere* mavis : : nimio liquido Libero.
702   : : *strategum* te facio huic convivio.

This makes even Gods subject to the slave-protagonists.

Greek mythology is pillaged not only for the glorification of the slave, but as a general decorative form of metaphor. Some examples without glorifying purpose are the following: *Capt.* 615, *Aiacem* cum hunc vides, *ipsum vides* (in his madness he is a veritable Ajax); *Epid.* 604, abi intro atque hanc adserva, *Circam solis filiam*; *Men.* 854, hunc impurissumum/barbatum tremulum *Tithonum* (or Titanum; so Mss) qui cluet Cygno patre; *Mer.* 689-90, ut videas semul/tuam *Alcumenam paelicem, Juno mea.* But, on the whole, mythological figures occur more often in comparisons whose form dilutes the element of imagery; cf. *Mer.* 469-70;

Pentheum diripuisse aiiunt Bacchas; nugas maximas
fuisse credo praeut quo pacto ego divorsus distrahor,

Men.
200-1   meo quidem animo ab *Hippolyta* subcingulum haud
          Hercules aeque magno umquam apstulit periculo.

Per.
1-2   qui amans egens ingressus est princeps in amoris vias
          superavit aerumnis suis aerumnas *Herculei* ...

Very often Plautus fastens on a (temporary) activity of a stage character, and uses it to compare his character to a professional, or a skilled craftsman. Apart from the intellectual use of ἰατρός and διδάσκαλος, this is largely absent from Greek New Comedy, and totally avoided by Terence. Thus, "I will bring out my thoughts from my own breast," becomes (*Trin.* 81) ego meo sum *promus* pectori; "Is any stranger listening to our words," becomes, via the verb-based metaphor *aucupare* (cf. *As.* 881; *Men.* 570 etc.), *St.* 102: numquis hic est alienus nostris dictis *auceps* auribus, or, *Mil.* 608: nequis .../ nostro consilio *venator* adsit cum *auritis plagis* ("eared snares" by a comic twist for "ears as snares"). I alone was sitting still in the market-place is "I alone was besieger of the market-place"; *Ps.* 807, hoc ego fui hodie solus *obsessor* fori. In *Ps.* 606, Pseudolus speaks as advocate of the door-way; nam ego *precator* et *patronus* foribus processi foras (here the door is implicitly personified). The germs of this professionalism are latent in the elaboration of *cor salit*, at

Aul.

626   continuo meum cor coepit *artem facere ludicram*
         atque in pectus emicare,

or in the transformation-joke addressed to the door-bolts;

Cur.

150–1   *fite* caussa mea, *ludii barbari*,
          sussilite, obsecro.

But Plautus clearly delighted in allusions to human crafts and trades for their own sake; thus the concept of the *messis mali* (*Epid.* 718; *Rud.* 637) gives rise to the description of Tyndarus in *Capt.* 661 as

sator scelerum *sartorque* et *messor* maxume,

with the facetious reply

non *occatorem* dicere audebas prius?
nam semper accant priu' quam sariunt rustici;

sator and *messor* belong together proverbially[19]; *sartor*, for *saritor*, is here only to provide the joke based on the role of the *occator*.

I have tried to show some of the patterns which emerge from the diversity of Plautus' own contribution to the imagery of his comedies. It is not just the free range of the images themselves, although these know no limits, but more perhaps his presentation – the syntactical flexibility, the extravagant indulgence in transformations and identifications – which creates a world of quick-change and flux to dazzle and at times intoxicate the hearer.

19 Cf. Otto, *Sprichwörter* 221, *metere* (2) and (3) and p. 77 and n. 8 above.

5

Beyond *sermo familiaris*:
the imagery of rhetoric

It might be expected that the imagery of Cicero's speeches would be highly coloured by rhetoric, displaying elaboration of syntax and expression beyond that acceptable in the *sermo familiaris* of the letters. To investigate the nature of this distinction I have concentrated on the speeches of one period – that immediately after Cicero's restoration from exile, the years 57 and 56. From this period come a pair of speeches delivered almost simultaneously on a related topic – *Post Reditum in Senatu* and *Post Reditum ad Quirites*, more or less equal in length – where the significant factor is the difference in the audience. The imagery of these two short speeches is treated separately because they offer both coincidences and illuminating contrasts. There are two full-scale speeches: *De Domo Sua ad Pontifices* and *pro Sestio*. The latter is a mine of political rhetoric, and its imagery is as emotive and fulsome as that of any Ciceronian speech extant. Since the imagery of *pro Sestio* is so abundant and highly developed, I have reserved an analysis of this speech for section III of the discussion.

The borderline of *sermo familiaris* and formal eloquence is best marked by *pro Balbo*, a speech essentially concerned with the technical aspects of Roman citizenship, in which Cicero has made it his first consideration to render a complex legal situation intelligible. The imagery of this speech is sparse and simple, and very little of it goes beyond the range of figurative language available in the run of the correspondence. This simplicity is thrown into relief by comparison with a work which pretends to be a private letter, but whose content and imagery alike reveal it to be a public utterance, *ad Fam.* 1.9, written to Lentulus Spinther in 54 BC, in defence of Cicero's change of political loyalty in 56, during the period from which our speeches are drawn. In this, alongside the traditional figurative usage of *sermo familiaris*, there occur formal metaphors and analogies found elsewhere in the speeches and rhetorical works, which mark the official nature of this supposedly private letter.

There are approximately thirty instances of figurative language or metaphor in *pro Balbo*, of which one third consists merely of the figurative use of a verb. In 4, ei succedo orationi quae non *praetervecta* sit auris vestras, sed in animis omnium penitus *insederit, praetervehi* might be taken as a living visual image of ship or vehicle, if the conflicting *insederit* did not show that the preceding verb must be colourless; this is simply a survival of the traditional metaphor of Homer, tragedy, and comedy, whereby speech travels or flies to the ears of the hearer, and enters into them. Similarly in 56: quos ut accusator *incenderet*, ut aliqui sermones ... etiam ad vestras auris *permanarent* et in iudicio ipso *redundarent*, idcirco illa in omni parte orationis summa arte *adspergi* videbatis, *incendere* is already a dead metaphor (cf. *Imagery of Terence*, p. 10), but the representation of the gossip as liquid, implied by *permanare*, is kept alive by the development with *redundare* and the use of *adspergere* in the same context. Yet liquid metaphors of this type are so commonplace that Cicero usually employs them in pairs; cf. *Dom.* 121: etsi *effluunt* multa ex vestra disciplina quae etiam ad nostras auris saepe *permanant*.

In 5, non in aliquo impudenti mendacio *delituisse*, non *inrepsisse* in censum, the verbs combine to suggest an animal allusion. Similar is 57, "more hominum invident, in conviviis *rodunt*,[1] in circulis *vellicant*: non *illo inimico, sed hoc malo dente carpunt*," based on the "tooth of envy" (cf. *Imagery of Terence*, s.v. *mordere*), but where *rodere* definitely suggests animal associations.

Other verbs are used figuratively in the traditional way: (39) mentis suas ... *flexerunt* (cf. *Imagery of Terence* s.v. *reflectere*); (35) Gaditanorum causa ... gravissimis ... et plurimis rebus est *fulta*;[2] (60) qui nostris familiaritatibus *implicantur* (originally of beasts snared in the hunt, but in Cicero's day the most colourless of the available synonyms);[3] (61) cur ea quae mutare non possumus *convellere*[4] malumus quam tueri; (62) cum ducibus ipsis, non

---

1 *Delitiscere*: literally of beasts; *N.D.* 2.126, in invective against Clodius, represented as *iste serpens*; *Har.* 55; cf. *vipera* (50), *inrepere* (52); figuratively; *Tull.* 33, *Caec.* 61, 66, *Cael.* 62, *Phil.* 2, 77. Inrepere, always metaphorical in Cicero; cf. *Arch.* 10 (parallel to the context of *Balb.* 5), *Har.* 52. Rodere; cf. *adrodere, Sest.* 72.

2 For *fulcire*, cf. *Red. Sen.* 18 (below, p. 118), *Har.* 60, *Att.* 5.2.14; Thermum creberrimis litteris *fulcio*.

3 There are some twenty instances of *implicare* in the speeches, never with any development of the latent metaphor. Contrast *inretire*, used with its original force in *Mil.* 40 (combined with *beluam* ... *laqueos declinantem* to recall the literal application); add from our period *Red. Pop.* 11, *Har.* 7, *Vatin.* 2. inlaqueare, only *Har.* 7.

4 *Convellere*, commonly used of politically destructive action. Like *fulcire*, it is associated

cum comitatu adsectatoribusque *confligant*. This minimal military-type image
has been presented more fully in 59: a suorum ... *urgetur* inimicis; quos
quidem ... Cn. Pompeius ... secum, si vellent, *contendere* iubebat, ab hoc
impari certamine atque *iniusta contentione* avocabat. This is perhaps the com-
monest source of imagery in oratory, political conflict depicted as physical
attack, and both passages refer to the same issue – that the attack on Balbus
was really aimed at those powerful men of whom he was a lesser supporter.
But in the grand style of rhetoric, as we shall illustrate from *pro Sestio*, semi-
abstract phrases like *confligere, contendere, certamen,* etc. are replaced by physical
metaphors based on *impetus* or *telum*.

Metaphors based on nouns are fewer: "est enim haec saeculi quaedam
macula atque labes, virtuti invidere, velle ipsum *florem dignitatis infringere*" (15).
Here *macula atque labes* are clichés;[5] *infringere*, common in metaphor, (cf.
gloriam infringere, Mil. 5) *flos*, itself fairly common, are combined to give new
life to each other – "trampling on the flower of glory." More unusual is 39,
"qui et veterem illam speciem foederis Marciani semper *omni sanctiorem arce*
duxerunt." In 49 "imperatorius *ardor oculorum*" takes an image often applied
unfavourably to wild or mad characters, and gives it new dignity through the
application to the noun, of the epithet *imperatorius*.[6] In 31, *fundamenta firmis-
sima* is another familiar cliché; cf. *Fam.* 1.9.12; *Sest.* 5.

A group of metaphors is based on motion and access. The access to
citizenship is variously described: the image of 29 cum ex omnibus civita-
tibus *via* sit in nostram, cumque nostris civibus *pateat* ad ceteras *iter* civitates,
is developed in 43; ne *saeptum* sit iis *iter* in perpetuum ad hoc amplissimum
praemium civitatis; in 40 the same notion was represented as an ascent (based
on the cliché of *gradus dignitatis*), sit his *gradibus ascensus* etiam ad civitatem.

The nautical analogy of 61, neque esse inconstantis puto sententiam
tamquam aliquod navigium atque cursum ex rei publicae *tempestate moderari*, is a

---

with buildings; the most common application is to demolition during a siege (so Verg.
Aen. 2 446, 464) or the breaking off of statues from their bases. Cf. *Dom.* 143: dis
penatibus ... quorum si iste suis sceleratissimis manibus *tecta sedisque convellit; Pis.* 52;
ipsa Roma prope iam convolsa sedibus suis.

5 *Macula*, applied to an event, not a person, *Font.* 36; *Sest.* 63; *Imp. Pomp.* 7; *labes,
Sest.* 56; *Phil.* 7.15. See also p. 133 below.

6 *Ardor oculorum. Ardor* most often in Cicero refers to laudable enthusiasm (cf. *Imagery
of Terence* p. 8), but the connotation of *ardeo* applied to the eyes is madness and cruelty;
e.g. *Verr.* 2.4.148, cum spumas ageret in ore, *oculis arderet;* 2.5.161, ardebant oculi; toto
ex ore crudelitas eminebat. *Imperatorius* (cf. *Balb.* 51) is only associated with good
qualities, and corrects the sinister impression which *ardor* would otherwise leave.

traditional version of the statesman as pilot of the ship of state, kept in its simplest form, mitigated by simile, and far less striking than its functional equivalent in *Fam.* 1.9.21, below.

It is at the level of national glory that metaphors are most easily provoked; cf. 34: cum ... Carthago *nixa* duobus Hispaniis huic imperio *immineret*, et cum duo *fulmina* nostri imperi subito in Hispania, Cn. et P. Scipiones, *exstincti* occidissent. Otto Skutsch, *Studia Enniana* 147–8, has shown that *fulmina* was traditionally applied to the Scipiones, probably arising from a double pun in which *fulmen* √ *fulcire* represented the Greek σκῆπτ(ρ)ον, and *fulmen* √ *fulgere* the Greek σκηπτός, both related to *Scipio*. Such a pun is most likely to have been devised by the bilingual Ennius. As Skutsch saw, the propping sense of *fulmen* balanced the leaning imagery of *immineret* and *nixa* (and led to an echo in *fulta* in 35 below), but *exstincti* suggests rather the fate of a thunderbolt. He comments "altius igitur investigandum." For our purpose, it does seem necessary to go beyond Skutsch's conclusion that Cicero was fully alert to the rarer sense of *fulmen*, in order to ask whether he intended, by his use of *exstincti*, to make a play on words, and what would have been its effect on the audience. Since we have not *exstincti essent*, but *exstincti* added to the otherwise adequate word *occidissent*, we must believe that Cicero intended to recall the thunderbolt image; but rather than crediting him with a frigid double-conceit that would detract from the solemnity of the theme, I would suggest that he added *exstincti* to provide an ornament of speech for those who, ignorant of Ennius, would fail to recognize the metaphorical link of *imminere* and *nixa* with *fulmina*. (See also p. 45 above on *columen* and *columna* as support-metaphors.) The most striking accumulation of imagery is reserved for Pompey's achievements: 13, quae est enim ora ... qui locus, in quo non exstent huius cum fortitudinis tum vero humanitatis cum animi tum consili *impressa*[7] *vestigia*? and the personifications of 16, cuius res gestae omnis gentis cum clarissima victoria terra marique *peragrassent*, cuius tres triumphi *testes essent* totum orbem terrarum nostro imperio teneri ... followed by mors enim cum *exstinxisset* invidiam, res eius gestae sempiterni nominis gloria *niterentur*.

This speech contains 65 paragraphs; the letter to Lentulus Spinther, *Fam.* 1.9, only 25. Yet the images and figurative uses of the letter are as many, and at times more elaborate. There are three Greek-style analogies, from

---

7 *Imprimere* is a strong metaphorical word. For its literal use with *vestigia*, cf. *Caec.* 76, *Phil.* 13.30; it is metaphorical in a different construction, *Phil.* 2.58: horum flagitiorum iste *vestigiis* ... totam denique Italiam *impressit*. Contrast the weakened force of the same root in *Sest.* 13, *vestigia non pressa leviter ... sed fixa.*

navigation, medicine, and the visual arts, all developed at length. With *Balb.* 61, cf. *Fam.* 1.9.21:

> numquam enim in praestantibus *in re publica gubernanda viris* laudata est in una sententia perpetua permansio, sed *ut in navigando tempestati obsequi* artis est, etiam *si portum tenere non queas*, cum vero id possis *mutata velificatione adsequi*, stultum est *eum tenere cum periculo cursum* quem coeperis, potius quam *eo commutato, quo velis tamen pervenire*, sic ... non idem semper dicere sed idem semper spectare debemus.

This is much fuller than the allusion in *pro Balbo*. In the rhetoric of *pro Sestio*, the *tempestas rei publicae* and the theme of pilot and shipwreck are exploited in many forms.[8]

The medical and aesthetic analogies are combined to reinforce each other in 15: qui me homines quod *salvum* esse voluerunt, est mihi gratissimum; sed vellem non solum *salutis* meae, quem ad modum *medici*, sed ut *aliptae* etiam *virium et coloris* rationem habere voluissent. (Here the Greek technical name *aliptae* would have been avoided in the speeches.[9]) Nam ut *Apelles Veneris caput et summa pectoris politissima arte perfecit, reliquam partem corporis incohatam reliquit*, sic quidem homines *in capite meo solum elaborarunt, reliquum corpus imperfectum ac rude reliquerunt*. Here, the point of the analogy may arise from the political sense of *caput*; Cicero has his civil status restored, but his personal circumstances were never restored to his own satisfaction.

The remaining imagery of the letter is more conventional, but its distribution is of interest:

> 2 qui tibi ex me *fructus* debentur, eos *uberiores* et *praestantiores* praesens capere potuisses – *praestantiores* is not appropriate to the original meaning of *fructus* having the metaphor to be fossilized; cf. *fructum capere, ferre*, 20.
>
> in eis vero ulciscendis ... mirificem me tibi *comitem* praestitissem (cf. 22, me quidem certe tuarum actionum ... rerum denique omnium *socium comitemque* habebis):
>
> 5 rei familiaris *naufragia*;
> in meis damnis ex auctoritate senatus *sarciendis* – colloquial; cf. *Fam.* 3.1.1; 13.62.)

8 non potui magis in *arcem* illius causae invadere – a striking metaphor of taking by storm. As in *Balb.* 39, *arx* here symbolizes the "holy of holies."

10 quod inimicum meum sic *amplexabantur,* sic *in manibus habebant,* sic *fovebant* ... non illi quidem ut mihi *stomachum facerent* – simple transference from the physical to the psychological sphere (in 19, *amplexari* is probably literal).

circumspectis rebus meis omnibus, *rationibusque subductis summam* feci cogitationum mearum omnium – a financial image, natural to *sermo familiaris*; cf. Ter. *Ad.* 855, and parallels s.v. *subducere,* in *Imagery of Terence,* p. 69.

11 meamque voluntatem ad summi viri ... dignitatem *adgregassem* – transference from physical to psychological; for *adgregare* cf. *Vatin.* 25.

12 nobis consulibus ea *fundamenta iacta* – conventional; cf. *Balb.* 31, *Sest.* 5, *Mur.* 14, *Cael.* 5, etc.

13 non consules, sed *mercatores* provinciarum et seditionum *servos* atque *ministros* – a reminiscence of *Red. Sen.* 10 and *Red. Pop.* 21 (see p. 122). This style of abusive metaphor derives from comedy, where the agent noun expresses the alleged function of the person described.

iecit quidem casus *caput* meum quasi *certaminis causa in mediam contentionem. Caput* here in the political sense suggests the physical allusion in the conventional conflict-metaphor (cf. the analogy of 15 discussed above, p. 119).

15 monumentum vero senatus hostili nomine et cruentis *inustum* litteris; *inurere*[10] is a favourite figurative use of Cicero's to denote cruelty; cf. *Sest.* 17 volnera *inusta* rei publicae (not literally possible, as here), *inustum odium, Dom.* 92, *Har.* 55.

17 *hic meus vitae cursus* – conventional in Greek and Latin; cf. *Red. Pop.* 2, *Imagery of Terence,* s.v. *spatium.* p. 68.

18 *implicatus* tenebar – conventional; cf. *Balb.* 60, above. With section 19, the imagery becomes more concentrated.

19 cum ... eius petitionem ... *oppugnassem,* neque tam illius *laedendi* causa quam *defendendi* atque ornandi Catonis ... tamen defendendi Vatini fuit etiam ille *stimulus* – a stronger image; cf. *Sest.* 12; quos *stimulos* admoverit ...

in quo possem illorum animos *mediocriter lacessitus leviter repungere* (cf. 20, me disputantem, non *lacessentem laesisset*). This is conventional combat

10 Cf. *dolorem inurere,* Mil. 99, Att. 1.16.7.

imagery, but *repungere* occurs only here. *Pungere* is always metaphorical in Cicero except within the analogy of *Sest.* 24 (see p. 132). Compare *Imagery of Terence*, p. 31.

20 *exarsi* non solum praesenti iracundia ... sed sum *inclusum* illud odium ... quod ego *effudisse* me omne arbitrabar *residuum* tamen insciente me fuisset, omne repente apparuit. (*Exardesco* and other fire-words are conventionally associated with anger; cf. *Imagery of Terence*, p. 10.) The image of bottled-up resentment bursting forth is represented differently in *Red. Pop.* 1; quod odium scelerati homines et audaces in rem publicam ... *conceptum* iam diu *continerent* (cf. *inclusum*), id in me uno potius quam in optimo quoque et universa civitate *defigerent* (see p. 123 below).

21 is dominated by the nautical analogy discussed above; ut eum mihi *devinctum* putarem is conventional; cf. *Imagery of Terence*, s.v. *devincire*, p. 50.

With 22 the momentum subsides temporarily, but "nulla malevolentia *suffusum*" is original and striking, and "me *socium comitemque* habebis" is intended to recall the second paragraph of the letter. It rounds off the political narrative by reiterating the original declaration of loyalty. This is complemented by the last figurative uses of the letter to express Cicero's personal devotion and debt to Lentulus through the rhetorical medium of personification: "sunt enim libri 'de temporibus meis' *testes* et erunt sempiterni meritorum erga me tuorum meaeque pietatis" ... confirmed by "istam quidem partem vitae consuetudinisque nostrae totam ad te *defero*." Thus the last paragraph of the political section of this letter focuses through imagery on a protestation, three times expressed, of Cicero's personal obligation and loyalty to Lentulus.

II

The two speeches *post reditum* offer an interesting study in Ciceronian adaptation of imagery. They share several striking metaphors, but in the use of these metaphors there is a distinction between the simplicity of *ad Quirites* and the rhetoric and formality of *in Senatu*. The range and technique of metaphors employed also differs from one speech to the other; where *ad Quirites* limits its allusions to the simpler concepts of attack and defence, sickness (or wound) and cure, human relationships, and the usual transfer of physical words to abstract functions, *in Senatu* has a wider range of sources for figurative language and a more unusual vocabulary.[11]

I shall consider the shared imagery first: in *Red. Sen.* 4, the state is described as neque solum *parentibus perpetuis* verum etiam *tutoribus annuis* ... *orbata*: "deprived not only of the senate's continuous protection but even of that of the annual consuls." This appears in *ad Quirites* as a mere simile: (11) *orba res publica consulis fidem tamquam legitimi tutoris* imploravit; there is no reference to the Senate as *parentes*, both for obvious political reasons, and because in the next line Lentulus Spinther is to be hailed as *parens* in his relationship to Cicero. The symmetry and alliteration of *Red. Sen.* 4 is too formal for the *contio*; indeed, the same metaphor is diluted to a simile in *de Orat.* 3.3, *orbitatem senatus, cuius ordinis a consule qui quasi parens bonus aut tutor fidelis esse deberet* ... and *Brut.* 330, *orbae* eloquentiae *quasi tutores* relicti sumus.

In *Red. Sen.* 9, Cicero describes himself thus: non enim eguissem *medicina consulari*, nisi *consulari vulnere concidissem* (echoed in 17,[12] *consulari ictu concidissem*). This is very little changed in *Red. Pop.* 14: me confectum *consularibus vulneribus consulari medicina ad salutem redduceret*. Both *vulnus* and *medicina* are metaphors at home in the *sermo familiaris* of Cicero's day (see *Imagery of Terence*, p. 17). A more impressive image, meum reditum ... *flumine sanguinis intercludendum, Red. Sen.* 6; *Red. Pop.* 14, is common to both speeches. Here Cicero combines the concept of streams of blood with the favoured military metaphor of cutting off access or supplies (cf. Plautus, *Mil.* 223 ff.) to create a bold new metaphor.

In the abusive passages on Piso and Gabinius (*Red. Sen.* 10–18) for which class loyalty denied Cicero an equivalent in the speech to the people, the opening phrase, "non consules, sed *mercatores provinciarum* ac *venditores vestrae dignitatis*," is partly utilized in *Red. Pop.* 21, *mercatores provinciarum* revocando domum; the second part is rephrased as *dignitatem* eius imperii quod erat penes ipsos *vendiderunt*, to be more informal. Again the *dignitas* has become that of the Roman magistracy, not of the Senate. Cicero clearly relished *mercatores provinciarum*; we have seen (p. 120) that he used it again in the letter

---

11 For a general stylistic comparison of these speeches, see D. Mack, *Senatsreden und Volksreden bei Cicero* (Hildesheim 1967) section III. His only specific comment on the use of imagery is to single out the abundance of figurative language in *Red. Sen.* 14 as a means of achieving the *genus grande*.

12 The echo of imagery from *Red. Sen.* 9–17 is paralleled by a similar repetition of *me nudum a propinquis, nulla cognatione munitum* in *Red. Pop.* 7 and 16. This is an example of imagery used as structure to achieve greater impact on the audience.

to Lentulus Spinther, *Fam.* 1.9.13. One other metaphor is shared, the state in exile, in *Red. Pop.* 14, in the simple form *res publica exterminata*; this is extended in *Red. Sen.* 34: neque ego *illa exterminata* mihi remanendum putavi, *et illa, simul atque revocata est, me secum pariter reportavit.* Further personifications follow depicting constitutional government as sharing exile with Cicero. These personifications are in general more highly developed in the address to the Senate; cf. 3, *rem publicam lacerare;* 6, *civium vulneribus res publica cruentaretur, mutum forum, elinguem curiam, tacitam et fractam civitatem;* 12, *patriae preces repudiavit,* and 39, *me vestra auctoritas arcessierit, populus Romanus vocarit, res publica implorarit, Italia cuncta paene suis umeris reportarit.* The last corresponds to *Red. Pop.* 10, *suis decretis Italia cuncta revocavit.*[13]

In the speech to the people the imagery is generally of types conventional in *sermo familiaris.* I quote 2, *secundo vitae ... cursu* (here nautical; cf. *Imagery of Terence,* p. 68); 8, vestros oculos *inflecteret;* 19, nobis ... cum fortuna *belligerandum fuit;* 21, cum *custodes* rei publicae esse deberent; and 24, illa *monumenta* vestri in me benefici permanebunt. There are two simple analogies: from medicine, avoiding technical terms, 4, tamquam *bona valetudo* iucundior est iis qui *e gravi morbo recreati sunt quam qui numquam aegro corpore fuerunt,* sic haec omnia desiderata magis quam adsidue percepta delectant; and from finance – an analogy ex contrario: 23, *in officio persolvendo* dissimilis est ratio *pecuniae debitae* propterea quod *pecuniam qui retinet non dissolvit, qui reddidit non habet; gratiam et qui rettulit habet, et qui habet dissolvit.*

Otherwise the most impressive imagery is emotive in purpose; the initial image of the hatred of Cicero's enemies: 1, quod *odium* scelerati homines et audaces in rem publicam et in omnes bonos *conceptum* iam diu *continerent,* id in me uno potius quam in in optimo quoque et universa civitate *defigerent,* is balanced by 25, Cicero's devotion to the people: haec cura, Quirites, erit *infixa animo*[14] meo sempiterna. In the same way 5, a parentibus, id quod necesse erat, parvus sum procreatus, *a vobis natus sum consularis,* and its emotional equivalent, 12, P. Lentulus, consul, *parens, deus, salus* nostrae vitae, fortunae, memoriae, nominis, are balanced by Cicero's tribute to Lentulus

---

13 The emphasis on Italia in *Red. Pop.* (cf. *consensus* Italiae, 1 and 8; *Italia cuncta* 10 and 16 [bis], was politically desirable, since the upper class Italians were the major element in the *Comitia Centuriata* responsible for Cicero's restoration.

14 *Defigere* is properly used of weapons, as at *Cat.* 1.16 (sicam *defigere*); hence cf. *Har.* 57, dedecora ... in eo penitus *defixa* atque *haerentia: Infigere;* cf. *Phil.* 2.64, *infixus* haeret animo dolor and Verg. *Aen.* 4.4, *haerent infixi* pectore vultus. In this metaphor the verbs are interchangeable.

and the Roman people: 17, P. Lentuli sententiam ... vos secuti me *in eo loco*, in quo vestris beneficiis fueram, isdem centuriis quibus *conlocaratis reposuistis*, which combines the political events alluded to in 5 and 12.

Metaphor in *post Reditum in Senatu* is both more varied and more allusive; verbs are effectively used to suggest rather than express imagery. Examples are: 3, sub alieno scelere *delituisse* (where *delitisco*, cf. *Balb.* 5, and n. 1, belongs properly to reptiles and beasts); 19, privatam offensionem *oblitteraverunt* (cf. *Vatin.* 15), and the careful emphasis on *reportare* (whose proper objects are the spoils of war) in the triumph image 28, non reducti sumus ... sed *equis insignibus et curru aurato reportati*; and 34, illa (res publica) me pariter secum *reportavit*. A whole complex of allusions makes up 15; his utitur *quasi praefectis* libidinum suarum, hi voluptates omnes *vestigant et odorantur*; *conditores instructoresque convivi expendunt atque aestimant voluptates, sententiamque dicunt et iudicant* quantum cuique libidini tribuendum esse videatur. Here Piso's Greek advisers pass from being Roman magistrates to being hounds,[15] then caterers.[16] Their weighing and valuing of pleasures takes them into the realm of finance. Finally with *sententiam dicere* we touch on the consultative function of the senator to the consul (and Piso was consul), and *iudicare* suggests the *iudex* or *iudices* whose function it was *aestimare litem*.[17]

The image of Rome as *hac omnium terrarum arce* (1) employs the familiar *arx* symbol (cf. *Balb.* 39; *Fam.* 1.9.8), but significantly, as the *Arx* is to Rome, so Rome is to the world; the compressed phrase expresses a kind of proportion. Other images have comic associations; Clodius takes refuge *in aram tribunatus* rather than the usual *in portum* of, for example, *Sest.* 18;[18] like a suppliant slave in comedy, he has done wrong and needs to escape legitimate vengeance. The flavour of much of the abusive imagery is derived from comedy: in 11, *piraticam facere*, to play the pirate, echoes phrases like *medicinam facere* (Plaut. *Cur.* 162 etc.), or from Cicero's letters, *embaeneticam facere* (Caelius, *Fam.* 8.1.4); 16, frontis tibi *integimento* ... diutius uti non liceret, again uses a comic twist of a solemn word; cf. Plaut. *Bac.* 601-2, *Trin.* 313.

---

15 For *odorari*, cf. *de Orat.* 2.186; ut *odorer, quam sagacissime possim*, and see *Imagery of Terence* p. 41, n. 31 for its use in intimate letters.

16 *Conditor/instructor*. For *conditor*, which I would derive from *condire* here, cf. *Clu.* 71; ipse *conditor* totius negoti Guttam aspergit huic Bulbo (a pun on seasoning), followed by the verb *condire* in 72; the nearest parallel for *instructor* is the Plautine use of *instruere* for preparing food or drink, *Men.* 107, *Ps.* 742, *Rud.* 529.

17 On the role of *iudices* in the *litis aestimatio*; cf. Cic. *Clu.* 116.

18 On *in portum confugere*; see *Imagery of Terence*, p. 24 for examples from Cicero's correspondence.

The imagery based on light and darkness is prominent: 5, *ex superioris anni caligine et tenebris lucem ... dispicere*; 8, *lumen* consulatus sui; 10, *mentes ... oppletae tenebris* et *sordibus ... splendorem* illius honoris; 28, tantum *splendorem* Italiae. Three relatively unusual images deserve notice: 18, horum consulum *ruinas vos ... fulsistis*, derived from architecture; 23, amicitias *igni perspectas* tuear (cf. *Off*. 2.38, virum *igni perspectum*, and Catullus 100.6, *perspecta ex igni ... amicitia*); and 24, again of Lentulus, qui mihi primo *adflicto et iacenti consularem fidem dextramque porrexit*; *qui me a morte ad vitam ... vocavit*.[19] Here we have the language of Epic and Tragedy, which can only be outdone in pathos by the verbal resurrection of the Metelli from deepest Acheron, which follows in 25, as Metellus Nepos consults his dead *maiores*.

III

Political rhetoric; the speech pro Sestio

Of the speeches from the period immediately after Cicero's restoration from exile, the largely autobiographical *pro Sestio* is the fullest in length, in vehemence, and in the ornaments of rhetoric. The imagery is unstinted, with over one hundred metaphors, many based on the visually stronger nouns, rather than verbs, and often developed through a sequence of words reflecting the original metaphor. If the fields of metaphor are themselves traditional and predictable, and such as are found also in the more subdued idiom of the correspondence, their application and form is skilfully varied, and comparison with other speeches of this period, especially *de Domo sua*, *de Haruspicum Responso*, shows no repetition of any but the simplest images.

This speech occupies 73 pages of Oxford Classical Text; it is one of Cicero's longest, comparable within his output to Demosthenes' *de Corona*, yet in all 96 pages of *de Corona* there are only some 75 figurative uses, many of them expressed in the briefest form through the verb.[20] But because Cicero

19 Cf. Ter. *Hec.* 852, qui ab Orco mortuom me reducem in lucem feceris. Contrast Cicero's picture of Clodius' alleged downfall in *Red. Pop.* 10, inimicus ... spiritu dumtaxat viveret, re quidem *infra omnes mortuos amandatus esset*.

20 Cicero admired Demosthenes most of all Attic orators, and chose him as a model (*Brut.* 35, *Orator* 23,104, *Opt. Gen.* 6). The speech *de Corona*, which in *Orator* 26 he calls *longe optima* of Demosthenes' speeches, seems to have come closest to his ideal, and the *de Optimo Genere Oratorum* was written, ten years after *pro Sestio*, as a preface to Cicero's own translations of Demosthenes' *de Corona* and Aeschines' *in Ctesiphontem*. Yet although Cicero applies the vocabulary of the rich style (*Brut.* 35, *grande, incitatum, ornatum vel verborum gravitate vel sententiarum*; nihil ... quo quicquam esset *elatius*) to at least certain sections of Demosthenes' speeches, his criticism in *Orat.* 104: "tamen non semper implet

has used *pro Sestio* to parade his political philosophy, the *loci communes* offer him a rich scope for imagery; compare his own comment in *de Inventione* 2, 49:

> omnia enim ornamenta elocutionis in quibus et suavitatis et gravitatis plurimum consistit, et omnia quae in inventione verborum et senten-tiarum aliquid habent dignitatis, in communes locos conferuntur.

Thus it is no accident that in chapters 96–100, in which Cicero outlines his views on the definition and role of the *optimates*, the passage reaches a climax of imagery as it approaches its end. In particular, the traditional imagery applied to *the state* has its fullest development in this speech, and it will be useful to consider this first.

The oldest analogy for the state, going back through Plato (e.g. *Resp.* 488a) to Aeschylus and Pindar is that of the ship, piloted by the ruler or ruling class. Although this certainly was Greek in origin and appears in Greek oratory,[21] it was naturalized early in Roman rhetoric, e.g., *de Inventione* 1.3.4. cum ad *gubernacula* rei publicae temerarii atque audaces homines accesserant, maxima ac miserrima *naufragia* fiebant; and the analogy given in *Rhet. Her.* 4.57:

> uti contemnendus est qui in navigando se quam navem mavult incolu-mem, ita vituperandus qui in rei publicae discrimine suae plus quam communi saluti consulit. Nave enim fracta, multi incolumes evaserunt; *ex naufragio patriae* salvus nemo potest enatare.

This appears in *Sest.* 45–6 in a new guise. Cicero sees himself as a volun-tary sacrifice to appease the anger of those pirates who would otherwise attack the ship of state; like the author of *ad Herennium*, he begins with the image, and proceeds to its application:

> Etenim si mihi in aliqua nave cum meis amicis naviganti hoc, iudices, accidisset ut multi ex multis locis praedones classibus eam navem se oppressuros minitarentur nisi me unum sibi dedidissent, si id *vectores*

aures meas, ita sunt avidae et capaces et saepe aliquid immensum infinitumque desi-derant," and his concentration on Demosthenes' *ornamenta sententiarum* (*Orat.* 136) rather than *ornamenta verborum* provoke the suspicion that his own translation of *de Corona* would have contained a higher proportion of figurative language and developed the individual metaphors at greater length. If only the translations had survived, to make the difference of diction between the two orators apparent in every detail!
21 Cf. *de Corona* 194; the hurricane that befalls the careful ναύκληρος and the ensuing shipwreck.

negarent ac mecum simul interire quam me tradere hostibus mallent, iecissem ipse me potius in profundum, ut ceteros conservarem, quam illos mei tam cupidos non modo ad certam mortem, sed in magnum vitae discrimen adducerem. cum vero *in hanc rei publicae navem, ereptis senatui gubernaculis fluitantem in alto tempestatibus* seditionum ac discordiarum *armatae tot classes,* nisi ego essem unus deditus, *incursurae viderentur ...*

Here an additional detail has been suggested by the picture of the political situation which Cicero wished to present. The *vectores* are inserted to convey the supposed loyalty of the *boni* to Cicero, and their willingness to sacrifice themselves for him; the pirate attack is a better (and more topical) image for the assaults of Clodius than the neutral shipwreck which would seem rather an "act of God." The shipwreck theme has already appeared briefly: 15, totum superioris anni *rei publicae naufragium.* Another motif, that of the leaders at the helm, alluded to in *ereptis senatui gubernaculis*[22] is used repeatedly in the speech; cf. 97, *in gubernanda re publica* ...; 98, quid est propositum *his rei publicae gubernatoribus* quod intueri *et quo cursum suum derigere* debeant ...; 99, *in re publica fluctus excitantur* ut vigilandum sit *iis qui sibi gubernacula patriae depoposcerunt, enitendumque ut ... tenere cursum possint et capere oti illum portum et dignitatis.* A similar expansion occurs in 20, quis enim *clavum tanti imperi tenere* et *gubernacula rei publicae tractare in maximo cursu ac fluctibus posse arbitraretur* ... We have seen the same analogy exploited in the manifesto to Lentulus (p. 119 above). But if the *res publica* equivalent to "state" is normally the ship in these comparisons, *res publica* in its other sense of political life, is the sea beset by storms and breakers; this note is struck in the early picture of Sestius' exiled father-in-law: (7) *fluctibus rei publicae expulsum, in alienis terris*

---

22 Cf. *Dom.* 24 (and 137 quoted below), *cum senatum e gubernaculis deiecisses,* populum e nave exturbasses, ipse archipirata cum grege praedonum ... plenissimis velis navigasses. Cicero applies the same metaphor to himself: *Att.* 2.7.4, cum cogar exire de navi *non abiectis sed ereptis gubernaculis,* cupio istorum *naufragia* ex terra intueri. In Cicero's political thought the helm rightly belongs to the Senate, or to the consuls, as representatives of the Senate (cf. *Sest.* 20, *Prov. Cos.* 7, *Fam.* 16.27.1 below), or to himself (*Att.* 2.7.4) and the *principes civitatis* (*Sest.* 97, 98) as representatives of all true *optimates.* From *Inv.* 1.3.4 (quoted above) onwards, *gubernacula* and *naufragium* are the favourite symbols of Ciceronian political imagery. For *naufragium,* cf. *Dom.* 129, 137, quod in *naufragio* rei publicae, tenebris offusis, demerso populo Romano, *everso atque eiecto senatu,* dirueris; *Prov. Cos.* 7, in illo *naufragio* huius urbis, quam tu idem qui *gubernare* debueras, everteras. Add from the letters *Att.* 2.7.4; 3.15.7; 4.19.2; *Fam.* 1.9.5; (a private shipwreck) 4.13.2; 13.5.2; 16.27.1; consules, qui nisi a *gubernaculis* recesserint, maximum ab universo *naufragio* periculum est.

iacentem, quem in maiorum vestigiis stare oportebat. Here the man is a castaway, and the added detail *iacentem* passes on to another figurative usage, the contrast of *iacere* (both to lie, and to fail) with *stare* (both to tread in his ancestral steps, and to be successful). There are a series of briefer allusions: 61, *in tanta rei p. tempestate*; 73, *praesentis fluctus tempestatemque fugisse*; 140, *iniqui iudici procella*, and *tempestate populari*. Accordingly, political adversaries are seen as storms; Gabinius and Piso are (25) *duo rei p. turbines*, just as Clodius is *tempestas rei p.* (*Vatin.* 33) *procella patriae, turbo ac tempestas pacis atque oti* (*Dom.* 137).

The other most frequent image of the state is that of a person or body, conceived as sick and in need of medical treatment, or of a soldier, wounded, defeated, even captured. Inevitably, there is some overlap between the two categories, as can be illustrated from the standard use of *adflictus*. In the first chapter of the speech, *qui rem p. adflictam excitarint et latrocinio domestico liberarint*, and in 24, *tribuno plebis adflictam et constrictam rem p. tradidissent*, we have the defeated soldier; in 31, *ut adflictae et perditae rei p. quantum posset mederetur*, the sick man. In 43, the theme of political cure,[23] *medicina*, is introduced, *qui hac una medicina sola potuit a rei p. peste depelli*. The same motif in 51, *eorum periculorum medicina*, and in 55, *vim omnium remediorum ... res p. desiderarit*, acts as a frame for Cicero's description of the disorders of the year 58. But when his adversaries adopted the cliché, Cicero could turn it to his own account: (135) *cohortari ausus est accusator ... ut aliquando medicinam adhiberetis rei p.* He answers with his own definition:

> non est medicina, cum sanae parti corporis scalpellum adhibetur atque integrae, carnificina[24] est ista atque crudelitas; ei medentur rei p. qui exsecant pestem aliquam tamquam struma civitatis.[25]

In the context of political violence which gave rise to the prosecution of Sestius, the imagery of wounding was more rewarding than sickness; hence the *scelera vulneraque inusta rei p.* of 17; the general *vulneribus illis*, followed by

---

23 There are only two instances of medical imagery in *de Corona*: 45, αἱ δὲ πόλεις ἐνόσουν (compare the frequency of νόσος, νοσεῖν in New Comedy) and the analogy of 242, the doctor who refuses to diagnose, and then blames the patient for dying.

24 *Carnificina*: metaphorical also in *Tusc.* 3.27, "*carnificina* est aegritudo. habet ... maiora quaedam, tabem, cruciatum.*" This seems to be a Roman concept with no Greek equivalent; cf. also Plaut. *Cist.* 203, credo ego Amorem primum apud homines *carnificinam* commentum, and the verb *excarnificare*, Ter. *Hau.* 813.

25 With this analogy, cf. *Att.* 2.7.7, *medicina quae sanaret vitiosas partes rei p. quam quae exsecaret*. *Struma* itself is best taken as an allusion to Vatinius; cf. *Vatin.* 39, and Catullus 52.2, *Struma* Nonius sedet, for the personification.

the *maximum rei p. vulnus*, of 31, or the development in 78: *accepisset res p. plagam, sed eam quam acceptam gemere posset.*[26]

Perhaps the most developed instances of this metaphor are in 24, where the comparison of Gabinius and Piso to a child or old man armed with a sharp sword leads to the statement "ii summi imperi nomine armati rem p. *contrucidarunt."* The rare verb purposely seeks to inject new horror into the traditional image by its physical crudity. Then in 54, the state, butchered by Gabinius and Piso and bereft of Cicero its champion, is ready to be stripped by them for plunder, although still breathing:

> statim me perculso ad meum sanguinem hauriendum, et spirante etiam re publica ad eius spolia detrahenda advolaverunt.

The state is even credited with blood, which becomes by a Roman allusion the diet of Clodius' gladiators (78): qui ab illo pestifero ac perdito civi iam pridem *rei publicae sanguine saginantur.*[27] Finally they are seen as rushing to be in at the kill: 110, furiae concitatae *tamquam ad funus*[28] *rei p. convolant.*

This kind of embodiment of the state is quite different from the personifications of 52–3, me ... *rei p. esse voce* revocatum ...; 53, cum ego me *e complexu patriae* conspectuque vestro eripuissem; or 131, tamquam *totius Italiae* atque *ipsius patriae dextram* porrexerint Brundisini. Such a passage as 145, *lugenti patriae*, flagitanti senatui, *poscenti Italiae*, vobis omnibus orantibus, shows that this is, in fact, little more than the use of the collective state to represent the desire of its members.

Finally the state, so often identified with the city of Rome, is seen as so

---

26 *Plaga* is most common in the phrase *plagam accipere, plaga/plagis concidere*; cf. *Prov. Cos.* 16, et tamen *hac una plaga conciderit*; *Att.* 1.16.9, quoting a speech, ille locus est inductus a me divinitus *ne una plaga accepta* patres conscripti conciderent, ne deficerent. vulnus esse eiusmodi quod mihi nec dissimulari ... videretur; *Att.* 7.15.3, *sed accipienda plaga est.* The word (Greek πληγή) seems to have entered Latin from gladiatorial combat; cf. *Orator* 228, and *Sest.* 80, *plaga una illa extrema* defuit, in a context of gladiatorial gang attack. *Rei publicae vulnus* is naturally very frequent; cf. *Vatin.* 20, *ad cetera vulnera* quibus rem publicam putasti deleri hanc quoque *mortiferam plagam inflixisses*; 36 *exemplo rem p. vulnerasti Dom.*; 146, *vulnus patriae*; from the letters *Att.* 1.16.7, *tanto imposito rei p. vulnere.*

27 *Saginari*, a technical word associated with the gladiator's diet, occurs only here in Cicero's works. For the image of feasting on blood; cf. *Dom.* 124, *helluatus tecum simul rei p. sanguine.* This is intended to recall allusions earlier in the speech to Cicero himself: 25, *id autem foedus meo sanguine ictum*; and 54, me perculso *ad meum sanguinem hauriendum* ... advolaverunt.

28 Cf. *Dom.* 42, cum tua rogatione *funere elatam* rem p. esse dicerent ... *funus te indixisse* rei p.; *Prov. Cos.* 45, casum illum meum *funus esse* rei p.

many buildings,[29] subject to fire and ruin: 5, *in ruinis eversae atque adflictae rei p.* (here *adfligere* is used in the sense of demolish; cf. *Cael.* 78; *Dom.* 106); 28, oratio ipsa consulis perniciosa potest *rem p. labefactare*; and 73, *flammam quassatae rei p.*[30] The ironical *columen rei publicae*[31] applied to Piso in 19 is a traditional phrase from before the time of Plautus, in which the architectural image has lost its force, and is no longer intended. Closely related to these metaphors is the picture of the city of Rome as taken by storm: 35, *urbem nondum excisam et eversam sed iam captam atque oppressam videremus.* This too is found in other speeches of the period.[32]

Generally, we find Cicero employing the same categories of image in this speech as in the letters; it is the extension of treatment which distinguishes the rhetorical level. Thus the usual imagery of fire is applied to the emotions: 4, *iracundia ... quae me inflammat*; 140, *hunc flagrantem invidia*, with its opposite *restinguere invidiam*, 82, illustrate anger and hatred. Fire represents destruction in 73 above, and 99, *propter implicationem rei familiaris communi incendio malint quam suo deflagrare*; 121, *de illis nostris incendiis ac ruinis* is half metaphorical, half literal, as the subsequent allusion to *domum incensam eversamque* shows. A bolder extension of the usual range is 116: in illo *ardenti* tribunatu, "in that blazing tribunate of his."

The medical imagery is largely confined to the political situation, but again Cicero identifies with the state by applying to himself an image which he has already applied to the *res publica*: 44, *ac non accipienda plaga mihi sanabilis*, illi *mortifera* qui *imposuisset*; cf. *Vatin.* 20, si ad cetera *vulnera*, quibus rem publicam putasti deleri, hanc quoque *mortiferam plagam* inflixisses.

Although, as we have seen, nautical imagery chiefly functions as an analogy for the *res publica* and its pilots, there is one passage with a different and striking application (18): *ne in Scyllaeo illo aeris alieni tamquam fretu ad columnam adhaeresceret, in tribunatus portum confugerat.* "Gabinius fled to the safe harbour of the tribunate to avoid being posted as a defaulter in the Scylla

---

29 Cf. *Fam.* 2.8.1, ut ... cum formam rei p. viderim, quale *aedificium* futurum sit scire possim; and *Fam.* 9.2.5, ad *aedificandam rem p.*

30 *ruinae rei p.*, *Vatin.* 21, *Prov. Cos.* 43, *tenebrae rei p.*, *ruina atque incendium civitatis*; cf. *Red. Sen.* 18, horum consulum ruinas vos vestra virtute fulsistis.

　Labefactare; conquassare. Vatin. 19, *non labefactatam rem p. ... neque conquassatam civitatem, sed captam hanc urbem atque perversam putaris*; similar is *Sest.* 56, *nationes ... conquassatas.* Compare the use of *labefieri* in *Har.* 60, a variation of *Red. Sen.* 18 above: *Vix haec si undique fulciamus iam labefacta, vix, inquam nixa in omnium nostrum umeris cohaerebunt.* There are other, colourless uses of *labefactare* in *Sest.* 49 and 63.

31 For the ironical use of *columen*, see the discussion in *Imagery of Terence* s.v. pp. 45-6.

32 Cf. *Vatin.* 19 (n. 30 above), *Dom.* 53, *capta iam urbe.*

infested straits of debt." In *de Orat.* 3.163, Cicero counsels against the metaphorical use of Scylla and Charybdis as too remote from natural imagery,[33] yet he apparently disregards his own principles here and in his *amplificatio* on Clodius' greed at *Har.* 59,

> quae denique tam immanem Charybdim poetae fingendo exprimere potuerunt quae tantos exhauriret gurgites, quantas ibi Byzantinorum Brogitarorumque praedas exsorbuit; aut tam eminentibus canibus Scyllam tamque ieiunis quam quibus istum videtis, Gelliis, Clodiis, Titiis, rostra ipsa mandentem.

However the reference to Scylla in *Sest.* 18 is not a direct comparison with Gabinius and so does not violate the point made in *de Oratore.* As for *Har.* 59, this comparison would be justified in Cicero's eyes by the monstrous and unique wickedness of his personal enemy. When he comes to a lesser man, Clodius' supporter Gellius, he applies the recommended substitutes, *gurges* and *vorago*, in *Sest.* 111, *gurges ac vorago patrimoni*, and *Dom.* 124, *ille gurges helluatus tecum simul rei publicae sanguine.*

The inevitable military metaphors are applied by Cicero to himself, as to the state under attack: in general terms, 4, *qui cum omnibus meae salutis defensoribus bellum esse sibi gerendum iudicaverunt*; specifically of Clodius' hostility, 15, *intentus est arcus in me unum.* This is picked up again near the end of the speech in a contrast between heavy artillery and mere arrowshots: 133, neque putavi *cum omnibus machinis ac tormentis, vi exercitu copiis oppugnarer, de uno sagittario* me queri convenisse. Clodius is presumably depicted as an archer because this is the weapon of the coward (like Paris in the *Iliad*) shot from a safe distance, and itself relatively contemptible as a form of attack. Neither usage is repeated elsewhere in Cicero's works, but the artillery theme recurs in *Dom.* 27, *isdem machinis* sperare me restitutum posse *labefactari* quibus antea *stantem perculerunt*, in which Cicero conceives himself as a defensive tower in the fortifications of the state. Here military and architectural imagery converge.

I have already referred briefly to the analogy in 24, based on the consulship seen as a sword:

> si gladium parvo puero aut si imbecillo seni ac debili dederis, ipse impetu

---

33 Deinde videndum est ne longe simile sit ductum. "Syrtim" patrimonii "scopulum" libentius dixerim; "Charybdim bonorum" voraginem potius. See Wilkins on *de Orat.* 3.163 for other instances where Cicero disregards his own advice.

suo nemini noceat, sin ad nudum fortissimi viri corpus accesserit, possit acie ipsa et ferri viribus vulnerare; cum hominibus enervatis et exsanguibus *consulatus tamquam gladius* esset datus, qui per se *pungere* neminem unquam potuerunt, ii summi imperii nomine *armati* rem publicam *contrucidaverunt.*

The immediate function of the analogy is to explain how characters so contemptible as Piso and Gabinius are represented by Cicero could have done the great harm to the state which he describes.

Finally, as Cicero introduced his speech by a generalized image of warfare against his supporters (4, above), so he urges it to its close with the generalizing *nos ... ad eam rem publicam tuendam aggressi quae tanta dignitate est ut eam defendentem occidere optatius sit quam oppugnantem rerum potiri* (141).

Clodius' association with gladiators explains the several allusions to the world of the amphitheatre. We have already noted the unique metaphor *saginari* used in this context; so in 80, Sestius as the victim of attack by these thugs gives rise to the jibe, *num, ut gladiatoribus imperari solet, ferrum non recepit?* "Was Sestius at fault for not accepting the coup de grace?" Again actual games provoke the portrayal of Clodius as a *pantomima*: (116) ipse ille maximus *ludius*, non solum spectator sed *actor* et *acroama*[34] (the Greek word adds contempt, not meaning) qui omnia sororis *embolia* novit ... nec tuos ludos aspexit in illo ardenti tribunatu.

From the world of hunting the metaphors most commonly in use are those of nets and snares; so referring to Clodius (16), beluam *vinctam* auspiciis, *adligatam* more maiorum, *constrictam* in legum sacrarum *catenis solvit* subito lege curiata consul; similarly in 88, illum ... legum ... *laqueis constringeret. Constringere* itself is to be referred to human captives rather than to the hunt in 24, rem publicam adflictam et *constrictam* tradidissent; cf. *Dom.* 113, senatum tribuno furenti *constrictum* tradidissent; *Har.* 22, servorum eludentium multitudini senatum populumque Romanum *vinctum* ipso consessu et *constrictum* spectaculis atque *impeditum* turba ... tradidisset. The whole range of snaring verbs is explored in *Har.* 7, *inlaqueatus* omnium legum periculis, *inretitus* odio bonorum, exspectatione supplici iam non diuturna *implicatus*, feretur tamen haesitans et in me impetum *impeditus* facere conabitur. Other metaphors in *pro Sestio* which can be connected with hunting, *vestigia* (13) and *aucupari* (119) (bird-snaring), are traditional in Latin.

---

34 *Acroama*, cf. *Verr.* 2.4.49; hic *tamquam festivum acroama* ... emblemata evellenda curavit, makes a similar use of the disreputable profession to deride a bitter enemy.

The abusive element in this speech provides imagery derived from animals; Clodius as a *belua* (16, above) the consuls as *vulturii paludati* (71); more striking (72), *illa ex vepreculis extracta nitedula* rem publicam conaretur *adrodere*; 98, *qui discordiis civium ac seditionibus pascuntur* also treats the forces of Cicero's opponents as animals. In this connection, *pasci*[35] is often applied by Cicero to feeding on misfortune or suffering.

Most often Cicero denigrates his enemies by associating them with dirt, or identifying them with monsters in the Roman ritual sense: Clodius is *ex omnium scelerum conluvione natus* (15), a *labes ac caenum* (20, cf. 26). *Labes*, the most frequent expression of abuse, is also applied to situations: 56, omnem domesticam *labem*; as is *macula*, 63, illa in re publica *macula* regni publicati maneret, quam nemo iam posset *eluere*; cf. *maculare* 60 and 108, quis fuit qui non eius voce *maculari* rem publicam ... arbitraretur. A natural association is then the *sordes* of 60 and 112, ab horum turpitudine, audacia, *sordibus*.

In the second category, *pro Sestio* offers only 38, duo importuna *prodigia* – the consuls previously described as *rei p. turbines* (25), later as *vulturii paludati* (71 above). But in other speeches *portentum* is common.[36] The most general and least vivid of these epithets is *pestis*, occurring in *pro Sestio* alone at 33, *illa furia ac peste patriae*; 65, *duabus huius imperi pestibus*; 83, *nefariis pestibus*; 114, *omnes illae pestes*; 146, *pestem suam et patris sui*. Few identifications of this type are found in the correspondence; in, e.g., *ad Brut.* 23.4, *magna pestis erat depulsa per vos, magna populi Romani macula deleta*, Cicero is dealing with hypothetical situations, not with a person or political group.

Three personifications in *pro Sestio* seem to be coined for the occasion: Piso's philosophical brow is described in 19 as non supercilium sed *pignus* rei publicae ... ut illo supercilio annus ille niti tamquam *vade*[37] videretur – the only legal imagery in the speech; in 21, Piso is "nobilitate ipsa, *blanda conciliatricula* commendatus;" his aristocratic name is seen as a marriage broker. The same metaphor, without the diminutive, is applied to nature in *de Natura Deorum*, 1.77. The effect of the diminutive, as of the feminine noun, is to

35 *Pascere*, cf. cruelty; cf. *Verr.* 2.5.65; *Pis.* 45, and *Mil.* 3, parallel to *Sest.* 98: quos P. Clodi furor rapinis et incendiis et omnibus exitiis publicis *pavit*.

36 Identifications in abuse: *labes, Dom.* 107, *Har.* 46; *labem atque eluviem, Dom.* 54; *labem pestemque, Vatin.* 25; *O caenum, o portentum, o scelus, Dom.* 47; *portentosa pestis, Dom.* 72; *portenta ac paene fulmina rei p., Prov. Cos.* 2. I add two samples of fuller listings: *Vatin.* 33, *pestem* illius anni, *furiam* patriae, *tempestatem* rei publicae; *Prov. Cos.* 13, duplicis *pestis* sociorum, militum *cladis*, publicanorum *ruinas*, provinciarum *vastitates*, imperi *maculas*, teneretis.

37 For *vades* here, cf. *ad Brut.* 26.3, cum me pro adulescentulo res p. accepisset *vadem*; similar is *pignus, Att.* 1.19.3, ut nos duo quasi *pignora* rei p. retineri videremur.

express contempt; in *Vatin*. 4, Gellius is by a similar coinage called *nutricula*[38] seditiosorum omnium.

Naturally the vice of Cicero's adversaries is associated with *tenebrae*; cf. *Sest*. 9, cum illa coniuratio *ex latebris atque ex tenebris erupisset*; 20, *emersum ex diuturnis tenebris lustrorum ac stuprorum*. But *tenebrae* as a metaphor connotes not only haunts of vice, but also a time of disaster; compare *Dom*. 24, *illis rei p. tenebris caecisque nubibus et procellis*. Darkness and dirt are exploited in combination in *Vatin*. 11, *illud tenebricosissimum tempus ineuntis tuae adulescentiae patiar latere ... adulescentiae turpitudo obscuritate et sordibus tuis obtegatur*; and in 13, *praescribo ne tuas sordes cum clarissimorum virorum splendore permisceas ... te ex tuis tenebris extraham*. Here the two elements of imagery are chiastically arranged around the central core of argument occupying chapter 12. By contrast excellence and virtue are displayed in terms of light (60):

> M. Catonis *splendorem* maculare voluerunt, ignari ... quid denique virtus valeret, quae in tempestate saeva quieta *est et lucet in tenebris* et pulsa loco manet tamen atque haeret in patria, *splendetque per sese semper, neque alienis* umquam sordibus obsolescit.

Here metaphor of sea-storm, light and dark, and military steadfastness follow each other in accumulated polysyndeton, but it is the imagery of light which dominates, and is the more effective for being the only example in the speech.

In talking of his own procedure, Cicero several times resorts to metaphor to enliven his transitions; in 7, his excuse for abbreviating the account of Sestius' blameless youth is *sed mihi ante oculos obversatur rei p. dignitas quae me ad sese rapit, haec minora relinquere hortatur*. He repeats this device at the transition to Sestius' tribunate (13), *ad tribunatum qui ipse ad se iamdudum vocat et quodam modo absorbet orationem meam, contento studio cursuque veniamus*. Here the straight personification *vocat* leads into mixed imagery: *absorbet* conveys the suck of a current or eddy; compare *Brutus* 282, *sed hunc quoque absorbuit aestus quidam ... gloriae*, and *de Orat*. 3.145 (on the speaker carried away!), *te ... aestus ingeni tui procul a terra abripuit atque in altum e conspectu paene omnium abstraxit*. *Contento studio cursuque*, on the other hand, suggests more the race than the voyage, and recalls a similar use of *cursus* in *de Orat*. 1.161 (see 144 and n. 10).

---

38 Cf. Cic. *N.D.* 1.77, blanda *conciliatrix* ... natura; and, for *nutrix* applied to a male, Pl. *Cur*. 358, *invoco* almam *meam nutricem* – *Herculem*. The feminine *conciliatrix* is appropriate to the feminine abstracts, *nobilitas* and *natura*; with *nutrix*, the passage in *Vatin*. 4 probably intends to imply effeminacy, whereas Plautus in the *Curculio* is seeking a surprise effect – as the hiatus before *Herculem* shows; instead of a female patron deity, the parasite calls on Hercules, the most masculine of heroes, and patron of gluttons.

At 119, *non sum tam ignarus, iudices, causarum, non tam insolens in dicendo ut omni ex genere orationem aucuper et omnis undique flosculos carpam atque delibem*, in a defence of Cicero's digression on the theatrical demonstrations (118–27), the mixed imagery reflects the promiscuous scraping together of subject matter which he repudiates. The florid and dainty *flosculos carpam atque delibem* is different in tone from the conventional use of *flores* for rhetorical ornament in *de Orat.* 3.96.[39] In 123, *quoniam huc me provexit*[40] *oratio* (cf. *Dom.* 32, *vestra benignitas provexit orationem meam*) serves to shift the blame for the length of speech from the speaker himself.

At the simplest level of metaphor, Cicero uses many verbs figuratively in such a way that, without suggesting an independent, visual image, they still enrich their context; often he substitutes an unexpected, drastic or violent verb for a milder one; such are *exstinguere iura*, 17; *vulnera inusta rei p.*, 18; *verbum ipsum … devorarat* 23; *nemo est quin non modo ex memoria sed etiam fastis evellendos putet*,[41] 33; *vitam exhausisse*, 48; (cf. *luctum hausimus* maiorem, 63) *unus me absente defluxit*, qui cognomen sibi ex Aeliorum imaginibus *arripuit*, 70; here *Clu.* 72, using the verb *delegerat* in the same phrase, provides a control to illustrate the more ordinary expression. A similar effect is achieved by applying physical verbs to mental or moral states; 67, *non sopitam* sed *retardatam* consuetudinem; 68, *res erat et causa nostra eo iam loci ut erigere oculos et vivere videretur*; 71, *respirasse homines videbantur*; 139, *sudandum* est iis pro communibus commodis, where *sudari* is more vivid and vigorous than the routine *laborare* or *eniti*; 114, *populum ipsum … qui ita vehementer eos … respuat*; 139, *qui largitione caecarunt mentes imperitorum*.[42] But the proportion of verb-based metaphors is small in comparison with the abundance of imagery based on nouns; at the same time metaphors depending on a single word (*in verbo simplici*: *de Orat.* 3.152) are less frequent than those developed through a sequence of words or even phrases, such as the characterization of Sestius' exiled father-in-law in 7, or of Cato as the symbol of brilliant *virtus* in 60.

39 The poetic flavour of this phrase can be judged from the Ennian quotation, *flos delibatus* populi, *Ann.* 308v discussed by Cicero himself in *Brutus* 57.

40 *Provehi* is most commonly used of ships putting out to sea; cf. *Verr.* 2.5.87, *paulum provecta classis est*. The speech or speaker then is implicitly compared to a ship. Compare the similar, but explicit, use of *praetervehi* in *Cael.* 51, *quoniam emersisse iam e vadis et scopulos praetervecta videtur oratio mea*, and *Balb.* 4 (p. 116 above.)

41 For this use of *evellere*, cf. *Fam.* 5.8.3, ea sint *evulsa* ex omni memoria vitaque nostra.

42 *Caecare*. *Dom.* 60, *cupiditate esse caecatum*. With *Sest.* 139 this is the first metaphorical use of the verb recorded in Thesaurus. The first literal use, *Lucr.* 4.325, need not be much earlier in date.

The greater scale of *pro Sestio* allows imagery to assume functions beyond mere local ornament, and creates relationships between metaphors, and between systems of metaphor. The thematic metaphors applied to the *Res Publica*, based on the ship of state and storms of politics, on the ills of a sick state, on military attack in combat or siege, are each kept in play. By their double application to the *Res Publica* and to himself (see n. 27 and compare metaphorical *plaga*, inflicted on Cicero (44) and the state (78)), Cicero affirms the identity of his interests with those of his country.[43] This is most conspicuous in the two parallelisms marked each by a formal analogy resumed in a later section by a prolonged ἀλληγορία. The formal analogy which introduces Gabinius and Piso wielding the sword of *imperium* to slaughter the state in 24 is renewed in 54 by a metaphor that unites their destruction of Cicero with the plundering of the state. The longer formal analogy in 45–6, representing Cicero as saviour of the ship of state by his voluntary sacrifice, is recalled by the extensive allegory of the *optimates* as pilots in 97–9. Because of their formality and extent these stand out from the running threads of metaphors based on combat and navigation in the body of the speech. In 51 and 55 we have a minor example of the use of imagery with variation (*medicina* equals *remedium*) to frame a digression or separate section. This is comparatively rare in speeches (but compare *Vatin.* 11 and 13, p. 134 above), but a frequent feature in the composition of the contemporary *de Oratore*.

Finally, it is characteristic of *pro Sestio* that metaphors correspond in their field to the literal actions described in their context. The *plaga* to be inflicted on the state in 78 precedes the gladiatorial attack on Sestius in 78–80 and the literal use of *plaga* in 80. The games from which Clodius was absent in 116 are followed by an image of Clodius as a *ludius*; the metaphorical *ruinae atque incendia* of 121 introduce Cicero's *domum incensam eversamque* in the same sentence. On a larger scale in the general climate of violence, the frequent imagery of bloodshed in *pro Sestio* is no longer a metaphor, but a symbol and an evocation of the hysterical and nightmarish politics of 56 B.C.

43 Compare the way in which he relates Sestius' victimization by Clodius' followers to the victimization of the state, by repeating (literally) in 79 the rare verb *contrucidare* applied in the dramatic analogy of 24.

6

Imagery in the literary dialogue:
Cicero's *de Oratore*

To illustrate the contrast between Cicero's use of imagery in the speeches and in the literary works, I have chosen to examine the *de Oratore*, a work largely concerned with style. It is generally believed that Cicero began this work in 56 B.C., soon after the speeches considered in the previous section. He completed it for copying in November 55, before the letter to Spinther, *Fam.* 1.9, which we had cause to examine alongside these speeches.[1] Thus the material of this chapter is as nearly contemporary with them as possible.

De Oratore is a pioneer work, for Cicero, and for the growth of Latin literature. It was Cicero's first comprehensive and artistic theoretical work; his first prose writing intended for reading, not oral presentation; for he regarded the *de Inventione* as a mere manual or text book.[2] He was uniquely well read in classical and contemporary Greek prose literature, and took pains to find and read all available Latin authors. Thus he was aware of the formal limitations and the historical development of all the literary genres.

Each genre implied an appropriate stylistic colouring, and the *Orator* of 46 B.C. provides us with Cicero's judgments on the relation between the *genera eloquentiae* and the tone and style of prose. It is useful, then to consider how Cicero would conceive *de Oratore* in terms of genre. The letter to Spinther

1 The date of completion is guaranteed by *Att.* 4.13.2, written before 20 November 55, authorizing Atticus to have the Ms copied for publication. From the reference in *Fam.* 1.9.23, "scripsi igitur Aristotelio more ... tres libros in disputatione ac dialogo *de oratore*," we may perhaps assume that Cicero was sending Lentulus a copy of the completed Ms. Lily Ross Taylor, *C.P.* 33, 1949, 217–21 identifies *de Oratore* with the *Hortensiana* of *Att.* 4.6, and dates both the letter and the inception of the dialogue to April 55.
2 For Cicero's estimate of *de Inventione*, cf. *de Orat.* 1.5, "quae pueris aut adulescentulis nobis ex commentariolis nostris incohata ac rudia exciderunt." Much of this is *dissimulatio*, but the classification as *commentarii*, as in Antonius' allusion to his *libellus* (*de Orat.* 1.208; *illa quae in commentarium meum rettuli*) implies a work of record or instruction rather than literary art.

(n. 1) above, describes the work as written *Aristotelio more in disputatione ac dialogo*, each element of this description suggesting certain conclusions. The reference to Aristotle is a clue to structure – continuous exposition and *disputatio in utramque partem* leading to a final assessment – rather than to localized form or style, but it does make clear that Cicero saw himself as writing in the philosophical tradition. *De Oratore* itself, both in the first proemium (1.28, *cur non imitamur Socratem illum ... qui est in Phaedro Platonis*) and the final salutation to Hortensius (3.228–30 = Plato, *Phaedr.* 278e–9b with a salute to Isocrates), acknowledges Cicero's position as *Platonis aemulus*. The praise he lavishes on Plato in *Orator* 62 as *longe omnium* (philosophorum) *et gravitate et suavitate princeps* suggests that Cicero considered Plato the model of philosophical style. Unfortunately, his further comments on this genre are too general to show what formal stylistic character he associated with either Plato, or philosophical writing as a whole. He emphasizes the aim of *docere*, and the subsidiary aim of *delectare*, with the consequent avoidance of forensic vehemence and then proceeds to a new distinction:

> mollis est enim oratio philosophorum ut umbratilis, nec sententiis nec verbis instructa popularibus, nec vincta numeris, sed soluta liberius ... *itaque sermo potius quam oratio dicitur.*

The definition as *sermo* corresponds to the last element in Cicero's description of *de Oratore*, "in disputatione ac *dialogo*" – actual conversation, in naturalistic conversational style; the other element, *in disputatione*, suggests another genre-tradition, that of Epideictic. To some extent all theoretical and protreptic writing came under the heading of Epideictic, but Cicero associated this genre with the works of the sophists, and above all with Isocrates. His encomium of Isocrates in *Orator* 41–2 culminates in a brief sketch of the genre:

> dulce igitur orationis genus et solutum et adfluens, sententiis argutum, verbis sonans est in illo epideictico genere, quod diximus proprium sophistarum.

Later, in the full portrait of Epideictic at *Orator* 65, he gives detailed recommendations, first emphasizing the aim of the genre – *delectare* – then deducing from this the formal stylistic features which will be appropriate:

> concinnas magis sententias exquirunt quam probabilis, a re saepe disce-dunt, intexunt fabulas, *verba altius transferunt, eaque ita disponunt ut pictores varietatem colorum*, paria paribus referunt, adversa contrariis, saepissimeque similia extrema definiunt.

Of these features the carefully balanced sentence structure and the use of rhythmic devices like isocola are incompatible with the naturalism required of dialogue, but the comment on figurative language, endorsing a bolder use of metaphor artistically applied as an ornament, is appropriate to *de Oratore*, which contains such relatively artificial forms of imagery as developed analogies, and the personification of abstract concepts.

In Greek terms, Cicero was attempting a blend of philosophical dialogue and Epideictic; but Cicero was a Latin writer, conscious of his own language and literature. What tradition of dialogue writing was available to Cicero in the literature of his own country?

We know of one Latin work in the form of prose dialogue which is definitely prior to *de Oratore*, the three books *de Iure Civili* of M. Iunius Brutus, from which Cicero's Crassus quotes in *de Orat.* 2.224; this was a didactic dialogue between father and son, and the brief quotations do not suggest a high level of literary artistry. Another dialogue work, this time political and partisan, is described with scorn in *Brutus* 218–19. But this work of the elder Curio was written in the late fifties, since it *reprendit eas res quas idem Caesar anno post et deinceps reliquis annis administravit in Gallia*, so that it should be dated after *de Oratore* itself. Only one author in Latin using dialogue form had earned Cicero's praise, the poet Lucilius, who wrote "ludus ac sermones" (1039M) in hexameter and other verse. If the difference of genre eliminated them as a precedent for the form of *de Oratore*, their easy *sermo*, at least, offered a stylistic model for the more informal passages of Cicero's dialogue. Evidence is advanced below that Cicero was in fact influenced by Lucilius in forming the style of his dialogue works.

There is another respect in which *de Oratore* has no precedent. Before 55 most Roman writers who attempted large scale prose works were historians, writing annalistically with an open-ended structure, to which the course of time added books to cover events occurring during composition. The rhetorical treatise *ad Herennium* (traditionally dated[3] to 86–82 B.C.) comes near to *de Oratore* in scale, but like *de Inventione*, it observes the didactic arrangement of a manual, without regard for the architecture of the complete work. *De Oratore*, in contrast, was conceived as a balanced structure, with its topics and arguments arranged so as to observe harmonious proportions within the body of the work. Its scale and balance permit Cicero to evolve two uses of imagery barely represented in the forensic speeches we have considered; the thematic use of an image to represent the focus of an argument, and the

3 For the dating, based on internal evidence, see Caplan, *ad C. Herennium de ratione dicendi* (Cambridge, Mass. 1954), p. xxvi.

architectonic use (which may overlap with thematic imagery) of a developed image or analogy to mark the beginning or end of phases in thought, to link a speech with the preceding speech which it answers, to frame digressions and mark transitions to a new or renewed topic.

Since figurative language can be employed in any given passage for both local and general effect, relating both to the immediate context, and to more remote sections, it is almost impossible in discussing Cicero's techniques to isolate single aspects of imagery. Within examples chosen to illustrate one point, individual words and phrases will have to be considered in the light of another function. For this reason I have thought it useful to present in advance these differing aspects of figurative language in *de Oratore* which will be found occurring constantly in combination.

I singled out the use of analogy as characteristic of epideictic writing; although in the strict sense analogy (*similitudo*[4]) is not imagery (since it differs in syntax and stylistic formality), it resembles imagery in its psychological function. Unlike metaphor, it expresses in full the relevant aspects of both objects or events compared; thus technical arguments can be made both clear and persuasive by means of non-technical analogies. Like metaphor, it is usually more vivid and attractive than its context, offering a pleasing diversion from abstract or jejune topics, and introducing a refreshing appeal to the visual imagination or social interests of the readers. The ancient world was conscious of the affinity: thus the author of *Rhetorica ad Herennium* deals with *similitudo* (translated by Caplan as comparison) at 4.59–61 in the same group with *exemplum* and *imago* (simile), 4.62, and introduces his illustrations in these terms:

> *Similitudo* est oratio traducens ad rem quampiam aliquid ex re dispari simile. ea sumitur aut *ornandi* causa aut *probandi* aut *apertius dicendi* aut *ante oculos ponendi*."

Of the analogies in *de Oratore*, some are primarily didactic, resembling Platonic *epagoge*, others primarily decorative, their function being *delectare* rather than *docere*; again while some are recognizably drawn from spheres of

---

4 *Similitudo* is the technical term used for analogy in *Rhet. Her.* 4.59–61. However, despite the arguments of Marsh McCall, *Ancient Rhetorical Theories of Simile and Comparison* (Harvard 1961), 90–114, I do not believe Cicero recognized *similitudo* as a rhetorical term. He uses the word in the general sense of resemblance and comparison, but when he applies it in a context of metaphor or rhetorical comparison, it is in order to explain these figures by their logical relationship, not as a defining term. The one passage in *de Oratore* in which *similitudo* needs to be technical in meaning, 3.157, should be rejected as an interpolation on other grounds (see Appendix, n. 1).

life dear to the Greek philosophical and rhetorical tradition, others, being expressed in terms of Roman society, represent the independent invention of Cicero himself.

Thus the references to athletics and the fine arts suggest a Greek origin for the analogies of 1.73; the orator reveals his liberal education, just as ball-players reveal their training in the *palaestra* by their movements, and sculptors reveal in sculpture their training in draftsmanship. Typically Cicero welds this analogy into his contexts by the subsequent metaphors from the *palaestra*: 74, non *luctabor* tecum ... id enim ipsum ... *artificio quodam* es consecutus ut ... ea ipsa nescio quomodo rursus *detorqueres* atque oratori propria *traderes*; and 81, when Antonius refers to the style of the epideictic orator as *nitidum quoddam genus* ... verborum et *laetum* et *palaestrae magis et olei* quam huius civilis turbae ac fori. To say that the analogy is Greek in origin, is not, of course, to claim that Cicero is here translating or adapting argument and analogy together from one Greek source, although this possibility cannot be excluded; merely that Cicero has derived the analogy from his extensive familiarity with Greek rhetorical theory. As an example of the orator-athlete analogy in Greek, we may refer to the specific parallel made by Isocrates, *Antidosis* 183 ff., between the physical training of the *paidotribes*, and the rhetorical training which he himself offered; for the orator-sculptor analogy, compare the judg-ment of Dionysius of Halicarnassus (*Isocr.* 3) that Isocrates was comparable in style to Polyclitus or Pheidias, whereas Lysias was closer to the bronze-caster Calamis. Dionysius is later than, but independent of, Cicero, and such detailed refinements of synaesthetic criticism presuppose a long tradition of analogy between the arts.[5]

Our general conclusions about these analogies are confirmed by 1.153, which is a complex and revealing case. Cicero writes:

> ut concitato navigio, cum remiges inhibuerunt, retinet tamen ipsa navis motum et cursum suum intermisso impetu pulsuque remorum, sic in oratione perpetua, cum scripta deficiunt, parem tamen obtinet oratio reliqua cursum scriptorum similitudine et vi concitata.

---

5 Compare Cicero's use of the evolution of Greek sculpture and painting to explain the evolution of Rhetoric in *Brutus* 70-1, imitated by Quintilian, 12.10.1-9. These accounts show the same relative valuation of artists as is implied by Dionysius above. In *Brut.* 70, Calamis represents the second stage or generation of sculpture, two stages before the *plane perfecta* (*signa*) of Polyclitus. With the loss of Greek rhetorical criticism of the centuries before Cicero and Dionysius, it is futile to argue whether this parallelism of the arts was Peripatetic (cf. Oltramare, *R.E.L.*19, 1941, 94) or Pergamene doctrine (so Desmouliez, *R.E.L.*30, 1952, 177 and n.).

He is comparing the ability of a well-prepared orator to extemporize on the basis of his written preparation, with the ship which keeps in motion when the oarsmen cease to row after a stretch at full speed. Here then is a nautical analogy for which we would tend to suspect a Greek origin; but in a letter of 45 B.C., *Att.* 13.21, Cicero has cause to discuss this same nautical analogy with Atticus, who had suggested that Cicero should use *inhibere remos* as a figurative translation for the Greek technical term ἐποχή. Cicero rejects the suggestion because he has now discovered by watching oarsmen that *inhibere* refers not to resting the oars, but to a different technique of rowing: *inhibitio autem remigum motum habet et vehementiorem quidem remigationis navem convertentis ad puppim.* Thus the analogy of *de Orat.* 1.153, is based on a misunderstanding of the technical application of *inhibere* in nautical practice, a misunderstanding unlikely to have been committed by a Greek. It would seem that we have in this case a comparison worked up by Cicero himself.

But the letter to Atticus reveals more about Cicero's general method in using imagery, for he supports his own original phrase in preference to Atticus' suggestion by two arguments: (1) nec est melius quicquam quam ut Lucilius *sustineas currum ut bonus saepe agitator equosque,* and (2) semperque Carneades προβολὴν pugilis et retentionem aurigae similem facit ἐποχῇ.

The passage discussed is from the *Academica posteriora,* already published and in Varro's possession, and it must coincide with the earlier form preserved in the *Academica priora, Lucullus* 94.

ego enim *ut agitator* callidus priusquam ad finem veniam *equos sustinebo* ... sic me ante *sustineo.*

This is spoken by a supporter of Carneades; hence Cicero's justification of his simile in terms of Carneades' habitual practice. Since it is habitual, we can deduce that Cicero is not translating a specific allusion in Carneades, but recalling his general technique. At the same time, the finished simile chooses the image of Carneades which coincides with the good Latin precedent of Lucilius, and uses the Lucilian *sustinere,* not Cicero's own verb *retinere* (as in *retentionem aurigae* above). In *Lucullus* 94 Cicero has the best of both worlds, the metaphor of the Greek philosophical source, and the reminiscence of an admired[6] Latin literary source. We cannot tell how often this bicultural

---

6 Lucilius is quoted by Cicero at *de Orat.* 1.72; 2.25, 253, and 263; 3.86 and 171. Cicero had two special motives for concern with Lucilius in the composition of this dialogue. From 1.72 it is clear that Lucilius wrote, however briefly, on the education required of an orator: *ut solebat C. Lucilius saepe dicere* (masking literary citation behind the

experience underlies the images and analogies in Cicero's writing, but we can perceive the immense artistic concern he had for even a brief figurative flight, and for its accuracy in representing the concept he wishes to make vivid. In considering further instances of analogy we should not let Greek content blind us to the possibility of a Roman precedent.

The analogy of 1.73 above is recalled in 2.69–73. Cicero argues from the practice of painters and sculptors that the man with a thorough training in the most difficult aspects of an art such as rhetoric will have no trouble with minor undertakings. Antonius' example in 2.70, the Hercules of Polyclitus, leads to an interruption by Catulus, after which the main argument is resumed by a variation of the same theme when Antonius reasserts his case in 73:

> si quis illam artem comprehenderit ut tamquam Phidias Minervae signum efficere possit, non sane quem ad modum, ut in clipeo idem artifex, minora illa opera facere discat laborabit.

Here is a neat example, on a small scale, of the architectural function of analogy.

Cicero's range in 2.186 is more varied; the major analogy is from the orator–audience to the doctor–patient relationship, and its close resemblance to Plato, *Phaedrus* 270b (noted by Wilkins, *ad loc.*) confirms its ultimate Greek origin. But it is reinforced by a great variety of minor imagery: from running (not necessarily the foot-race[7]) *facilius est enim, ut aiunt, currentem incitare quam commovere languentem*; then, after the major analogy, from hounds, *ut odorer quam sagacissime possim, quid sentiant*; then a more extended metaphor based on a man yielding, or leaning under physical pressure. Speaking still of the jurors, Antonius comments (187) *si se dant et ... sua sponte quo impellimus inclinant[8] atque propendent ...*, but interrupts with a nautical image in the apodosis, *ad id, unde aliquis flatus ostenditur, vela do*. This in itself seems to

---

dialogue convention of oral record) *neminem esse in oratorum numero habendum qui non sit omnibus eis artibus, quae sunt libero dignae, perpolitus* (1241M); compare also the rhetorical criticism of 84M, 1133M. Secondly, as an older contemporary and acquaintance of Crassus and Scaevola, Lucilius was part of the historical colouring of *de Oratore*.

7 This seems to be proverbial and Roman; cf. *Q.fr.* 1.1.16, *ut currentem incitasse videatur*. For Greek influenced metaphors from the footrace, especially those based on the race of life motif, compare p. 68 above s.v. *spatium*, and from *de Orat.* 1.1, *decursu honorum etiam aetatis flexu constitisset (flexus* equals καμπτήρ); and 1.147, non vobis; *vos quidem iam estis in cursu, sed eis, qui ingrediuntur in stadium.*

8 The pair *impellere/inclinare* is found again in 2.324, *sed tantum impelli iudicem primo leviter, ut iam inclinato reliqua incumbat oratio;* cf. also 1.31; 3.55, *ut eos qui audiant quocunque incubuerit, possit impellere.* For the same pair in a military context such as would suggest the transition made by Cicero to the *imperator* image, cf. Livy 2.20.11, tum demum *impulsi* Latini perculsaque *inclinavit* acies.

conflict with the previous relationship, since we would expect the orator to be equated with the active wind, and the jurors with the sailors; instead their response is identified with the wind, and the orator is now the reactor. He returns to the push and yield image and continues *ut non modo inclinantem excipere aut stantem inclinare*, but recalling the military use of *inclinare*, again changes his metaphorical reference, *sed etiam adversantem ac repugnantem, ut imperator ... bonus, capere possit*. Here, then, the Greek-style analogy leads finally to military imagery of a more Roman flavour.

An example of analogy for *epagoge* is 3.98 f. the dangers of excessive charm in style are illustrated from the surfeit caused by the florid style of new-fangled painting and lyric poetry, from sickly perfumes (99) or food. In 3.178, to support the maxim *in oratione ... ea quae maximam utilitatem in se continerent plurimum eadem haberent vel dignitatis vel saepe etiam venustatis*, the beauty of functionalism is invoked in the Cosmos itself, in man, in trees (analogies from nature), and in ships and architecture. Here as in 2.187, the climax is provided by a Roman comparison; the *fastigium* of the Capitol devised for the utili-tarian purpose of draining heavy rains is intrinsically a source of *venustas* and *dignitas*. Yet the choice of comparisons, with the careful distinction between examples from *natura* and *artes* (180, *init.*) suggests a Greek, philosophically inspired, source.

Other analogies may very well be original to Cicero himself. The com-parison, 1.161–2, of the orator's store of cultural equipment (*instrumentum*) to the rich furnishings[9] of a house, is introduced by a metaphor comparing Crassus' swift flow of speech to the gallop of a racehorse (161, *init.*).[10] Both

---

9 Cf. *Orator* 80, verecundus erit usus oratoriae *quasi supellectilis; supellex est* enim quodam modo nostra, *quae est in ornamentis*, alia rerum alia verborum. See n. 27 below on the comparable application of κατασκευή as equivalent to *ornamenta orationis*.

10 Wilkins in this passage declares "the figure is taken from a horse at full speed." But what exactly is our metaphor? The words sustaining it are *cursus, evolavit, vim et incita-tionem, vestigia ingressumque*. Of these, *cursus*, in the sense of *cursus verborum*, "flow of eloquence," is the neutralized metaphor restored to life by the others. The image of a speed so intense that the tracks are indistinguishable demands not a human runner but a race horse or chariot, and the verb *evolare* confirms this. Crassus' speech has rushed out ahead like horses released from the starting gates (cf. Ovid, *Am.* 3.2.78, *evolat admissis discolor agmen equis*), and Crassus is playing charioteer. The key word *cursus*, whether applied to rhetorical fluency or political career, can generate imagery of the footrace (as in 1.147, n. 7 above), the chariot race, or the voyage; it can even provoke an irrational blend of the last two as in de Orat. 3.7. (p. ooo below). Consider these four "racing" images in the *Brutus*. In 233, *verborum ... cursu quodam incitato* barely colours the neutral *cursus*; in 272, the exceptionally rapid progress of C. Piso *ut evolare non excurrere videretur* is described in terms similar to de Orat. 1.161. Cicero says of his own *cursus*

are intended to convey the same theme – a richness and flow of eloquence only partially perceived by the hearers, and the verbs of the main image (*refertam*; *non explicata*) become metaphor in Cotta's comments of 163: "perfice, ut Crassus haec, quae *coartavit et peranguste refersit* in oratione sua, *dilatet* nobis atque *explicet*."

The diversions of men released from work are explained by the analogy in 2.23 of birds who fly away after the toil of nest-building; these games become the analogy in 3.58 (the Roman diversions of *pila, tali,* and *tesserae* are quoted) for the absorption of Greek intellectuals in forms of cultural activity when excluded from political life.

In 2.88 the long and detailed analogy from the pruning of over-luxuriant vines to the disciplining of an exuberant young orator is probably Roman. It is used by Antonius to introduce a digression related to the occasion of the dialogue through the person of Sulpicius. The digression leads from Sulpicius' training to the principle of *imitatio,* and then to a brief survey of Greek oratory illustrating the effect of *imitatio* on succeeding generations, returning to Sulpicius in 96. A second analogy drawn from agriculture, (97) *ut in herbis rustici solent dicere: in summa ubertate inest luxuries quaedam stilo depascenda est,* marks the end of the digression by repeating the theme of 88 from which it departed, with a new twist, the emphasis on writing as a form of control. Thus 2.88 and 2.97 have a structural function, but it can also be said that the agricultural imagery is thematic, since Antonius later (2.131) compares the trainee orator to a ploughed field in which the teacher is to sow. Crassus, too, in 1.113–14, demanded that his pupils should be *uberes,* for the necessary talents *inseri et donari ab arte non possunt. Inserere* here alludes to the grafting of the cultivated fruit tree onto its wild counterpart. This same natural fertility which is essential, since it cannot be increased by grafting, will (2.88) have to be controlled by pruning in its early stages in order to achieve proper maturity.

(career) in 307, *simus in spatio* Q. Hortensium *ipsius vestigiis persecuti,* implying the relay footrace. But the fullest treatment is in 331–2; he grieves for Brutus' *adulescentiam quasi quadrigis vehentem,* damaged by the veering onslaught of national disaster. Resuming this in 332 he continues "*etsi cursum ingeni tui ... premit haec importuna clades ... effice ut te eripias ex ea ... turba patronorum.*" Brutus is to pull forward out of the crowd of rival charioteers and draw ahead. While Cicero accepted the inherited Greek image of life as a relay, he developed more fully the metaphor of the chariot race, which appealed to Roman sporting preferences. Tacitus, who comments in *Dialogus* 29 on the *peculiaria huius urbis vitia ... histrionalis favor et gladiatorum equorumque studia,* himself adapts the analogy (*ibid.* 39)

quo modo nobilis equos cursus et spatia probant, sic est aliquis oratorum campus, per quem nisi liberi et soluti ferantur, debilitatur et frangitur eloquentia.

It will be seen that the relationship of 1.113 to 2.88 is closer than to the later examples (2.97 and 131); a continuation of the strictly arboricultural image would have seemed too artificial, whereas the variations sustain the agricultural analogy less conspicuously.[11]

As a last example of Roman analogy, I would refer to 3.69, where the derivation of philosophy and rhetoric from the same educational source provokes a comparison with the Italian watershed of the Apennines, from which philosophy flows eastwards to the safe Greek sea full of harbours, but rhetoric flows to the rocky and violent *Mare Etruscum*. Thus philosophy found its home in Greece; but rhetoric in Rome. Clearly from its argument, as well as the Italian reference, this analogy is original to the Roman writer.

This wide range of illustrations is in striking contrast with the limited analogies of Cicero's earlier *de Inventione* (from medicine 1.5.6–7; 1.38.68, and from navigation 1.3.4; 1.30.47) or the *Rhetorica ad Herennium*. In book 4 of the latter, the writer introduces into his prooemium analogies from the Olympic footrace (4.4), from hucksters who advertise their merchandise with borrowed samples (4.9), from the absurdity of a man parched with thirst claiming to control precious springs of water (here the basic image of the *fons* of knowledge is invoked), and from named Greek sculptors. Later he chooses as examples of *similitudo* the statesman seen as helmsman of the ship of state (4.57); the slackening of speed by the runner in the torch-race as he relays his torch (4.59); the need for a horse to be broken in, and a runner to be trained (60); his fullest comparison (60 again) is between the man of prestige and ability but no virtue, and the handsome and richly dressed *citharoedus* with the dreadful voice. Both are alike rejected by the disillusioned public. In none of these cases is there any reason to suppose original invention rather than a traditional Greek comparison.

The other form of figurative language common in Cicero's literary and

11 With 2.88 compare *Cael.* 76, *amputanda plura sunt adulescentiae quam inserenda.* *Amputare* and *circumcidere* are paired in *Fin.* 1.44 as in *de Orat.* 1.65: *inserere* is used figuratively in *Brut.* 213; o generosam ... *stirpem et tamquam in unam arborem plura genera*, sic in istam domum multorum *insitam* sapientiam. With *de Orat.* 2.97, compare *Orator* 48, nihil est enim feracius ingeniis, eis praesertim quae disciplina exculta sunt. sed ut segetes fecundae et uberes non solum fruges verum etiam herbas effundunt inimicissimas frugibus ... Larue Van Hook, *The Metaphorical Terminology of Greek Rhetoric and Literary Criticism* (Diss. Chicago 1905) 32–3 relates the pruning image, especially Quintilian's use of *castigare* (10.1.115) to the Greek κολάζειν, used of pruning by Theophrastus, *H.P.* 2.7.6; but, whereas κολάζειν can be extended from its normal use to include pruning, *circumcidere* is literal in arboriculture, and figurative in the moral and aesthetic field.

philosophical writings but rare in the speeches and absent from the letters (see "Imagery of Terence," pp. 37–8) is the Greek-style personified abstraction. Such expressions as πενία διδάσκαλος, ἰατρὸς χρόνος, in Greek New Comedy, which found no echoes in the Roman adaptations, represent a turn of thought natural to Greek rhetoric and popularizing philosophy. From *de Oratore*, compare:

1.9 omnium laudatarum artium *procreatricem* quandam, et quasi *parentem* eam, quam φιλοσοφίαν Graeci vocant

1.18 *thesauro* rerum omnium memoria. quae nisi *custos* ... adhibeatur (here one suspects direct reminiscence of Greek theory; cf. *Rhet. Her.* 3.28, ad *thesaurum* inventorum atque ad omnium partium rhetoricae *custodem*, memoriam)

1.38 ista praeclara *gubernatrice* ... civitatum eloquentia.

1.75 (artes) *comites ac ministratrices* oratoris.

1.150 stilus optimus ... dicendi *effector et magister* (cf. 1.257; quem tu vere dixisti *perfectorem* (sic) dicendi esse ac *magistrum*)

2.36 historia vero *testis* temporum, *lux* veritatis, *vita* memoriae, *magistra* vitae, *nuntia* vetustatis ...

These personifications are altogether more artificial in effect than such a direct statement as 3.74, cui *disciplina* fuerit forum, *magister* usus et leges et instituta populi Romani, and they are typical features of didactic prose. Thus in the early and summary *de Inventione*, one may pick out *caeca ac temeraria dominatrix* animi cupiditas (1.2.2); commoditas quaedam *prava* virtutis *comitatrix* (1.2.3); *moderatrix* omnium rerum sapientia (1.2.3, the same conception as *de Orat.* 1.38); and 1.41.76, similitudo est satietatis *mater*, which like *de Orat.* 3.74 above, mitigates the boldness of the identification by presenting it as a full statement. Since most abstractions in Latin, as in Greek, are feminine in gender, they lend themselves to comparison with females, and one may contrast with these rather sexless personifications the witty comparison by Scaevola (1.234–5) between jurisprudence and a "virgo indotata" (see p. 171 below), whose final fate is to be (236) *eloquentiae tamquam ancillulam pedisequamque*.

In discussing the use of analogy I have touched several times on the extension and complexity of the material, and the use of imagery drawn from mixed spheres. Four passages from *de Oratore* will illustrate how far Cicero indulges his figurative language in this genre beyond its narrower scope in even the fullest of his speeches.

Let us begin with 1.41. Here Scaevola takes Crassus to task for attributing to oratory alone the subject matter of so many disciplines.

> id, nisi hic in tuo regno essemus, non tulissem, *multisque praeissem, qui aut interdicto tecum contenderent aut te ex iure manum consertum vocarent, quod in alienas possessiones tam temere inruisses. Agerent enim tecum lege primum Pythagorei omnes atque Democritii ceterique in iure sua physici vindicarent,* ... *quibuscum tibi iusto sacramento contendere non liceret*; urgerent praeterea philosophorum greges iam ab illo fonte et capite Socrate ... et cum universi in te impetum fecissent tum singulae familiae *litem tibi intenderent*; instaret Academia ... Stoici vero nostri disputationum suarum atque interrogationum laqueis te inretitum tenerent.

As is appropriate to the jurisconsult Scaevola, the main metaphor is legal, based on the various procedures to dispute possession or ownership of property. I have adopted *praeissem*, rather than *praeessem* of the Oxford text, because this correction provides another element in the legal language; *praeire* (cf. *Mil.* 3) is technical of the prefatory recitation of legal formulae by the magistrate, or of the drafting performed by a jurisconsult such as Scaevola for his client. But the complex legal imagery is prefaced by a minor metaphor – Crassus' estate as his *regnum* – related to the main issue (*in alienas possessiones inruere*) and then diversified by language suggestive of physical combat. The *greges* and *familiae* of the philosophers recall the private gladiatorial establishments of wealthy contemporaries; *urgere, impetum facere,* and *instare* imply military attack; Socrates as the *fons et caput* of the philosophical schools represents the favourite image of learning as derived from a source or wellspring (more often applied to source materials than human agents, as we shall see in considering 2.162 below). Finally, *laqueis inretitum* alludes to the hunt and the animal ensnared by the noose of the hunters. The legal and gladiatorial imagery is purely Roman; the subsidiary figurative language, while not without Greek equivalents, is at home in Roman prose imagery, and can be paralleled from Cicero's speeches and letters.

This speech of Scaevola represents the formal challenge to Crassus' claim for the wider scope of oratory, and its right to deal with universal issues. Only when Crassus has established the validity of this claim through his historical account in book 3 of the *discidium ... quasi linguae et cordis* (61) and subsequent

usurpation by philosophy, does the theme return; in a preliminary form at
3.108, *quoniam de nostra possessione depulsi in parvo et eo litigioso praediolo relicti
sumus*, et ... nostra tenere tuerique non potuimus, ab eis ... *qui in nostrum
patrimonium inruperunt*, quod opus est nobis mutuemur. The dispossessed
orators should borrow from the intruders. Cicero illustrates in 109 how recent
philosophers have offered rhetoricians new scope in elaborating the *quaestiones
infinitae*, but the response has been tentative (110) *ita non ut iure aut iudicio, vi
denique, recuperare amissam possessionem, sed ut surculo defringendo usurpare
videantur*; that is, they have laid a symbolic claim to handle the *quaestiones*,
without actually entering into possession. This metaphor prefaces an account
of the *quaestiones* and their divisions, from 111–21; at the end of the account,
it is modified and reformulated in a final triumphant assertion of the orator's
rights, and his intent, 122–3

> nostra est, inquam, nostra, omnis ista prudentiae doctrinaeque *possessio
> in quam homines quasi caducam et vacuam* abundantes otio, nobis occupatis,
> *involaverunt* ... quae quoniam iam aliunde non possumus, sumenda sunt
> nobis ab eis ipsis a quibus expilati sumus.

Socrates' attack had led the orators to let their right of possession lapse; while
they were kept occupied with their role as statesmen, idle philosophers had
become squatters on their territory. Thus orators had now every right to a
compensatory revenue from the philosophers' moral and political themes.
Structurally 1.41 and 3.122–3 mark the challenge and the vindication, major
moments in the dialogue, while 3.108 and 110 play a subordinate role, herald-
ing the formal analysis of the *quaestiones*. In this they combine with 3.122–3 to
form a framework for a crucial theoretical section, like the images 2.162 and
174 discussed below. At the same time these fully developed ἀλληγορίαι
(cf. 3.166) are closely related to the thematic imagery of *fines, termini, regio*,
denoting the range or scope of the orator; since these are diffused more widely
throughout the work, I shall discuss them separately (pp. 162–3 below).

My second example comes from Antonius' discussion of *Inventio* at 2.162:

> Ego autem, si quem nunc rudem plane institui ad dicendum velim his
> potius tradam adsiduis uno opere *eandem incudem diem noctemque tundenti-
> bus, qui omnes tenuissimas particulas atque omnia minima mansa ut nutrices
> infantibus pueris in os inserant*; sin sit is qui et doctrine mihi liberaliter

institutus et aliquo iam *imbutus* usu et satis acri ingenio esse videatur, *illuc eum rapiam ubi non seclusa aliqua acula teneatur, sed unde universum flumen erumpat*; qui illi *sedis et quasi domicilia* omnium argumentorum commonstret et ea breviter inlustret verbisque definiat.

In one paragraph Antonius passes through five, perhaps six, images. Thus the hack teachers of rhetoric are described first as blacksmiths, the monotony of their methods brought out by threefold repetition, *adsiduis, uno opere*, and *eandem incudem*;[12] without transition, they become wet-nurses, weaning their babies with morsels of food; the last five words, are appropriate to both the literal and the metaphorical situation; the untrained speaker is *infans* (cf. *Rhet. Her.* 2.16; Cic. *Inv.* 1.4; *Brut.* 77, 90, 108, 305; *Orat.* 56) in one sense, as the baby is at a lower level; *in os inserere* is as applicable to "putting words into one's mouth," as inserting scraps of food. Although both these images are classified as proverbial by Otto (*Sprichwörter*, 174, 247), this is their first appearance in Latin in this form. The use of *tundere* for monotonous speech recalls the traditional *aures/aliquem obtundere* of *sermo familiaris*. (cf. *Imagery of Terence, s.v. obtundere*, p. 61). The nurse-simile, on the other hand, is probably Greek inspired; not only do τροφός and τίτθη feature largely in Greek popular humour (cf. Thrasymachus' mockery of Socrates, *Resp.* 343a), but an allusion very similar to this occurs in Aristophanes, *Eq.* 715–18, and Aristotle, *Rhet.* 3.4.3, 9–10, quotes as a classic example of simile ὡς ὁ Δημοκράτης εἴκασε τοὺς ῥήτορας ταῖς τίτθαις αἳ τὸ ψώμισμα καταπίνουσαι τῷ σιάλῳ τὰ παιδία παραλείφουσιν. Antonius has just mentioned his knowledge of Aristotle's rhetorical works, (160) *in quibus ipse sua quaedam de eadem arte dixit*. Is this metaphor a reminiscence of the *Topica* which Cicero adapts in the following sections?

12 The basic image here is that of the *acies ingenii*; cf. *acie mentis* in 2.160 above. Both intellect and tongue are conceived as weapons or tools of oratory to be sharpened by training, and the hack rhetoricians are the smiths who beat out the blade on the anvil. With *tundo* the emphasis is placed on the monotony of the process; more usual is play on the concepts of sharpening and blunting. Compare *de Orat.* 3.93, *non quo ... acui ingenia adulescentium nollem, sed contra ingenia obtundi nolui*, and 121, *non enim solum acuenda nobis neque procudenda lingua est*, or *Tusc.* 1.73, *mentis acies ... hebescit*, and 80, *multa quae acuant mentem, multa quae obtundant*. Tacitus in *Dial.* 20, *iuvenes ... studiorum in incude positi*, is imitating *de Oratore* 2.162, as he does many other metaphors of this book. In *Ars.* 304–5 Horace offers a variant to express the critic's role, *fungar vice cotis, acutum/reddere quae ferrum valet*.

The metaphor occurs in comedy also; cf. Plaut. *Ps.* 614, *haec mihi incus est; procudam ego hodie hinc multos dolos*. The dupe is himself the anvil on which the slave will beat out the weapon of his wiles.

Passing to the more educated student, Antonius describes him as *aliquo iam imbutus* usu; in this case *imbutus* (literally dipped; the metaphorical association with learning goes back to Plaut. *Trin.* 293-4, neve *imbuas* ingenium (artibus)) is in harmony with the succeeding, developed, image based on the traditional theme of drinking from the springs of knowledge. The contrast is made between the inferior *seclusa acula* and *unde universum flumen erumpat*. Wilkins (*ad. loc.*) interprets *acula* as a pool, contrasted with the flowing river, but there is no reason why *acula* should not be a stream here as in 1.28 (applied to the Ilissus). The antithesis is between a small remote stream and, not the *flumen*, but the *fons unde ... flumen erumpat* – the source of all knowledge; thus this allusion offers no conflict with 2.117 (tardi ingenii est *rivulos* consectari, *fontis* rerum non videre; et iam aetatis est usque nostri *a capite* quod velimus arcessere et *unde omnia manent* videre) or typical Hellenistic literary symbolism, as in Prop. 2.10.25-6, where *Ascraei fontes* are superior to *Permessi flumen*.

But how is the transition made from the source of knowledge to the next metaphor? There is no masculine antecedent to supply the subject of *qui ... commonstret*, nor can we derive an antecedent from the previous phrase logically reconcilable with showing the seat of all the orator's *argumenta* as a man would show another the way.[13]

Instead the imagery itself ensures that the reader will follow the argument. Both *illuc* and *unde* must refer to Aristotle, who was praised in 160 as the possessor and source of universal knowledge – the *universum flumen* of 162. Similarly the image of showing the way recalls the first reference to Aristotle by Catulus in 152: sed Aristoteles posuit ... quosdam locos ex quibus omnis argumenti *via* ... *inveniretur*, a quo quidem homine ... *non aberrat* oratio tua, sive tu similitudine illius divini ingeni *eadem incurris vestigia*, and its resumption by Antonius in 160: a cuius inventis tibi ego videor non longe aberrare. *Inventio*, which Cicero traces back to Aristotle, is indicated by the imagery of finding a path; the recurrence of the metaphor in 152, 160, and 162 enables the reader to follow the thread of discussion without any need for specification of the masculine pronoun *qui*.

13 Of the two elements in this image the nouns *sedes et quasi domicilia* are less significant than the verb *commonstrare*, since *domicilium* is most often metaphorical in Cicero; cf. 1.105, *domicilium imperi et gloriae*; Balb. 13, *gloriae domicilium*; Prov. Cos. 34, *numquam haec urbs summo imperio domicilium ac sedem praebuisset*. Commonstrare (*monstrare, demonstrare*) are the *voces propriae* for showing a person the way (cf. Plaut. As. 381, Cur. 404, 467; Enn. Sc. 321v, 398v; Ter. Ph. 305-6), and so the verb revives the original physical force of the nouns dimmed by the traditional metaphor.

For the combination of images, cf. 1.203, equidem vobis, quoniam ita voluistis, *fontis unde hauriretis atque itinera ipsa* ita putavi esse *demonstranda*, non ut ipse *dux essem ... sed ut commonstrem tantum viam, et*, ut fieri solet, *digitum ad fontes intenderem*. Here Crassus is speaking of the sources of the orator's general education; in book II, Antonius' dominant theme from 116 to 176 is *inventio*, and the technical sources of argument (πίστεις ἔντεχνοι) provided by Aristotle's *Topica*. These are summarized in the ten chapters introduced by our passage (163–73). But from the beginning Antonius keeps the *Topica* before the reader by a sequence of *fontes*-imagery; 117, *rivulos* contrasted with *fontes*;[14] 130, *aperiamus autem capita ea, unde omnis ... disputatio ducitur*; 142, argumentorum *fontes*, and the final allusion here in 162. At the same time, the second image, that of showing the way, serves as a marker for the opening of the ten chapters of *Topica*, matched, at their close, by a modified version of the same image in the analogy of 174:

> si aurum cui ... *commonstrare* vellem, satis esse deberet *si signa et notas ostenderem locorum*, quibus cognitis ipse sibi foderet et id quod vellet parvo labore, *nullo errore*, inveniret; sic ego *has argumentorum notavi notas*, quae quaerenti *demonstrant ubi sint*.

Here *locorum* too performs a double function, for Cicero, wishing to refer to the τόποι of Aristotle, returns to the literal meaning of their Latin equivalent (the genitive is common to abstract *loci* and physical *loca*) as the focus of his analogy. A whole network of thematic and structural relationships can be traced from the one sentence of 2.162.

A more obvious pattern of thematic imagery runs through my third example, the section from 2.188–205, illustrating the inflammatory power of *movere* from Antonius' great defence speech for Norbanus. We have already examined the two chapters (186–7) of general introduction to the theme; in these Cicero drops no hint of fire-imagery, drawing instead from racing, medicine, hunting, sailing, and military tactics. This must be a conscious artistic decision to reserve the basic fire-motif, for with the trial narrative in 188, there begins a series of allusions to inflaming the audience which is continued through

---

14 For the contrast of inferior, derivative *rivuli* and original creative *fontes*, cf. *Cael.* 19; ... ex *quo* iste *fonte* senator *emanet*. nam si ipse *orietur* et nascetur ex sese, fortasse, ut soleo, commovebor; sin autem est *rivolus arcessitus et ductus ab ipso capite* ... and *Acad. Post.* 8 (Varro is speaking) meos amicos ... ad Graecos ire iubeo, ut *ex fontibus potius hauriant quam rivolos consectentur*.

seventeen paragraphs; cf. 188, ut mihi non solum tu *incendere* iudicem sed ipse *ardere* videaris; 190, nisi te ipsum *flagrantem* odio ante viderit ... ut enim nulla *materies* tam facilis ad *exardescendum* est quae nisi *admoto igni ignem concipere possit*, sic nulla mens est tam ad comprehendendam vim oratoris parata, quae possit *incendi*, nisi ipse *inflammatus* ad eam et *ardens* accesserit; 193, ut ex persona mihi *ardere* oculos hominis histrionis viderentur; 194 poetam bonum neminem ... sine *inflammatione* animorum exsistere posse et sine *quodam adflatu* quasi furoris (the wind to fan the flames); 197, qui in accusando sodali meo tantum *incendium* non oratione solum sed etiam ... vi et dolore et *ardore* animi concitaras, ut ego *ad id restinguendum vix conarer accedere*. This is recalled by Sulpicius in 202, tibi ego non iudicium sed *incendium* tradidissem and leads to a new variation in 205, nam neque parvis in rebus *adhibendae sunt hae dicendi faces* ... Even after the main sequence, there is a late echo; 209, quae si *inflammanda* sunt.

At the same time the dominant motif is diversified by other figurative language: 199, dolorem ... *refricabam* (rubbing a sore or wound); 203, quam tibi ... *munisti* ad te audiendum *viam, serpere* occulte coepisti; 205, ad eorum mentes oratione *flectendas* ... si aut *tragoedias agamus* in nugis aut *convellere* adoriamur ea quae non possint commoveri. Within the fire imagery itself there is great variety. Cicero plays on a range of five "fire"-verbs and four nouns[15] and three related metaphors – the mind as *materies* (fuel or timber), *furor* as a fanning wind, and the more common *restinguere* of calming inflamed emotions. Such imagery can be found in Greek prose, but it is far more at home in Latin; see *Imagery in Terence* p. 11.

The fourth and last example illustrates Cicero's use of imagery as an element of structure in the social framework of book 2 – imagery as part of the *sermo*

15 These often occur in combination elsewhere in *de Oratore*. I list usages of single words also: 1.15, *flagrare*; 60, *inflammare* and *exstinguere*; 97, *incendere*; 134, *flagrare* and *ardor*; 219, *inflammare* and *restinguere*. There is a run of such words in the description of civil chaos in 3.4–11; 4, *faces* and *exardescere*; 8, *flagrare* and *ardere*; and 11, *flamma*.

From *Orator* compare 26–7 on the *vis* of Demosthenes: "post sensim *incendens* iudices, ut vidit *ardentis*, in reliquis exsultavit audacius ... facile est enim verbum aliquod *ardens*, ut ita dicam, notare, idque *restinctis* iam animorum *incendiis* inridere"; and 132, on Cicero's own emotional response: "nulla me ingeni sed magna vis animi *inflammat*, ut me ipse non teneam; nec unquam is qui audiret *incenderetur* nisi *ardens* ad eum perveniret oratio." The examples of Van Hook, *op. cit.*, p. 14 suggest that the application of fire imagery to style is very rare in Greek rhetoric, while Demetrius in his section on δεινότης praises Demosthenes with the imagery of close combat, 274, ἐγγύθεν πλήττουσιν ἔοικεν (with which compare p. 156 below). Longinus comments on τὸ διάπυρον (12.3).

facetus of this aristocratic houseparty. This involves two related sections, 2.233–4 and 2.290.

In introducing the wit Caesar Strabo to discuss the nature of humour and its place in oratory, Cicero permits himself an exchange of metaphorical fantasy, which is resumed as neatly at the end of his excursus. Strabo begins with an urbane allusion to the Greek-style subscription dinner *quoniam conlectam a conviva ... exigis ...* He then modestly deprecates himself by an adaptation of the proverb "sus Minervam docet" *docebo sus, ut aiunt, oratorem eum quem cum Catulus nuper audisset, fenum alios aiebat esse oportere,* which is take up by Crassus, with a deft compliment to Catulus, *cum ita dicat ipse, ut ambrosia alendus esse videatur.* Antonius, in turn, coins the motif of the *deversorium,* the rich man's travelling lodge, to describe Strabo's excursus:

> defessus iam labore atque itinere disputationis meae requiescam in Caesaris sermone quasi in aliquo peropportuno deversorio. "Atqui," inquit Iulius, "non nimis liberale hospitium meum dices, nam te in viam simulac perpaulum gustaris, extrudam et eiciam."

Antonius then is to content himself with a light meal; *gustare,* appropriate to the metaphorical context, coincides happily with the frequent use of the verb for drawing intellectual nourishment. When Strabo ends his discourse, the motif is resumed: (290)

> sed iam tu, Antoni, qui hoc deversorio sermonis mei libenter acquieturum te esse dixisti, tamquam in Pomptinum deverteris, neque amoenum neque salubrem locum, censeo ut satis diu te putes requiesse et iter reliquum conficere pergas. ego vero, atque hilare quidem a te acceptus.

Thus the dialogue is again set in motion, and the image of the *deversorium* given a new and tactful twist by a Roman allusion; Antonius is to set out again after a brief pause, as if the lodge were in a malarial region; Strabo again combines implied modesty with courtesy in his reason for suggesting that his guest should now depart. But the Roman dress conceals a Greek motif. From Plato *Politicus* 267a onwards, a digression within a work could be called ἐκτροπή,[16] Latin *deverticulum* (cf. Livy 9.17.2; Quint. 10.1.29, depulsa recta via necessario ad eloquendi quaedam deverticula confugiat); literally this was a side turning from the road (Ter. *Eu.* 635), or an inn. *Deversorium* does not have this metaphorical application, but from a fragment of Varro's *Menippea* 418 Buecheler (quoted by Nonius as from περίπλους, book II περὶ φιλοσοφίας),

16 Compare Van Hook, *op. cit.,* p. 34.

et ne erraremus, *ectropas* esse multas, omnino *tutum esse sed spissum iter*, and from the metaphor in Demetr. *de Elocutione* 47, καθάπερ γὰρ τὰς μακρὰς ὁδοὺς αἱ συνεχεῖς καταγωγαὶ μικρὰς ποιοῦσιν, αἱ δ' ἐρημίαι καὶ ταῖς μικραῖς ὁδοῖς ἔμφασίν τινα ἔχουσι μήκους, ταὐτὸ δὴ κατὰ τῶν κώλων ἂν γίγνοιτο, we can be confident that Cicero was familiar with the rhetorical application of ἐκτροπή and its metaphorical potential. This does not detract from the freshness of his own adaptation in which the *deversorium* image coincides with the courtesy that his noble conversationalists would naturally show each other in providing overnight accommodation on their way from one villa to another. He has revitalized a technical term to provide a fine example of the *urbanitas* which is the theme of the digression itself. These four passages contain some of the most striking and elegant imagery of *de Oratore*, and it is remarkable that in each case there is good reason to assume that it is predominantly original to Cicero.

As in the earlier analysis of metaphor in Terence (chap. 1) it is useful to examine figurative language in *de Oratore* in terms of the categories and activities from which the imagery is drawn, but the following discussion should be regarded as selective. I have aimed at examining categories which have some systematic role in the dialogue, omitting others whose appearance is casual and unsystematic. Even within the selected categories (warfare and single combat, navigation, architecture, weaving, the theatre, springs and sources, land and boundaries), I have omitted minor figurative uses. For convenience and continuity the rather disparate Greek parallels have been relegated to the footnotes, and material from Cicero's later rhetorical works which goes beyond, or diverges from the practice of *de Oratore*, will also be found in the footnotes rather than in the text, in order not to distract the reader from the language of *de Oratore* itself.

Although Cicero's philosophical education had led him to claim eloquence as an art, his practical career as orator and statesman made him well aware of its role in the battlefield of public life; imagery of combat repeatedly presents this aspect of oratory. The emphasis in Crassus' opening eulogy is primarily on oratory as a defensive weapon, but the need for (justified!) aggression is recognized:

> quid autem tam necessarium quam *tenere semper arma quibus vel tectus ipse esse possis vel provocare integer vel te ulcisci lacessitus* (1.32)?

This image and the contrast of defence and offence occupy a dominant position in the prooemium of *de Inventione* (1.1, *qui vero ita sese armat eloquentia ut non oppugnare commoda patriae sed pro his propugnare possit*), and are likely to have been part of the traditional apologia of the rhetorician. But in *de Oratore* the figurative language of warfare and single combat is particularly associated with the person of Antonius who dominates book II. His skill as a rhetorical tactician is similarly emphasized in the characterization of *Brutus* 139:

> omnia veniebant Antonio in mentem; eaque suo quaeque loco, ubi plurimum proficere et valere possent, *ut ab imperatore equites, pedites, levis armatura*, sic ab illo in maxime opportunis orationis partibus conlocabantur ... imparatus semper *aggredi* ad dicendum videbatur, sed ita erat paratus ut iudices illo dicente non umquam viderentur satis parati ad cavendum fuisse.

The first application in *de Oratore* is 1.172. Crassus courteously declares that Antonius' eloquence is so great that *videtur etiam si hac scientia iuris nudata sit, posse se facile ceteris armis prudentiae tueri atque defendere*. But such allusions are concentrated in the final section of book 2, in which Antonius deals with *tractatio*, itself a noun commonly associated with *armorum* (cf. *de Orat*. 3.200, 206). From 292, *a malo autem vitioque causae ita recedam non ut me id fugere appareat*, he proceeds to aggression; 293, *omnia in illum tela conferam*. The metaphor of tactical flight is developed by further details in 294–5:

> *confiteor me ... ita cedere solere ut non modo non abiecto sed ne reiecto quidem scuto fugere videat, sed adhibere quandam in dicendo speciem atque pompae et pugnae similem fugam, consistere vero in meo praesidio sic ut non fugiendi hostis sed capiendi loci causa cessisse videar.*

The motif is not allowed to lapse: Catulus in 296 compliments Antonius as *unum in dicendo tectissimum*. When he resumes the exposition in 303 he first recalls his feigned flight, then contrasts others' rash aggression – *versanturque in hostium castris ac sua praesidia dimittunt*.

It is Antonius who in 316 compares the stylish use of spears and decorative preliminary skirmishes of gladiatorial combat in his comment on Philippus' dictum "cum bracchium concalefecerit, tum se solere pugnare;"[17] but Crassus too takes his imagery from the arena in presenting the σχήματα λέξεως:

---

17 From Van Hook, *op. cit.*, p. 24, it appears that this derives from Aristotle's προεξαγκωνίζειν, *Rhet*. 3.14.12, comparing the use of a proemium before the speech proper to boxers raising their arms before fighting. As Philippus was *in primis ... Graecis doctrinis institutus* (*Brut*. 173), his famous saying could be Romanization of a Greek source.

3.200: hic nobis orator its conformandus est ... ut ei qui *in armorum tractatione* versantur, ut quemadmodum qui utuntur armis aut palaestra, non solum sibi vitandi aut feriendi rationem esse habendam putent, sed etiam ut cum venustate moveantur.

He repeats this in a modified form to mark the end of the catalogue of tropes and figures at 206:

orationis autem ipsius *tamquam armorum* est vel ad usum comminatio et quasi petitio vel ad venustatem ipsam *tractatio*.

These standards combine the requirement of beauty for the art, and efficacy for the combat.[18] The concern for beauty and the reference to the *palaestra* in 200 betray the underlying Greek theory; armed combat is the analogy suggested by Roman taste and the visible gestures accompanying oratory. This is the implication of *Rhet. Her.* 4.27, comparing the rhythmic effect of different *articuli* (*commata*):

itaque in illo genere ex remotione bracchi et contortione dexterae gladius ad corpus adferri, in hoc autem crebro et celeri corpus vulnere consauciari videtur.

Thus in Latin as in Greek, *actio* is one link suggesting imagery transferred from physical to intellectual combat.

More casual, shorter allusions to armed attack appear in 1.40, quem tu adulescentum *perculisti*; 242, a quo, *cum hastas amentatas acceperit, ipse eas oratoris lacertis viribusque torquebit*; or 2.72, *ubi adest armatus adversarius qui sit et feriendus et repellendus*. Because of the traditional association of, e.g., *emittere* and *iactare* with utterance, it is the long-distance weapon which typifies speech: *telum* is used figuratively at 1.202; 2.293; 3.220. It is implied in the description of the orator's *argumentum*; 2.214, idque simul *atque emissum est adhaerescit*; cf. 219, ante illud facete dictum *emissum haerere debeat*[19] ... Arma

18 The same analogy is applied in *Orator* 228: "ut enim athletas *nec multo secus gladiatores* videmus nihil nec vitando facere caute nec petendo vehementer in quo non motus hic habeat palaestram quandem, ut quicquid in his rebus *fiat utiliter ad pugnam* idem *ad aspectum etiam sit venustum*, sic orator nec plagam gravem facit, nisi petitio fuit apta, nec satis tecte declinat impetum, nisi etiam in cedendo *quid deceat* intelligit." Here too the Greek illusion to the σχήματα of the *palaestra* is Romanized by a secondary reference to gladiatorial combat. On, σχήματα, see below p. 164 and n. 26.

19 The metaphorical use of *aculeus* for "stinging" abuse is an alternative to *telum* at 2.64, sine sententiarum forensibus aculeis; 222, in quo nulli aculei contumeliarum inerant; and 3.138, ut in eorum mentes qui audissent quasi aculeos quosdam relinqueret. From *Brut.* 38 we know that this description of Pericles was a famous quotation from Eupolis, KI, 281, fr. 94, τὸ κέντρον ἐγκατέλειπε τοῖς ἀκρωμένοις; the same comparison is applied to Socrates in Plato *Phaedo* 91c, ὥσπερ μέλιττα τὸ κέντρον ἐγκαταλίπων.

has the same function in 1.32 and 172, and 3.206 above, and *hastae* in 1.242 and 2.317.

But if comparison with the gladiator was appropriate, comparison with the general was more glorious; this occurs once explicitly in *de Oratore* (2.187, above p. 144) and, as we have seen, is applied to Antonius in *Brutus* 139. If the orator is general, and the courts are real warfare, then both the preliminary *exercitatio*, and the private genre of epideictic oratory can be represented as mere practice or demonstration combat. In these analogies the battlefield and the arena alternate or are combined. For this view of *exercitatio*, cf. the Greek title Προγυμνάσματα for rhetorical manuals such as those of Theon and of Hermogenes. In *de Oratore*, cf. 1.147, 157 (especially the phrase *aciem forensem*), and 2.84, *aliud enim pugna atque acies, aliud ludus campusque noster desiderat, ac tamen ars ipsa ludicra armorum et gladiatori et militi prodest aliquid*. Similar is Cicero's qualification to his praise of Isocrates in *Orator* 41, *pompae quam pugnae aptius, gymnasiis et palaestrae* dicatum, *spretum et pulsum foro*, or *de Opt. Gen.* 17, non enim *in acie* versatur *nec ferro*, sed quasi *rudibus* eius *eludit* oratio, followed by a gladiatorial image.

Imagery from navigation and the sea is less important to the main theme of the orator's training.[20] The ship of state is the source of the routine figurative use of *gubernare, gubernaculum* etc. in 1.8; 39; 46; and 3.131. There is a more sophisticated image in 1.3, hoc tempus omne ... obiecimus *eis fluctibus* qui per nos a communi peste *depulsi in nosmet ipsos redundarent* (the statesman attempts to block the passage of the waves or flood and, in saving the state, suffers the onslaught himself); 1.153 above and 186, refer to rowing and trimming the sails. More interesting is 1.174: Scaevola claims that the speaker ignorant of legal technicalities should not attempt the major task of a defensive speech:

> illa vero deridenda arrogantia est, *in minoribus navigiis rudem esse se profiteri, quinquiremis autem aut etiam maiores gubernare didicisse* ... citius hercle is qui *duorum scalmorum naviculam in portu everterit in Euxino ponto Argonautarum navem gubernarit.*

The first form of the comparison is based on the scale of the vessel, the second

---

20 Compare Van Hook *op. cit.*, p. 26, "critical terms of nautical origin are few." He adduces only χειμάζεσθαι "to be in stylistic difficulties" and ἐποκέλλειν (Longinus 3.4) "to run aground." With the latter, compare the use of *ad scopulum appellere*, *de Orat.* 2.154, "valde timide *tamquam ad aliquem libidinis scopulum* sic tuam mentem ad philosophiam *appulisti*"; Caesar, *ap. Gell.* 1.10.4, "*tamquam scopulum* sic fugias inauditum atque insolens verbum;" and chap. 2, p. 42 on the figurative use of *appellere* and *applicare* in Terence. None of these uses are examples of rhetorical criticism.

version on the difficulty of the voyage. The analogy is taken up, and rightly rejected by Antonius in his reply (1.237); the relationship between steering a small and a large vessel is not the same as that between knowledge of civil law, and the ability to present a case depending on that law. Other marine imagery is that based on *portus*, conventional in 1.255; more startling in 3.7, where the metaphor changes in mid-course from that of the racing chariot to the shipwreck, under the influence of (*navem*) *frangere* ... inanis nostras contentiones *quae medio in spatio saepe franguntur et corruunt, aut ante in ipso cursu obruuntur quam portum conspicere potuerunt.*

Finally at 3.145 Cotta reproaches Crassus, repente te quasi quidam *aestus* ingeni tui *procul a terra abripuit atque in altum e conspectu paene omnium abstraxit*; he has been carried beyond their comprehension by the swift current of this thought; here we have an alternative expression for the racing-metaphor used with the same function in 1.161, discussed above (p. 144).

For the construction of a speech or argument, architecture and weaving supply metaphors; cf. 1.164, ne graveris *aedificare* id opus quod instituisti; 2.63–4 haec scilicet *fundamenta*[21] nota sunt omnibus, ipsa autem *exaedificatio*, posita est in rebus et verbis, and 3.151–2; verum tamen hoc quasi *solum* quoddam atque *fundamentum* est, verborum usus et copia bonorum. sed quid ipse *aedificet* orator ... id esse nobis quaerendum videtur. From weaving, cf. 2.145 (parallel in function to 1.164), *pertexe modo, inquit, Antoni, quod exorsus es*; 158, *ante exorsa et potius detexta prope retexantur*; add 3.226 (of political conspiracy), quamquam ea tela *texitur* et ea in civitati ratio vivendi posteritati ostenditur.[22] From the casual use of *exordiri* and *ordiri* in 1.30 and 98,

---

21 *Fundamenta* is particularly common; cf. chap. 5, p. 117 above, and compare with de Orat. 3.151, Brut. 258, solum quidem ... et quasi fundamentum oratoris ... locutionem emendatam et Latinam, Cicero's restatement of the same principle, that diction is the foundation of eloquence.

Dionysius, de comp. 6, uses the architect or mason as his basic analogy for the writer, distinguishing three functions common to them both: that of selecting materials, arranging them in combination, and trimming the individual units. He is concerned above all with position of words in the sentence, for which the architectural term ἕδρα provides an analogy; later, in discussing his three styles, he compares words to columns set apart, visible on all side and set on broad firm bases (22 and 23). Both his selection and application of architectural imagery differ from that of Cicero.

22 Add to these 2.68, in causa intexere (cf. Orator 65, fabulas intexere) of the speaker weaving loci communes into his speech like ornamental thread into the background of plainer cloth. Cicero uses intexere (Att. 13.12.3 and 22.1) and probably detexere (Att. 13.23.2, see app. crit.) casually in the letters to describe literary composition. Weaving is Dionysius' basic image in de Compositione for the arrangement of individual words; cf. πλέκειν (3, 19), συμπλέκειν (15, 18), συμπλοκή (16, 19), ἐγκαταπλέκειν τε

it is clear that 2.145 and 158 are reviving a dead metaphor; other dead meta-phors from weaving are the use of *subtilis* (cf. λεπτός) to describe the plain style 1.17 (with Wilkins' note *ad loc.*) and the description of the orators Critias, Theramenes and Lysias, 2.94, *retinebant illum Pericli sucum, sed erant paulo uberiore filo*. *Filum* appears only here in *de Oratore*, and its clumsy com-bination with the physiological metaphor *sucus* suggests that it was inherited not felt. (See, however, n. 35 below on *Orator* 124.)

Like Aristotle (cf. *Rhetorica* 3, ch. 1), Cicero was acutely aware of the importance of delivery; unlike Aristotle, Cicero noted with sympathy what the orator could learn from the actor or entertainer. The Roman orator was both creator and interpreter. Hence comparisons with actors in 1.118–130, or 3.83, are more than analogies. In 2.338, *quia maxima quasi oratoris scaena videtur contio esse ... quemadmodum tibicen sine tibiis canere, sic orator nisi multitudine audiente eloquens esse non possit*, we have the nucleus of a major critical digression in *Brutus* 184–200. For the audience as the orator's instru-ment, compare *Brut.* 192 (*tibiae*) and 200 (*fides*). The word *tragoediae* is applied to melodramatic rhetoric in 2.205, 219 and 228. Another obvious instance of this minor category is the use of *palma*, when Catulus awards Crassus the prize for wit (2.227) and by Crassus himself in the triumphant summing up of 3.143, *docto oratori palma danda est*. But the most ambiguous usage is that of *primae* with ellipse of the noun, which occurs twice in *de Oratore*. At 2.147 speaking of the three essential qualities, *ingenium, ars, diligentia*, Antonius declares *non possum ... non ingenio primas concedere*. Similarly 3.213 tells the anecdote (repeated in *Orator* 56) in praise of *actio* in oratory: *huic primas dedisse Demos-thenes fertur, ... huic secundas, huic tertias*. I believe we have here an ellipse of *partes* as in Ter. *Hau.* 402 (cf. chap. 1, p. 33; *partes* is used metaphorically with *priores* in *Eu.* 151; *durae, Eu.* 354). Of the *three* roles of protagonist, deutera-gonist, and tritagonist, Antonius gives the first to natural talent, and Demo-thenes credits *actio* with playing them all; we may compare a more natural personal application, *Brut.* 317, *cum Cotta princeps adhibitus esset, priores tamen agere partes Hortensium* (as in *Eu.* 151). In *Brut.* 84, however, *denique etsi*

καὶ συνυφαίνειν (12), and συνυφαίνειν alone (16, 17, 23). ὑφαίνειν is not found. In 23 he compares samples of the rich style to εὐητρίοις ὕφεσι (cf. *tela*), but he does not appear to offer parallels for the use of *filum*. This is the more remarkable in view of the frequency of the adjective λεπτός, related to fine texture, in Greek criticism. Cicero's use of these weaving metaphors, as of architectural imagery (n. 21 above) is general, relating to the work as a whole, and not to detailed composition.

For *tela, exordiri*, and *detexere* in Plautus' vocabulary of intrigue and invention, see chap. 4, p. 106.

utrique primas, priores tamen libenter deferunt Laelio, as in *Att.* 1.17.5, Douglas sees an allusion to the first prize (πρωτεῖα), and Cicero's use of the verb *deferre*[23] favours this interpretation. However, we do not know what feminine noun is assumed by the ellipse (*palma* is normally singular) and in none of the later passages (*Brut.* 84, 183, 308, *Orat.* 18, etc.) is the sense of leading role impossible. It seems clear that the theatrical role could be applied figuratively both to men who were *principes* and to abstract qualities. But the very relevance of theatrical values to the discussion of oratory explains why *de Oratore* contains many allusions, but few images derived from that sphere.

I have had occasion already to refer to one category of imagery drawn from nature: metaphors deriving from springs and streams. This characteristic image for the orator's sources was already a cliché in its basic form, as is shown by the elaborate analogy of *Rhet. Her.* 4.9:

> si qui se fontes maximos penitus absconditos aperuisse dicat et hoc sitiens quam maxime loquatur, neque habeat qui sitim sedet, non rideatur? Ipsi cum non modo dominos se fontium sed se ipsos fontes esse dicant et nimirum rigare debeant ingenia, non putant fore ridiculum si arescant ipsi siccitate?

The seclusion of the springs (found also in the Callimachean apparatus) features in *de Orat.* 1.12, *studia fere reconditis atque abditis e fontibus hauriuntur*, and is implied by 1.87, *haec enim esse penitus media philosophia retrusa atque abdita quae isti rhetores ne primoribus quidem labris attigissent*. The opening up of the springs is exploited in 2.130, *aperiamus autem capita ea ... unde omnis ... disputatio ducitur*. Besides the routine references to *fontes* (1.42, 94, 193, 203; 2.45, 330; 3.123) Cicero makes the distinction between the true *fons* and the inferior *rivus/rivulus*: 2.117, *tardi ingeni est rivulos consectari, fontes rerum non videre*; and 3.23, *rivis est diducta ratio, non fontibus*. We saw above (p. 151) that 2.162, *illuc ... ubi non seclusa acula teneatur sed unde universum flumen erumpat*, is consistent with the usual relative values of *fons* and *rivus*.

Many verbs are associated with the *fons*-imagery: of the knowledge itself, *manare*, to seep down, 2.117, 3.62, and 68; cf. *de Inv.* 2.7. Of the seeker after knowledge, *haurire* is the most common; 1.12, 193, 203; 3.123. *Libare* and *gustare* are perhaps less directly dependent, but maintain the concept of

23 For *palmam dare* in Comedy, see p. 34. Volcacius Sedigitus (*ap.Gell.* 15.24) uses *palmam deferre*, with the verb of *Brut.* 84, *Att.* 1.17.5, which supports the identification of *primae* with πρωτεῖα equivalent to *palma*, in these passages. The absence of *palma* from Cicero's later rhetorical works also argues in favour of taking *primae* as a translation of πρωτεῖα.

drinking in knowledge. For *libare*, compare *de Inv.* 2.2.4, *ex variis ingeniis excellentissima quaeque libavimus*; *de Orat.* 1.159, *libandus est etiam ex omni genere urbanitatis facetiarum quidam lepos quo tamquam sale perspergatur omnis oratio*; 1.218, *neque ea ut sua possedisse sed ut aliena libasse*. The emphasis with this verb is on fastidious selection. *Gustare*, too, implies a more restrained approach; cf. 1.145, 223; 2.153; in these passages the original force of *gustare* may be little felt, since it is combined with no other liquid associations, but 2.75, *paulum sitiens istarum artium ... gustavi*, is more vivid.

Finally the student orator must be dipped in culture, 2.85, *sit enim mihi tinctus litteris*, and in experience, 2.162, *aliquo iam imbutus usu* – but here as in the use of *imbuere* in 2.289, it is more likely that the imagery of the dyer's craft is intended.[24]

Cicero's use of *flumen* (*orationis/verborum*) and *fluere*, belong to another topic, the theme of style and rhythm in speech, and will be considered separately.

Just as the topic of sources led to water imagery, so the topic of subject matter is associated by Cicero with the language of landed property. This first appears with Scaevola's introduction of the *possessio* and trespass (*in alienas possessiones ... inruere*, 1.41) motif. Subsequently, Cicero operates with simpler figurative terms, none of which, however, seem to be represented in the traditional imagery of Greek rhetoric and criticism.

The subject matter of the orator is seen as a territory or region which others wish to limit; *circumscribere, terminus, finis, saepire, regio,* repeatedly appear in discussion of the scope of oratory. But there is a conflict between Crassus who comprehends all arts within the sphere of oratory, and Antonius who takes a narrower interpretation, and this conflict is reflected in their use of this metaphor. Crassus rejects *forensibus cancellis circumscriptam scientiam* (1.52) and prefers 1.70, *nullis ut terminis circumscribat aut definiat ius suum quo minus ei liceat eadem illa facultate et copia vagari quo velit* (here *vagari* is recommended, in contrast with 209, *ne vagari et errare cogatur oratio*). Crassus himself is depicted as *oratoris facultatem non illius artis terminis sed ingeni sui finibus immensis paene describere*, 214, just as he reproaches Antonius; 264, *quoniam exiguis quibusdam finibus totum oratoris munus circumdedisti*.

The concept of a limited *regio* is introduced and rejected by Cicero in person, 2.5, *bene dicere ... non habet definitam aliquam regionem cuius terminis*

---

24 The metaphor of dyeing is more explicit in *Fin.* 3.9 "iam *infici* debet iis artibus quas si dum est tener *combiberit*, ad maiora veniet paratior"; the young man is like cloth which when dipped, drinks in the dye of education.

saepta teneatur, but reasserted by Antonius, 2.68, *sed ita ut sit circumscripta modicis regionibus*; later in the same book it is adapted for the more specific question of *inventio*. In composition the orator's task is to *nosse regiones intra quas venere et pervestiges quod quaeras; ubi eum locum omnem cogitatione saepseris, nihil te effugiet atque omne ... occurret atque incidet* (2.147). Here the figurative use of *regiones* is related to a new sphere – that of hunting; the game is to be cordonned off (*saepire*) and then it will fall into the hunter's hands. In 3.24, the application of *regio* receives another twist, *una est enim ... eloquentia, quascunque in oras disputationis regionesque delata est*; eloquence is like a ship, or passenger, unchanged no matter what topic is its landfall. But 3.70 sees a new variant of the imagery: Crassus reasserts his claim for a wider scope with the symbol *campus*; the orator is like a horseman, whom Antonius confines to a small circuit, *ex ingenti quodam* oratorem *immensoque campo in exiguum* (cf. 1.264) *sane gyrum compellitis*. The word *gyrus* is found in Propertius 3.3.21, recommending the small scope of the elegiac poet's material, and is probably a Hellenistic legacy from Callimachus; it is one of the few Greek words in *de Oratore*.[25] Again in 3.124, after his final assertion of the orator's right of *possessio* (122–3), Crassus invokes the *immensus campus; in hoc igitur tanto tam immensoque campo cum liceat oratori vagari libere atque ubicunque constiterit consistere in suo ...* But Cicero has not exhausted the variety of his expression. Catulus thanks and praises Crassus, two sections later, in these terms, (126) *quantisque ex angustiis oratorem educere ausus es et in maiorum suorum regnum collocare*. Crassus is the general who has successfully led his troops from a dangerous defile, and, by a change of image, restored them to the possession of their ancestral land. Is it design that *regnum*, the most authoritative and absolute word for possession, rounds off the last allusion to this theme of subject matter, as, in a different application, it introduced the first challenge to the orator's claim, in 1.41?

Before discussing Cicero's application of figurative language to rhetorical style and relating his vocabulary to that of Greek rhetoric, I feel it is necessary to recognize the limitations imposed by the loss of most Hellenistic rhetorical theory. With the failure of Greek rhetorical works of the third and second centuries B.C. to survive, it has become customary to deduce the Greek vocabulary of style from the extant treatises of Dionysius of Halicarnassus,

---

25 Compare the quotation attributed to Panaetius in *Off.* 1.90, sic homines secundis rebus ecfrenatos sibique praefidentes tamquam in *gyrum* rationis et doctrinae duci oportere. For Panaetius as for Propertius *gyrus* symbolizes a desirable limitation or control.

writing a generation after Cicero, and Demetrius *de elocutione* whose date
is still disputed. Yet Cicero himself approached rhetoric from a wider and
more philosophical standpoint, and constantly acknowledges his debts to
Plato (especially the *Phaedrus*, as the Platonic work most constructive in its
attitude to rhetoric), to Aristotle, and to Isocrates; whether for literary or
theoretical reasons, he seems to have preferred the Hellenic to the Hellenistic
sources. Thus rather than hypothesize Hellenistic precedents from what
survives in Dionysius and Demetrius, I would prefer to look for coincidence
of language with his acknowledged classical Greek models.

Greek rhetorical theory evolved comparatively late (compare *Brut.* 26,
and 39) in a civilization already enjoying well-developed plastic arts, sculpture,
and painting, and fully developed drama, with its accompaniment of dancing
and choral movement. Thus, behind the dominant rhetorical vocabulary
based on analogies with the human body, lies the Greek admiration for that
body, whether static in the visual arts, or mobile in dance, and of course in
athletics. The use of $\sigma\chi\acute{\eta}\mu\alpha\tau\alpha$[26] for conventional rhetorical figures of ornament,
the characterization of style by epithets like $\iota\sigma\chi\nu\acute{o}s$ and $\acute{\alpha}\delta\rho os$ should be seen
within this context of aesthetic values drawn from athletics, drama, and fine
art. Besides the parallel treatment of the evolution of the plastic and verbal
arts in *Brutus* 70–1 (expanded by Quintilian 12.10.1–9), we have seen this
tendency to represent rhetoric in terms of the visual arts in the analogies of
de Oratore. When 1.73 compares the style of the trained orator to that of the
ball-player with athletic training, and the sculptor trained in draftsmanship,
we can see how the common element of the two paralleled activities is the
human body. Rhetorical arguments are illustrated from the visual arts in
2.69–73, and again in 3.26.

26 The most significant illustration of this analogy drawn between rhetorical figures and
physical $\sigma\chi\acute{\eta}\mu\alpha\tau\alpha$ occurs at Isocrates *Antidosis* 183; the $\sigma\chi\acute{\eta}\mu\alpha\tau\alpha$ of the $\pi\alpha\iota\delta o\tau\rho\acute{\iota}\beta\eta s$
are like the $\iota\delta\acute{\epsilon}\alpha\iota$ of the rhetorician. This analogy was fundamental to his teaching
method (see R. Johnston, *A.J.P.* 80, 1959, 26 f.) but since Isocrates uses $\iota\delta\acute{\epsilon}\alpha\iota$ for the
figures, it is likely that the technical usage of $\sigma\chi\acute{\eta}\mu\alpha\tau\alpha$ came later, perhaps with
Theophrastus, as suggested by Caplan, *op. cit.*, p. 191, note b, following Stroux. The
word relates to posture and gesture, not only in athletics but also in dancing (Plato
Leg. 669d, cf. Hdt. 6.129, $\sigma\chi\eta\mu\acute{\alpha}\tau\iota\alpha$) and the performance of actors (cf. the verb
$\sigma\chi\eta\mu\alpha\tau\acute{\iota}\zeta\epsilon\iota\nu$, Xen. *Symp.* 1; Arist. *Poetics* 1), and rhapsodes (Plato, *Ion* 536c,
$\epsilon\grave{\iota}s \ \grave{\epsilon}\kappa\epsilon\hat{\iota}\nu o \ \tau\grave{o} \ \mu\acute{\epsilon}\lambda os \ \kappa\alpha\grave{\iota} \ \sigma\chi\eta\mu\acute{\alpha}\tau\omega\nu \ \kappa\alpha\grave{\iota} \ \rho\eta\mu\acute{\alpha}\tau\omega\nu \ \epsilon\grave{\upsilon}\pi o\rho o\hat{\upsilon}\sigma\iota\nu$). Athenaeus,
14.629b, traces the traditional $\sigma\chi\acute{\eta}\mu\alpha\tau\alpha$ from individual to choral dancing and thence
to the wrestling schools, but further connects these disciplines with sculpture, claiming
that archaic statuary was treated as evidence for the gestures of the earliest dancing.
Cicero too, at *Orator* 83, explains the Greek term as *quasi aliquos gestus orationis.*
Quintilian 10.1.4, presents the analogy of *Antidosis* 183 as a metaphor, representing
$\sigma\chi\acute{\eta}\mu\alpha\tau\alpha$ by *numeri.*

But in the analogy between the speech and the human body which underlies so many of the figurative epithets to be discussed, the Roman prejudice
against nudity intervenes. Cicero (*Tusc*. 4.70, cf. *de Rep*. 4.4) saw the nudity
of the gymnasia as a cause of homosexuality, quoting with approval Ennius'
flagiti principium est nudare inter cives corpora (*Sc*. 395v). He shows similar
prudery in recommending the gentleman's physical appearance in *de Officiis*;
first urging concealment of the naked body as grounded in nature (1.126–7)
he passes to general comments on physical *decorum* and deportment (130):

> cum autem pulchritudinis genera duo sunt, quorum in altero venustas
> sit, in altero dignitas, venustatem muliebrem ducere debemus, dignitatem
> virilem. ergo *et a forma removeatur omnis viro non dignus ornatus et huic
> simile vitium in gestu motuque caveatur*. Nam *et palaestrici motus sunt saepe
> odiosiores et histrionum non nulli gestus ineptiis non vacant*, et in utroque
> genere quae sunt recta et simplicia laudantur. *Formae autem dignitas coloris
> bonitate tuenda est, color exercitationibus corporis.*

We sense from this passage the suspicion and reserve with which in ordinary
life the Romans viewed the athletic and performing arts. Cicero himself might
have greater sophistication and tolerance, but he obviously stood to gain in
persuasiveness if he dissociated his stylistic recommendations from the too
Greek esteem for both these activities. At the same time, the sentences I have
italicized show in their literal context the values of physical decorum which
will be reflected when Cicero applies the same vocabulary figuratively to the
style and form of oratory.

The presupposition of speech as a body which relates these physical values
to those of rhetoric and gives coherence and relevance to the analogies from
sculpture and athletics, is already to be found in Plato, *Phaedr*. 264c; a speech
must be an organic whole; its parts are compared to elements of anatomy:

> δεῖν πάντα λόγον ὥσπερ ζῷον συνεστάναι σῶμά τι ἔχοντα αὐτὸν αὑτοῦ,
> ὥστε μήτε ἀκέφαλον εἶναι μήτε ἄπουν, ἀλλὰ μέσα τε ἔχειν καὶ ἄκρα,
> πρέποντα ἀλλήλοις καὶ τῷ ὅλῳ γεγραμμένα.

This anatomical imagery is taken over freely both by *Rhet. Her*. 4.58: hic
locus non est a tota causa separatus *sicuti membrum aliquod, sed tamquam sanguis
perfusus est per totum corpus orationis*, and by Antonius in Cicero's section on
dispositio; *de Orat*. 2.318, haec ... *ex ipsis visceribus* causae sumenda sunt; 2.325,
conexum autem ita sit principium consequenti orationi, ut ... *cohaerens* cum
omni corpore *membrum* esse videatur; cf. 2.358, verba quae *quasi articuli
conectunt membra* orationis. Where anatomy offers parallels for structural

analysis, physiology is even more fertile in imagery for stylistic qualities of oratory, and provides much of the figurative vocabulary applied to *elocutio* in book 3.

But Cicero's own critical values affect both his choice of imagery, and the colouring of praise or blame which he imparts to these figurative stylistic epithets.

A His interest in style as a diffused and unifying element within the speech is in contrast to the preoccupation of Hellenistic rhetoricians with occasional and detachable ornament. He opposes to the itemization of σχήματα and τρόποι a value system based on the health and physiology of speech as a whole.

B Cicero's principal word for ornament of style, *ornatus*, has a different semantic range from *ornamenta*, which he also uses, and *exornationes*, the equivalent in *Rhet. Her.* 4.18 for σχήματα. The dominant Greek terms for ornament (as a collective) are κατασκευή and κόσμος.[27] In the most general sense of a state in which something is presented, *ornatus*, κατασκευή, and κόσμος coincide. Now κατασκευή commonly means equipment, furnishings, represented in *de Oratore* 1.161–4, by *ornamenta, supellex* (cf. *Orator* 79–80), whereas κόσμος and *ornamenta* can be used in the sense of costume, wardrobe. Indeed *ornamenta* is the technical term of comedy for wardrobes and stage properties.

27 κατασκευή, properly applied to physical properties or equipment, is probably Theophrastian, but is found as rhetorical terminology in Dionysius, who uses it at, e.g., *Isocr.* 2 τοιούτων σχημάτων κόσμος πολύς ἐστι παρ' αὐτῷ καὶ λυπεῖ πόλλακις τὴν ἄλλην κατασκευήν without differentiation from κόσμος. It is certainly the inspiration for the full-scale analogy of *de Oratore* 1.161–5 which passes from the *divitiae atque ornamenta eius ingeni* (161) to the metaphor of a *domum plenam ornamentorum* (162; cf. 163, *copiam ornamentorum suorum*) and meets the final comment *in oratoris vero instrumento tam lautam supellectilem numquam videbam*. As with *deversorium* representing ἐκτροπή, pp. 154–5 above, a Greek technical term has been restored as a living metaphor, socially appropriate to the company and helping to bridge a transition by giving direction to a conversational interlude. Cicero avoids the metaphor elsewhere, either from aversion to its implication of detachable and extraneous "stage properties," or because of a positive preference for the closer association with the human body provided by κόσμος.

The association of κόσμος with rhetoric has a longer history. In Plato's *Ion* the literal κόσμος of Ion's dress (530 b6) is juxtaposed with his adornment of Homer (530 d7), ὡς εὖ κεκόσμηκα τὸν "Ομηρον. Socrates in the *Apology* (17c) rejects the orator's trick of κοσμεῖν. In Euripides' *Medea* the chorus, while praising Jason's eloquence (576, εὖ ... ἐκόσμησας λόγους), go on to reject his words as unjust. Isocrates provides the expected contrast of attitude, emulating οἱ δυνάμενοι τὰ τῶν παλαίων ἔργα κοσμεῖν (*Euag.* 5), and declaring enviously τοῖς μὲν γὰρ ποιηταῖς πόλλοι δέδονται κόσμοι (*Euag.* 9). Aristotle too associates κόσμος with poetic style (*Poetics* 22; *Rhet.* 3.2.2.) μὴ ταπεινὴν δὲ ἀλλὰ κεκοσμημένην, but deprecates its presence in prose (*Rhet.* 3.7.2). No Greek writer seems to use κόσμος as a basis for metaphor or

But *ornatus*,[28] Cicero's preferred phrase, is particularly so used, and this metaphor of clothing is developed by Cicero so that imagery of clothing and grooming assumes a more dominant role in his figurative vocabulary than in surviving Greek works. Here Roman distaste for nudity plays some part.

c Cicero's high esteem for the rich style means that language denoting the richly clothed will be associated with praise, whereas language denoting plain clothing or grooming will be associated with criticism, or at best faint praise. This set of values is applied alongside the traditional Greek opposition of the well-rounded healthy body (rich style) and the lean and spare physique of the plain stylist.

Thus stylistic preferences, social prejudices, and semantics combine to produce a new and original pattern of figurative vocabulary in Cicero's theory of *elocutio*.

A good starting point for analysis is 3.96, a passage which contains most of the essential figurative uses.

(a) ornatur igitur oratio genere primum et quasi colore quodam et suco suo; nam ut gravis, ut suavis, ut erudita sit, ut liberalis, ut admirabilis, ut polita, ut sensus ut doloris habeat quantum opus sit, non est singulorum articulorum; in toto spectantur haec corpore.

(b) Ut porro conspersa sit quasi verborum sententiarumque floribus, id non debet esse fusum aequabiliter per omnem orationem sed ita distinctum ut sint quasi in ornatu disposita quaedam insignia et lumina.

In this section Crassus distinguishes two aspects of *ornatus*. (a) The speech as a whole body must have its own general style, evenly diffused. This is the *color sanguine diffusus* of 3.199 below, and to it are related the metaphorical use of

allegory. In particular, I have looked in vain for a developed analogy of rhetorical ornament with clothing; the nearest instance is perhaps Dion. Halic. *Isocr.* 3, τοσοῦτον δὲ αὐτοῦ λείπεται κατὰ ταύτην τὴν ἀρετήν (sc. χάριν) ὅσον τῶν φύσει καλῶν σωμάτων τὰ συνερανιζόμενα κόσμοις ἐπιθέτοις. Cicero's successors, Tacitus (*Dial.* 26) and Quintilian (10.1.33) extend and specify the metaphor of style as clothing with allusions to *vestes fucatae et meretriciae*, and *versicolorem illa ... qua Demetrius Phalereus dicebatur uti vestem*. Peterson is probably right in assuming a Greek origin for the latter phrase with its allusions to ποικιλία (see also n. 32 below).

28 *Ornamenta* refers to the stage wardrobe at Plaut. *Cur.* 464, *Per.* 159, *Trin.* 858. Cicero uses it for rhetorical ornament and decorative commonplaces at *de Orat.* 1.43; *Brut.* 261; *Orator* 81 and 234. Crassus, speaking for Cicero, clearly prefers *ornatus* in his account of *elocutio*, *de Orat.* 3.23.24, 149, and 210. The singular *ornatus* is particularly appropriate to express the continued and homogeneous beauty of style which is the Ciceronian ideal, and contrast with the individual and localized *ornamenta*. Thus Ciceronian *ornatus* corresponds to *dignitas* in *Rhet. Her.* 4.18, dignitas est quae reddit ornatam orationem varietate distinguens.

physiological terms: *sucus, sanguis, color, valetudo, nervi*, etc; (b) *ornament* in the narrower sense of stylistic embellishment, should not be evenly distributed (*fusum aequabiliter*) but locally applied as highlights in selected passages.

The two functions of *conciliare* and (*per*)*movere* – the affective side of oratory, are conceived as part of the *genus, color, sucus*, for in 2.310, Antonius asserts that they *sicuti sanguis in corporibus,...* in perpetuis orationibus *fusae esse debebunt*. So too in 3.199, the *color* of a speech must derive from its *sanguis*; sed si *habitum orationis et quasi colorem aliquem requiritis*, est et plena quaedam, sed tamen teres, et tenuis, non sine nervis ac viribus, et ea quae particeps utriusque generis quaedam mediocritate laudatur. His tribus figuris insidere quidam venustatis non fuco inlitus, sed sanguine diffusus debet color.

The speech has then, as a body, a physical appearance – *figura, habitus*. Whether this be full and round, or lean and spare, or of intermediate build, it must have the complexion and beauty of health, not of cosmetics. The language anticipates the judgments in the social context of *de Officiis* 1.130, quoted above.

We must distinguish *color*, singular from the figurative use of *colores* meaning pigments. Natural *color* is contrasted with *fucus*, not only in 3.199, but by implication in 2.188 (sententiae) tam *sine pigmentis fucoque puerili*, and 3.101, in oratoris cincinnis *ac fuco* offenditur ... *infucata* vitia noscuntur. This sense of *color* underlies the analogy of 2.60, ut cum in sole ambulem ... fieri natura tamen ut *colorer*, sic cum istos libros ... studiosius legerim, sentio illorum tactu *orationem meam quasi colorari*.

Paired with *color* is *sucus*, in 3.96, physiologically more difficult to define.[29] In 2.88, *sucus* occurs within the analogy between orators and vines, and so is naturally equated with sap; on the other side of the equation is the orator, and *sucus* describes his vitality; shortly after, Pericles' rich eloquence is described as *illum Pericli sucum*. *Sucus* and *sanguis* are paired in *Brut.* 36 and *Att.* 4.18.2, but *Orator* 76, etsi enim *non plurimi sanguinis est, habeat tamen sucum aliquem oportet ut* etiam si illis maximis viribus careat, *sit*, ut ita dicam, *integra valetudine*, seems to assume a differentiation of meaning, since the plain style can have *sucus* while lacking *sanguis*. From *de Orat.* 3.199, *sanguine diffusus color*; 3.96, *colore et suco suo*; and *de opt. gen.* 8, non sunt contenti *quasi bona valetudine sed viris lacertos sanguinem quaerunt, quandam etiam suavitatem coloris*, I would deduce

---

29 On the relationship of *sucus* and *color*, compare Chaerea's ideal girl in Ter. *Eu.* 318, *color veru' corpu' solidum et suci plenum*, and Donatus' comments: 1. color verus; quia non de cura est ac de fuco ... 3. suci plenum ... *nam sucus est humor in corpore quo abundant bene valentes* ... 6. sucus est interior pinguedo membrorum (Wessner 1, p. 339).

that *sanguis* supplied *color*, while *sucus*, distinct from *sanguis*, supplied energy (*nervi*) and health (*valetudo*). Yet it is reasonable to doubt whether Cicero had formulated this refinement of terminology at the time of *de Oratore*, in which *sucus* seems no more than a synonym of *sanguis*.

In the second section (b) occur most of the images applied in *de Oratore* to the individual ornaments of the rich style. They are described in terms of lights, flowers, pigments (*colores* pl.) and decorations. The use of *lumina* for σχήματα is a metaphorical innovation in *Rhet. Her.* 4.32, si raro interseremus has exornationes, et in causa tota varie dispergemus, commode *luminibus distinctis inlustrabimus orationem*, but becomes conventional in the terminology of Cicero's later rhetorical works;[30] from *de Oratore* compare 2.120; ut *certis dicendi luminibus ornentur*, 3.201 and 206. The motive behind Cicero's adoption of the image is suggested by *de Orat.* 3.19–20, neque verba sedem habere possunt si rem subtraxeris, neque res *lumen* si verba semoveris; and 25, neque esse ullam sententiam *inlustrem sine luce verborum*. (He continues with illa ... quibus orationem ornari atque *inluminari* putem.) Yet *lumen* differs from *lumina*, as *color*, from *colores*. By *lumen* Crassus intends a general vividness and clarity (ἐνάργεια), whereas the *lumina* of 2.120 and 3.96, 201, 206 are individual figures, which by their brilliance shed light on their context. The rarer *stellae*

---

30 Compare *Orator* 67, *clarissimis* verborum *luminibus* utatur; 83, quae verborum conlocationem *inluminat eis luminibus* quae Graeci quasi aliquos gestus orationis σχήματα appellant; 85, illa sententiarum *lumina* adsumet, quae non erunt vehementer *inlustria*. This leads to the figurative use of *luminosus* in *Orator* 125, *luminosae partes orationis*. But although *lumina* may be regarded as settled terminology in *Orator*, the earlier *Brutus* bears witness to Cicero's embarrassment over the translation of σχήματα. Three times he introduces the Greek term in explanation of his own idiom: to explain *formae* in 69; *sententiarum ornamenta et conformationes* in 141 (he had coined *conformationes* in *de Orat.* 3.200 parallel with the use of *lumina*, 201, 206); and *lumina* ... quibus tanquam insignibus in ornatu distinguebatur omnis oratio in 275.

Schema, although Greek, had already enjoyed a long existence in Latin. In Naevius *Trag.* fr. 9 Marmorale, *Bacchico cum schemati*, the noun may denote merely *ornatus* (as in Plaut. *Am.* 117, *cum servili schema*; *Per.* 463, *tiara ornatum lepida condecorat schema*) or, if taken more closely with *pergite*, describe choral movement. In Caecilius, 57R and 76R, *sat hilara schema*, and in Pomponius 150R, *puls in buccam betet: sic dixin schema?* the reference seems to be more general, "deportment." Plautus' application of *euscheme* to an elegant pose or stance (*Mil.* 213; *Trin.* 625) and Lucilius 804M, *in gymnasio ut schema antiquo spectatores retineas*, are more close to the Greek *schemata* of formal posture and motion. Thus the word was well established in Latin in its physical, visual sense. Cicero need not have feared that the metaphor in its rhetorical application would be missed by a Roman reader. Rather his choice of Latin substitutes – *formae, conformationes, lumina* and its extensions – suggests that he wished to avoid the associations of *schema*, or the Latin equivalent *gestus*. Not just the word, but the entire concept, was alien to his critical approach.

occurs once in *de Oratore*: 3.170 (verbum), translatum quod maxime *tamquam stellis* quibusdam notat ac *inluminat* orationem; and in the same connection, at *Orator* 92, *inlustrant* eam *quasi stellae* translata verba. In both cases, *stella* is presented in the mitigatory form of a simile, but the verb used shows its equivalence with *lumina*.

With *insignia* in 3.96, compare 2.36, variare ac distinguere *quasi* quibusdam verborum sententiarumque *insignibus*. It is equated with *lumina* in *Brut.* 275, and *Orator* 134, quasi lumina magnum adferunt ornatum orationi; sunt enim similia illis quae in amplo ornatu scaenae aut fori appellantur *insignia*, non quia sola ornent sed quod excellant (they "stand out"). eadem ratio est horum quae sunt orationis lumina et *quodam modo insignia*. Thus *insignia*, like *stellae*, is a bolder extension of the image expressed in *lumina*.

Flores is more rare. It occurs here only in *de Oratore*. Compare *Brut.* 66, Origines eius *quem florem aut quod lumen* eloquentiae non habent, and 233, where it is again paired with *lumen*. In association with the style of the sophists at *Orator* 65, *flores* recalls the Isocratean ideal of a diction that was ἀνθηρόν (*floridum*). It may have been felt by Cicero as rather precious. This is suggested by his deprecatory use of *flosculi* (but the diminutive is naturally mocking) in *Sest.* 119, omnes undique *flosculos* carpam atque delibem.

Colores is used as a simile for rhetorical adornment in *Rhet. Her.* 4.16, distinctam *sicuti coloribus* orationem; with this, cf. *de Orat.* 2.54 (distinguere), *varietate colorum* and 3.217, hi sunt actori *ut pictori* expositi *ad variandum colores*. This is echoed in *Orator* 65, the sophists verba altius transferunt eaque ita disponunt *ut pictores varietatem colorum*. The persistent association with *variare* or *varietas* reflects the attempt to translate ποικιλία (cf. Isocr. *Phil.* 27, Dion. Halic. *de Comp.* 11), ποικίλλειν (*ibid.* 12, etc.) into Latin.[31]

31 It should be noted that Cicero does not seem to employ the later sense of *colores*, found in, e.g., Seneca the elder, for the different psychological interpretations available to the rhetorician presenting a factually given situation. In this later sense *colores* takes over some of the meanings of ἤθη or ἠθοποιία, an aspect of oratory which Cicero neglects in *de Oratore*. Thus while *color* in *de Oratore* and the later rhetorical works denotes health, or bloom, the *colores* of *de Orat.* 2.54 are undefined, and elsewhere the word is still dependent on the painter-metaphor. Only in 3.217 are *colores* related to mood or characterization, and there the specific reference is to vocal "colour" *aliud enim vocis genus iracundia sibi sumat, acutum incitatum, crebro incidens.*

Brutus 171 is an interesting case: urbanitate quadam *quasi colorata oratio* and *urbanitatis color*, like *sapore vernaculo* in 172 following, are merely metaphors using bloom and flavour as merits appealing to the senses; *urbanitas* is not seen as one of several *colores* each reflecting a different mood or approach. This is confirmed by Cicero's comment in *de Orat.* 3.161, nam et "odor urbanitatis" et "mollitudo humanitatis" ... sunt ducta a ceteris sensibus; illa vero oculorum multo acriora.

In 3.155 Crassus explains the origin of metaphor itself by analogy with clothing:

nam *ut vestis* frigoris depellendi causa reperta primo, post adhiberi coepta est ad *ornatum* etiam corporis et *dignitatem*, sic verbi translatio instituta est inopiae causa, frequentata delectationis.

I would like to return now to the theme of *ornatus* and *ornare*, and their role in relating stylistic ornament as clothing to the speech as body. *Ornare*, like κοσμεῖν in Greek, is applied to two functions of oratory: stylistic enrichment, with the speech as object, and amplification, the building up of a theme or person, with that theme as object. The former sense leads by a transference from the speech to the speaker in the words of Antonius in 2.123: He will equip the pupil in *inventio*, *dispositio*, and *memoria*, but hand him over to Crassus for training in *elocutio*: tradam eum Crasso *et vestiendum et ornandum*. In the latter sense Scaevola accuses Crassus of inexpedient *ornatio* of Jurisprudence; 1.234, cuius artem cum *indotatam* esse et *incomptam* videres, verborum eam *dote locupletasti atque ornasti* ... 235, vide ne dum *novo et alieno ornatu* velis *ornare* iuris civilis scientiam, *suo quoque eam concesso et tradito spolies atque denudes*. Within this passage *ornare* moves from generalized equipping and enriching in 234 to specific clothing in 235. It is in this sense that *ornare*, *ornatus* are most fertile in stylistic metaphor. Antonius in 2.341 speaks of the brevitas *nuda et inornata* of a formal affidavit; similarly, in a rare concession to the plain style, Cicero in *Brut*. 262 praises Caesar's *commentarii* as *nudi ... recti et venusti, omni ornatu orationis tamquam veste detracta*.[32] But in

---

32 Comment is needed on the quite exceptional phrase in *Brut*. 274, praising Calidius' diction: ita reconditas exquisitasque sententias *mollis et perlucens vestiebat* oratio. Douglas, *op. cit*., p. 201, rightly points out that clinging transparent garments were as admired in sculptural representation as they were deprecated on the living individual, and deduces that the image derives (like 327, *ingeni quaedam forma elucebat?*) from art, not life. The entire portrait of Calidius seems to employ criteria normally alien to Cicero, eulogizing an example of the *genus floridum* (ἀνθηρόν) to the extent of giving as praise the phrase with which Lucilius condemned the effeminate Albucius, tamquam "in vermiculato emblemate" ... structum. Only in 276 does Cicero express his own reservations based on Calidius' lack of *vis*. I am inclined to suspect that 274 derives from a Greek source – perhaps an adaptation of a Greek critic's assessment of Demetrius of Phalerum, and is presented (a) as a foil and counter to Calvus, the supreme Atticist (played down in *Brut*. 283, following below) and (b) as a tour de force exhibiting Cicero's ability to adapt this type of criticism into Latin. (For Calidius as representative of the *genus medium*, see Douglas, *C.Q.n.s.5*, 1958, 240–7). This passage cannot be related to any allusions to style as clothing in *de Oratore*; in Greek criticism also we draw a blank. Larue Van Hook *op. cit*., pp. 22–3, offers nothing remotely similar to *mollis et perlucens vestiebat oratio*.

general his attitude to the plain style varied from moderate praise of its elegant simplicity of dress to the accusation of neglected grooming. So both *incomptus* and *incultus* are used of unrefined or unadorned speech; *incultus* only as a criticism; cf. *de Orat.* 3.97; *Brut.* 117, *durus incultus horridus*: but in *Att.* 2.1.1: *quamquam tua illa ... horridula mihi atque incompta visa sunt, sed tamen erant ornata hoc ipso quod ornamenta neglexerant, et ut mulieres, ideo bene olere quia nihil olebant videbantur*, and in *Orator* 78: *nam ut mulieres esse dicuntur inornatae quas id ipsum deceat, sic haec subtilis oratio etiam incompta delectat*, lack of rhetorical embellishment is seen as a virtue. Both passages follow their comments with more elaborations based on cosmetics and jewelry and allow for the Atticist viewpoint with its cultivation of *elegantia* and *munditia*.

Certain adjectives of style relate to the grooming of the body, rather than actual clothing, and so form a transition to the vocabulary of physique. The fuller style of Epideictic characterized by a free use of *ornatio* is described by Crassus in 1.81 as *nitidum* quoddam genus verborum et *laetum*; again in 3.51, Antonius praises Crassus' speech as "de horridis rebus *nitida*, de ieiunis *plena*." These words, *nitidus* and *laetus*, are combined with the visual *conlustratus*, to describe richly coloured paintings in *Orator* 36 and contrasted with *horrida*, *inculta*, opaca atque abdita; even the noun *nitor* is associated with the "bloom" of good style: In *Brut.* 36 *naturalis non fucatus nitor* is connected with *sucus et sanguis incorruptus*; so too in *Att.* 13.19.4 and *Orator* 115 (written in the same year) the *nitor* of eloquent style is contrasted with dialectic subject matter which is *squalidiora*. Thus *nitidus, laetus, ornatus* convey praise; *inornatus, incomptus* are neutral and susceptible of praise or blame; *incultus, horridus, squalidus* are words of unqualified condemnation, all derived from the analogy between speech and grooming. Although *nitidus* itself can be interpreted as generally as the popular word *lautus*, originally "having bathed," then generalized as "smart," its connection in 1.81 with *palaestra et oleum* seems to point to the gleaming oiled torso of the athlete as the exemplar.

How far is that torso as a physical ideal a paradigm for Ciceronian ideals of style? It is easy to identify in Cicero critical epithets based on the scrawny and undeveloped physique; thus 1.50, philosophers are condemned as writing *ieiune et exiliter*, or speaking *tenui quodam exsanguique sermone* (1.57); a Stoic speaker produces *spinosa et exilis oratio* (1.83). In 1.218 Cicero declares explicitly, *dicendi facultas non debet esse ieiuna atque nuda, sed aspersa atque distincta multarum rerum iucunda quadam varietate* – but here the literal meaning of *ieiunus* must be lost, in its combination with different figurative concepts. To *exilis* as the main adjective of condemnation Cicero adds in 2.159 *aridus*;[33] here he coincides with *Rhet. Her.* 4.16, *aridum et exsangue genus orationis quod non alienum est exile nominare.* While *exilis* and *exsanguis* need no explanation, *ieiunus* and *aridus* should perhaps be diagnosed as due to lack of *sucus*, which we have seen paired with *sanguis*.[34] But whereas these adjectives unequivocally damn, *tenuis* is susceptible of a more favourable interpretation.[35] In *de Orat.* 3.199, the plain style is *tenuis, non sine nervis et viribus*, "slim but not without sinews and power"; it seems that this is the equivalent of the Greek ἰσχνός; so also in *Orator* 81, *ille tenuis* is the good representative of a particular *genus*, and in *Brut.* 64, *tenuitas*, as the merit of the Attic Lysias, is part of a more explicitly physical stylistic portrait.

> ... studiosos, qui non tam habitus corporis opimos quam gracilitates consectentur, quos, valetudo modo bona sit, tenuitas ipsa delectat – quamquam in Lysia sunt saepe etiam lacerti, sic uti fieri nihil possit valentius; verum est genere toto strigosior.

Cicero's emphasis is on *vis*. Only in so far as slimness is compatible with strength can he tolerate it as an ideal. Here, it is relevant to draw the corollary of a point made by Van Hook (*op. cit.*, pp. 19–20): such images as *sanguis, sucus, ossa, lacerti, nervi* have no equivalent in the Greek metaphorical vocabu-

---

33 *Aridus* (Greek ξηρός), always unfavourable in Cicero, can be contrasted with *siccus*, whose figurative use in Cicero implies relative praise; cf. *Brut.* 202, nihil erat in eius oratione nisi *sincerum*, nihil nisi *siccum* et *sanum*; *de Opt. Gen.* 8, *sani et sicci* dumtaxat habeantur; and 12, eos solos Atticos dicere, id est quasi *sicce et integre*. In these passages Cicero applies *siccus* to the plain style, but in its best form. Later, in Tacitus (*Dial.* 21) and Gellius (14.1.32), we find *siccus* associated with *ieiunus, aridus*, and *durus* in obvious reproach. For *siccus* of physical health, cf. Afranius 61–3 R; "vigilans ac sollers, *sicca, sana sobria*/virosa non sum, et si sum non desunt mihi/qui ultro dent; *aetas integra est, formae satis.*" Uncertainty of text prevents any deductions from the apparent juxtaposition (disjunction?) of *siccam sucidam* in Plaut. *Mil.* 787.

34 Quintilian adds his own coinage; 12.10.15, *aridi et exsuci et exsangues.*

35 We must distinguish between *tenuis* representing ἰσχνός in physical contexts, and *tenuis* (like *subtilis*) representing λεπτός. In the latter sense it is always a word of high praise; compare the Callimachean principles in Prop. 3.1.5, carmen ... *tenuastis*; 3.1.8, exactus *tenui* pumice versus eat (a transferred epithet); Hor. *Ep.* 2.1.225, *tenui deducta* poemata filo. Here, as in *Orator* 124, si *tenuis* causa est, tum etiam argumentandi *tenue filum* ... the metaphor is drawn from weaving fine cloth. The Atticist Dionysius has a similar esteem for λεπτότης, cf. *Isocr.* 3 comparing the λεπτότης of Lysias to that of Calamis or Callimachus. But in *Brut.* 64 below, Cicero explains the *tenuitas* of Lysias in terms of physiology, since he does not want to see this simplicity of diction as the absolute excellence which the other sense of *tenuis* would imply.

lary of the rich style; Greek employs the abstracts ὥρα, ῥώμη, τόνος, ἀκμή, or τὸ ἔμψυχον; but their Latin equivalents, *vires, robur, valetudo*, are always accompanied in Ciceronian criticism by some more concrete physiological term.

When he comes to express his own stylistic ideals, Cicero's words of approval do not relate to physique; the best style is instead, *gravis, ornatus, copiosus, sublimis, grandis, uber, plenus*. Of these only *plenus* approaches a visual value, contrasted with *exilis* in *de Orat.* 3.16, and combined with *teres* in 3.199, *plena quaedam, sed tamen teres*.[36] Physical vocabulary when used to recommend style, is not related to appearance, but to performance. Quintilian 12.10 offers a choice illustration of this Roman attitude. He quotes Atticists as criticizing the full style on aesthetic grounds, because it is unnatural: (41), sicut athletarum corpora, etiamsi validiora fiant exercitatione et lege quadam ciborum, non tamen esse naturalia, atque *ab illa specie quae sit concessa hominibus abhorrere*. His retort is practical: (44), *et lacertos exercitatione constringere et augere vires et colorem trahere naturale est*.[37] Greek aesthetic pleasure has been displaced by Roman emphasis on training and the strength which it produces; *vis* and *dignitas* as ideals replace beauty, and though τὸ πρέπον remains in the form of *decorum*, this most relative of value words survives by being adopted into a new family of values.

A separate comment is needed for the treatment of rhythm and movement in oratory. In this context the *flumen verborum* (*de Orat.* 2.188, *Orator* 53) or *flumen orationis* (*de Orat.* 2.62) is basic. Good oratory will be (2.64.) *fusum atque tractum et cum lenitate quadam aequabiliter profluens*, or (2.159), *liquidum ... fusum, ... profluens*; cf. *Orator* 66, *tracta quaedam et fluens expetitur oratio*. By

36 Van Hook, *op. cit.*, 36–7, compares *teres* here with στρογγύλος at Plato *Phaedr.* 234e, σαφῆ καὶ στρογγύλα καὶ ἀκριβῶς ἕκαστα τῶν ὀνομάτων ἀποτετόρνευται, and Dion. Halic. *Isocr.* 2, στρογγύλη δ'οὐκ ἐστιν καὶ συγκεκροτημένη καὶ πρὸς ἀγῶνας δικανικοὺς εὔθετος, ὕπτια δέ ἐστι μᾶλλον καὶ κεχυμένη πλουσίως. He derives the metaphor (even at *de Orat.* 3.199) from carpentry, in keeping with the Phaedrus passage. But G.M.A. Grube, *A.J.P.* 73, 1952, 257, n. 10, shows in a full discussion of στρογγύλος that in Dionysius it is combined with συστρέφειν at *Isocr.* 11 and 12, giving the sense of "rolled up," and suggests we refer the adjective to "things compact, well-rounded, with a distinct shape of their own." I believe this meaning is appropriate in *teres* in *de Orat.* 3.199 and in keeping with the anatomical context suggested by *habitus ... nervi*, etc. Thus Cicero uses *teres* quite distinctly from *rotundus* (*Brutus* 272, *Orator* 40), which relates to periodic structure, not, like στρογγύλος, to conciseness of presentation.

37 We may compare Quintilian's recommendation at 10.1.33, *non athletarum toris sed militum lacertis opus est*. Strength (*lacerti*) is preferred to visible muscle (*tori*) and the pragmatic soldier to the glamorous but useless athlete.

contrast, both *fluere* and *fluctuare* can denote uncontrolled speech; cf. *Rhet. Her.* 4.16: (genus) *quod appellamus dissolutum, quod est sine nervis atque articulis, ut hoc modo appellem fluctuans, eo quod fluat huc et illuc*, or *de Orat.* 3.190: *efficiendum est illo modo ne fluat oratio, ne vagetur ... ut membris distinguatur*. This, however, is considering speech from a different aspect, the rhythm and structure of the individual period, and this motivates the frequent use of *fluere* in *Orator*: 198, *ne ... aut dissoluta aut fluens sit oratio*; 220, *dissipata et inculta et fluens est oratio*; 233, *diffluens ac solutum*. In 228, *flumen* also is applied unfavourably: *ne infinite feratur ut flumen oratio ... quod multo maiorem habent apta vim quam soluta*. Basically Cicero's practice does not change from *de Oratore* to the later works. In both phases of his oratorical writings *flumen* gives rise to two senses of *fluere*, one critical, close to *diffluere* or *fluctuare*, the other favourable. Thus, even in the section of *Orator* dealing with rhythm, *fluere* can be desirable: (199), *ad hunc exitum iam a principio ferri debet verborum illa comprehensio, et tota a capite ita fluere ut ad extremum veniens ipsa consistat*.

In previous sections I had to choose between the alternatives of classifying by category of image, or by the category of objects to which the image was applied. In *de Oratore* the thematic use of imagery springing from the requirements and possibilities of a complex didactic composition promoted a large degree of coincidence between the two classifications. I have tried to select from the rich abundance of imagery such examples as will give the best general picture of the special techniques, topics, and applications to be found in the dialogue and to distinguish imagery which springs from cultivated conversation, the decorative metaphors of *belles lettres*, the figurative vocabulary of rhetorical criticism, and that of the teacher's *supellex*; those images in fact which help to distinguish the diction and texture of writing in this genre from that of both the letters and speeches.

APPENDIX II

Critical comments on the use of metaphor in *de Oratore* 3.155–68

We have seen that the element of imagery in *de Oratore* is provided either by metaphor or by full analogies. The simple simile of the Aristotelian type, "he rushed like a lion," is more useful for the emotional colouring of poetry than in persuasive or didactic prose, which argues by expressing likeness in the form of a full comparison. But neither simile nor comparison is relevant to the discussion introduced by Crassus in 3.152 of ornament *in verbo simplici*, since they are figures of thought rather than of vocabulary. Such ornament depends on *aut inusitatum verbum aut novatum aut translatum*, and of the three categories, Crassus gives preference to the last (cf. 170).

Crassus is concerned only with *translatio*, and then with its application, not the logic behind the figure. But he prefaces his recommendations with an account of the origin of metaphor in *catachresis* (155):

nam ut vestis frigoris depellendi causa reperta primo, post adhiberi coepta est ad ornatum etiam corporis et dignitatem, sic verbi translatio instituta est inopiae causa, frequentata delectationis.

He contrasts with this inartistic metaphor the literary and ornamental use, but passes over the methods of discovering imagery, and the categories of metaphor, just as Aristotle passes over in *Rhet.* 3.2.1405a4–7 what he had explained in the *Poetics*, about the four categories.[1] Instead, he proceeds in 157 to

---

1 I have omitted comment on 156, *similitudinis* to *repudiatur*, because I believe, despite Marsh McCall's attempt to vindicate the sentence (*op. cit.*, n. 4, pp. 106–11), that it did not stand in Cicero's text. Since I agree with McCall that it is a bold step to assert an interpolation in *de Oratore*, I should like to give the arguments which compel me to reject this sentence.

If we are to understand it at all, it must be related to the end of 155, *quod enim* to *similitudo*. Since this is a difficult sentence I will offer a translation:

For when what can scarcely be made clear by a technically correct word is expressed

consider what purposes are served by metaphor. Aristotle had listed τὸ σαφὲς καὶ τὸ ἡδὺ καὶ τὸ ξενικὸν ἔχει ... ἡ μεταφορά. In 157 Cicero covers τὸ σαφὲς, "ea transferri oportet quae *aut clariorem faciunt rem*"; imagery which makes the meaning more vivid, or (158), "*quo significatur magis* res tota sive facti alicuius sive consili," imagery by which the whole matter, whether consisting of action or motive, is explained more clearly. He adds as an afterthought, "nonnumquam etiam brevitas translatione conficitur, ut illud 'si telum manu fugit.' " Here Cicero's example is typical of the economy of expression achieved by the one-word metaphor, when that word is the verb – a feature we have noticed in the figurative language of Terence.

What appears to be a digression on the psychology of imagery, 159–61, illustrates the other Aristotelian points of τὸ ἡδύ and τὸ ξενικόν. Borrowed words, *aliena*, delight more than the correct, literal forms. One cause may be the pleasure of the hearer in testing his intelligence: "ingeni specimen est quoddam transsilire ... et alia longe petita sumere"; another cause, the pleasure of diversion, without losing the main theme "alio ducitur cogitatione, neque tamen aberrat." He adds to this, economy (as in 158), "quod in singulis verbis res ac totum simile conficitur," and appeal to the senses, especially to sight. It is probably with this in mind that he himself uses the metaphor *lumen* to

by a transferred word, the resemblance of the thing which we have set down by means of a borrowed word throws light on the meaning we wish to be understood.

In this sentence, consistent with the previous discussion, metaphor is seen as a borrowing of the metaphor-word to replace a missing literal word. Now in the disputed sentence 156, the viewpoint is quite different; *alieno loco* sees the metaphor-word as occupying a borrowed place as if it were its own, and claiming recognition (*agnoscitur*). Again, in this sentence it is the metaphor that is rejected if *simile nihil habet*. It lacks *similitudo*, whereas in 155 above, *similitudo* was predicated of the concept which the metaphor replaces. Thus the point of view is completely reversed from 155 and inconsistent with it. McCall's major claim for this passage, that Cicero "has coupled metaphor and comparison, but reversed Aristotle's procedure by superordinating metaphor to comparison (p. 111)," is one more argument against the sentence. For Cicero took *translatio* as his starting point and uses it as his defining term, whereas *similitudo* need not be technical in any passage of *de Oratore*, and is best translated with the ordinary meaning "resemblance," "likeness." The emphasis of McCall's interpretation reverses not only Aristotle's but Cicero's own approach to the whole topic of metaphor.

Attempts to interpret or emend the first words, *similitudinis est ad verbum unum contracta brevitas*, cannot overcome the difficulty of *brevitas*, and merely produce a definition occurring out of place. But the sentence as a whole makes only two points: the first, the achievement of *brevitas*, is expressed fully and clearly at the end of 158; the second, *si simile nihil habet repudiatur*, is made more effectively in 162, *quo in genere primum est fugienda dissimilitudo*, and made in terms which exclude the possibility that Cicero had already touched on this in 156. I would suggest that this sentence is not Ciceronian, but a later attempt, perhaps influenced by Quint. 8.6.8–9, to summarize the points made by Cicero in 158–62.

describe the effect of imagery on speech – imagery is a *source of vision*. His actual recommendations to the orator begin in 162:

Nihil est enim in rerum natura, cuius nos non in aliis rebus possimus uti vocabulo et nomine. Unde enim simile duci potest, potest autem ex omnibus, indidem verbum unum, quod similitudinem continet, translatum *lumen* adferet orationi. Quo in genere primum est fugienda dissimilitudo: "caeli ingentes fornices"; quamvis sphaeram in scaenam, ut dicitur, attulerit Ennius, tamen in sphaera fornicis similitudo inesse non potest.

> Vive, Ulixes; dum licet:
> oculis postremum lumen radiatum rape!

non dixit 'pete' non 'cape,' – haberet enim moram sperantis diutius esse victurum – sed 'rape': est hoc verbum ad id aptatum, quod ante dixerat, 'dum licet.' Deinde videndum est ne longe simile sit ductum: "Syrtim" 163 patrimoni, "scopulum" libentius dixerim; "Charybdim" bonorum, "voraginem" potius; facilius enim ad ea, quae visa, quam ad illa, quae audita sunt, mentis oculi feruntur; et quoniam haec vel summa laus est in verbis transferendis, ut sensum feriat id, quod translatum sit, fugienda est omnis turpitudo earum rerum, ad quas eorum animos, qui audient, 164 trahet similitudo. Nolo dici morte Africani "castratam" esse rem publicam, nolo "stercus curiae" dici Glauciam; quamvis sit simile, tamen est in utroque deformis cogitatio similitudinis; nolo esse aut maius, quam res postulet: "tempestas comissationis;" aut minus: "comissatio tempestatis;" nolo esse verbum angustius id, quod translatum sit, quam fuisset illud proprium ac suum:

> quidnam est, obsecro? Quid te adirier abnutas?
> melius esset vetas, prohibes, absterres, quoniam ille dixerat:
> ilico istic,
> ne contagio mea bonis umbrave obsit ...

165 Atque etiam, si vereare, ne paulo durior translatio esse videatur, mollienda est praeposito saepe verbo; ut si olim, M. Catone mortuo, "pupillum" senatum quis relictum diceret, paulo durius; sin "ut ita dicam, pupillum," aliquanto mitius: etenim verecunda decet esse translatio, ut deducta esse in alienum locum, non inrupisse, atque ut precario, non vi, venisse videatur.

For the purposes of oratory – the concern of his speaker Crassus – Cicero counsels negatively, in terms of restraint; the orator must avoid inappropriate (162) or far-fetched metaphors (163); from the examples of the latter given (cf. chap. 5, p. 131, n. 33), he seems to be recommending natural and general, rather than literary and specific allusions, as more appealing to the visual imagination. His criterion, used to introduce the next caution, applies also retrospectively to what preceded: "haec vel summa laus est in rebus transferendis *ut sensus feriat* id quod translatum sit." Because the appeal of figurative language should be directly to the senses, any obscene allusion should be avoided. The metaphor must not be more noble than what it describes, nor more trivial (164, *aut maius quam res postulet ... aut minus*). Finally if a metaphor seems too harsh, it can be softened by approximating it to a simile. Imagery must be restrained and modest (*verecunda*), so that it seems to have been decently introduced and not a gatecrasher, natural, not forced (165). As a postscript, he deals in 166 with the developed metaphor, *allegoria*, which "non est in uno verbo translato, sed ex pluribus continuatis conectitur"; 167–8 cover hypallage, synecdoche, metonymy, and related figures. Simile as such receives no separate treatment.

Although it is still disputed whether Cicero was familiar with Aristotle's *Rhetorica*,[2] there are in this section enough general points of resemblance to Aristotle's discussion in *Rhet.* 3.2–4 to suggest that Cicero was familiar, if not with the *Rhetorica* itself, at least with handbooks deriving immediately from it. Thus in Ar. *Rhet.* 3.2.5, γλώτταις μὲν καὶ διπλοῖς ὀνόμασι καὶ πεποιημένοις, which are to be discouraged in prose-writing, correspond to *inusitatum aut novatum* (*verbum*) *de Orat.* 3.152. τὸ ξενικόν (3.2.8), the foreign or imported element in metaphor, can be translated by "translata atque *aliena*," "*aliena* multo magis, si sunt ratione translata, delectant," of *de Orat.* 3.159. The primary need for μεταφορὰς ἁρμοττούσας. τοῦτο δ' ἔσται ἐκ τοῦ ἀναλόγου makes the same point as *fugienda ... dissimilitudo*, 162. In Aristotle's discussion of τὸ ἀπρεπές, his condemnation of the Telephus fragment (3.2.11) as ἀπρεπές, ὅτι μεῖζον τὸ ἀνάσσειν ἢ κατ' ἀξίαν corresponds to Cicero's *nolo esse* (aut) *maius* quam res postulet (164), and this section of the *Rhetorica* gives examples of metaphors more dignified and more trivial than their application. ἔτι δὲ οὐ

2 See F. Solmsen, *C.P.* 33, 1939, 401–2. (He favours belief in Cicero's direct acquaintance with the *Rhetorica*.) From *de Orat.* 2.160, Aristotelem, cuius illum legi librum, in quo exposuit dicendi artes omnium superiorum, *et illos, in quibus ipse sua quaedam de eadem arte dixit*, it is usually assumed that Cicero, for whom Antonius is speaking here, had read the τεχνῶν συναγωγή and the *Topica* (source of Cicero's *Topica*), but not necessarily the *Rhetorica*.

πόρρωθεν δεῖ, ἀλλ᾽ ἐκ τῶν συγγενῶν (3.2.12), apparently making the same point as *ne longe simile sit ductum* (*de Orat.* 163) in fact serves to introduce the topic of catachresis – the necessary metaphor of *de Orat.* 3.155-6. In 3.2.13, where Cicero has given the negative counsel *fugienda est omnis turpitudo*, Aristotle expresses his ideal positively: τὰς δὲ μεταφορὰς ἐντεῦθεν οἰστέον, ἀπὸ καλῶν ἢ τῇ φωνῇ ἢ τῇ δυνάμει ἢ τῇ ὄψει ἢ ἄλλῃ τινὶ αἰσθήσει (like Cicero, he gives priority to sight). Finally in 3.3.4 on τὸ ψυχρόν, Aristotle produces examples of tasteless simile which illustrate these prescriptions, and reflect the same standards as Cicero's briefer treatment of metaphor in *de Orat.* 3.162-5. But it is significant that Aristotle gives special attention to the simile after his comments on metaphor, whereas Cicero ignores it.

This section of *de Oratore* is the most extensive treatment of figurative language in Cicero's rhetorical works, and allusions in the works of his later phase – *Brutus, Orator, de Optimo Genere Oratorum* – are frustratingly scanty. Speaking of the Atticist Orator, Cicero in *Orator* 81 recommends that he be "in transferendis *verecundus* et *parcus*" ... and 82: "hoc ornamento liberius paulo quam ceteris utitur hic summissus, nec *tam licenter* tamen quam si genere dicendi uteretur amplissimo. itaque illud indecorum (τὸ ἀπρεπές!) hic quoque apparet, cum verbum aliquid altius transfertur, idque in oratione humili ponitur quod idem in altera deceret." But if the criticism of too lofty metaphor applies here only to the *tenuis orator* of 81, the recommendation of *verecundia* is more general in, e.g., *de Opt. Gen.* 4: perficiendum est ... in translatis (verbis) ut similitudinem secuti *verecunde* utamur alienis. As in *de Orat.* 3.155, Cicero classifies figurative language as (*Orator* 92) *translata* ... quae per similitudinem ab alia re *aut suavitatis aut inopiae causa* transferuntur. Later in *Orator* 134, he recommends that *translationes* should be the most frequently used of all forms of *singulorum verborum* ... *lumina*, "quod eae propter similitudinem transferunt animos et referunt ac movent huc et illuc, qui motus cogitationis celeriter agitatus per se delectat." Again, this recalls his psychological analysis of the pleasures of metaphor in *de Orat.* 3.159-61. But such comments neither add to, nor modify, the critical account of *de Oratore*, and one must regret its brevity. It is even more to be regretted that Cicero was limited by Crassus' official topic of metaphor *in oratory*, and prevented from discussing the far freer use of imagery in the genre in which he himself was writing – the work of literary and rhetorical criticism for the educated layman. For this genre, his principles can only be deduced from his practice, and this I have sought to do in chap. 6.

7

Some conclusions

In these studies it has been my aim to examine the role of imagery in Latin *sermo* and the formal prose-writing which developed from it. Terence's plays are the first body of evidence for a spoken Latin that was discriminating yet unaffected. Although he presents naturalistic rather than natural utterance and speech disciplined by art, metaphor, since it is primarily a figure of thought, will be less affected by the formalizing tendency of composed dialogue than pure "Klangfiguren," figures of diction. Yet a lover of paradox might delight in the fact that the first evidence for the style of Latin *sermo* is neither wholly Latin nor *sermo*, since it is in a verse form and adapted from Hellenistic drama by an author praised for his fidelity to the spirit and values of his Greek originals. So Terence's Latinity has to be seen as a reconciliation of good Latin speech in its quest for *urbanitas*, and the slightly over-ripe sophistication of third-century Athenian idiom.

No aspect of language is quicker to offend against taste than metaphor; hence the insistence of Theophrastus, and Cicero following him, on *verecunda tralatio* (*Fam.* 16.17.1). Taste in both the sources and the application of imagery must have differed between the two civilizations. When Terence came upon an effective metaphor in Menander's Greek, how did he decide whether to translate, replace, or omit the figurative element in the language? Under the influence of Euripidean tragedy, of Platonic and then Peripatetic philosophy, the Attic playwrights had inherited a tradition of imagery drawn from certain aspects of Greek social life, primarily those of navigation and medicine. In Terence the proportion of medical and nautical metaphor is highest in the early *Andria*, relatively low in the last play, *Adelphoe*, yet simple metaphors relying on the basic concepts of these activities persist throughout his plays. Many other metaphors are demonstrably Greek in origin: In *Adelphoe* we can recognize analogies familiar from New Comedy in Micio's use of *defervisse*

(*Ad.* 152) for the maturing of a young man like a new wine; the comparison is made formally in Alexis κΠ fr. 45. Micio's comparison of life to a game of dice (*Ad.* 739–41) is found in Alexis κΠ fr. 34 and before Alexis in Plato. Demea's allusion to the home stretch in life's race (*Ad.* 860) has precedents in the same authors. All these metaphors presuppose the existence of a Hellenized urban class in Rome which would appreciate such analogies. Because of their way of life, Romans up to this time would have tended to draw imagery from agriculture, warfare, or the magistracies and rituals of the state. In Terence, agricultural metaphors are almost absent and allusions to Roman institutions are confined to the most obvious (cf. p. 77). Of the major categories of metaphor which I have distinguished – fire, heat and cold; sickness and cure; navigation and storm; imagery of combat; imagery from the drama, from teaching and training, and from hunting, fowling, and fishing – only the first group seems to be favoured in Latin, while rare in Greek, and this category is free of such "local colour" as would impair the presentation of a neutral, non-national bourgeois world to the audience.

But in drama imagery should reflect characterization in terms of age, sex, and class; an important element in Terence's intrigues is provided by the parasites and slaves. Their roles account for other more colloquial figurative language. Vigorous metaphors come naturally and frequently to the uninhibited lower classes. Thus, particularly in *Eunuchus* and *Phormio* we find a greater abundance and variety of metaphor because of the many slave and parasite roles; in *Eunuchus* more is contributed by the hyperbolic idiom of young Chaerea. It is the deceptions and malice of slaves which chiefly give rise to the metaphors of hunting and attack. Yet there are more colourful idioms of deception in Plautus – *detondere, oblinere, emungere,* barely to be found in Terence; only *emungere* occurs once, at *Ph.* 862.

In general, we saw (pp. 42, 77) that Terence in comparison with Plautus plays down animal metaphors, whether in description or abuse; Gnatho's *ain vero, canis* (*Eu.* 803) is quite exceptional, to express exceptional vulgarity. Terence also avoids the specific sociological or technical image comparing a character with a craftsman. But in contrast with Menander or Philemon he excluded the personification of abstractions (cf. pp. 16, 35, 37) by which poverty is called a disease, or time a healer. The typical εἰκών, a developed simile or analogy, is found only once in Terence (*Ad.* 739–41 above). Both Greek and Roman traditions of imagery, then, are to some extent muted by Terence, in his search for an idiom that is neutral in time and place, but expressive of individual psychology. Considerations of taste combine with his psychological orientation to produce a usage that is restrained both in allusive content and form.

Terence's success in achieving this harmony of style is confirmed by the recurrence of the same vocabulary and categories of imagery in Cicero's correspondence a century later. The metaphors of Terence's citizens are frequent in Cicero's letters and I have illustrated their occurrence and variations upon them from the correspondence. It is worth pointing out here the complement of this relationship, that only a tiny minority of metaphors found in Cicero's letters are of new types not represented in Terence's plays.

In the Appendix to Part I, I attempted a different approach to Terence's practice. Given one common theme – love and the lover – by what metaphors did Terence express the condition? Again it was possible to compare his usage with both his Greek predecessors and the re-emergence of the tradition in Latin, in Catullus and Augustan elegy and lyric. Elegy, like comedy, was regarded as a genre less elevated in diction than tragedy or epic, and the same stylistic level is found in Horace's symposiastic or amatory lyrics. Catullan hendecasyllables are more down to earth, and Syrus' colloquial *deperire* (*Hau.* 525) is echoed in Cat. 35.12; cf. 45.5. But Catullus in his elegiac love poems and Tibullus and Propertius provide a body of poetry whose systems of erotic imagery can be matched against the elements found in Terence, and which shares with him the strong emphasis on passion as fire or heat, and a relative indifference to the Hellenistic cliché of wounds from Cupid's bow. Fire, fever, sickness, madness, torture, and battle are used to depict the suffering lover from Phaedria to Propertius. Only in Ovid's self-conscious exploitation of the tradition for humour and paradox does elegy take imagery beyond the practice of comedy.

The parallel Plautine material given in Part I showed how many metaphors were common to Plautus and Terence, because they had the same task of blending Greek and Roman idiom, but also pointed to a freer treatment by Plautus of the inherited imagery. In chap. 4 an attempt has been made to isolate certain features of Plautus' exploitation of metaphor for humour and fantasy. His images give life to the inanimate, personalities and purposes to the impersonal, and physical violence to almost everything. His handling of metaphor takes it far beyond its prosaic function of making vivid or psychologically clear motives and actions. The images themselves become points of departure for imaginative word-flights which seldom return to earth. Syntactically too the metaphor *in verbo simplici* based on a transferred verb or noun develops towards allegory in the accumulation of terms transferred from the same field, or generates a clash of words drawn from deliberately incongruous sources. One point of similarity – say a confused or twisted manner of speech – leads to complete identification of the speaker with a twisted creature, the caterpillar of *Cist.* 728–30. Hyperbole, mythology, and neologisms are drafted to reinforce the verbal onslaught, and in Plautus imagery performs as it never did on either the Greek stage of Menander, or the Roman street.

The remaining sections are concerned with Cicero, and his use of figurative language at different levels of prose. Certain of his letters are distinguished from the body of his correspondence by their formality of diction and publicist intent. The letter to Lucceius (*Fam.* 5.12) and the great manual of provincial administration sent to Quintus (*Q.fr.* 1.1) reflect their preoccupation with a wider public in style and imagery. The self-vindication addressed to Lentulus Spinther (*Fam.* 1.9) was chosen to illustrate the role of imagery when *sermo* has to be reconciled with formal apologetics; comparison with *pro Balbo*, a contemporary speech dealing with technical problems of citizenship, showed that the *genus tenue* applied a similar range of metaphors. The need for clarity of explanation accounts for a relatively low frequency in this speech, and innovative development of imagery is confined to the patriotic passages recording the military achievements of Pompey (13 and 16) and the past heroism of the Scipiones (34).

In *post reditum in Senatu* and *ad Quirites*, we have contemporaneous speeches on a common theme of gratitude for restoration and condemnation of Cicero's enemies. Only the audiences differ. The stylistic level of these, especially the speech *ad Quirites*, is achieved by other means as well as by imagery, by audible effects of alliteration, accumulation, and antithesis. But the coincidences of imagery (see pp. 122–3) are as interesting as the divergences, reflecting both political tact, and, in the *ad Quirites*, a conscious suppression of intellectual or aesthetic metaphors in favour of simple analogies from sickness (*Red. Pop.* 4) and the world of debt and credit (*ibid.*, 23). The brevity of these speeches prevents any organization of metaphor for structural effects, beyond one interesting pattern of repetition observable in both: in *Red. Sen.* 9, *consulare vulnus* is deliberately recalled by *consularis ictus* in 17; the use of *reportare* in 28 is similarly recalled at 34 and 39. In the *ad Quirites* the repetition is more conspicuous; two phrases, *me nudum a propinquis, nulla cognatione munitum*, are repeated verbatim from 7 to 16.

Pro Sestio has to cover many of the same themes, but the stylistic level is consistently the *genus grande*. Cicero was not only defending an ally on a capital charge that called for all the resources of emotive rhetoric, but he converted the speech into a partisan record of Roman political life and a personal manifesto of principle. The scale of the speech gave scope for variations and elaborations of each class of image. Two formal analogies (24 and 45–6) stand out from the context of the speech in a thematic role: the first expressing the wanton destruction of the state by the Consuls of 58 B.C.; the second the noble self-sacrifice of Cicero for the *boni*. This prolonged ship-analogy (45–6) marks Cicero's moment of decision and gives it a special intensity. Other metaphors of aggression and navigation resume the themes of these analogies and help to associate Cicero's personal fate with that of his country. The difference in development in the high style can be measured by juxtaposing *Red. Sen.* 17:

> ne unam quidem horam interesse paterere inter meam pestem et tuam praedam,

and Sest. 54:

> ne noctem quidem consules inter meum ⟨interitum⟩ et suam praedam interesse passi sunt; statim me perculso ad meum sanguinem hauriendum et spirante etiam re publica ad eius spolia detrahenda advolaverunt.

At the same time the violence of the imagery reflects acts of violence in contemporary politics. While the main categories of allusion are familiar from Terence and the correspondence, two new elements are the imagery of pollution and darkness (pp. 133–4) and the architectural metaphors related to the imagery of siege-warfare and to the reality of demolition which Cicero had personally suffered.

With *de Oratore* Cicero tackled what was virtually a new genre in Latin. The epideictic and protreptic content related it to the tradition of Greek philosophy with its use of didactic analogy, while the element of conversation related it to the more urbane dialogue in comedy, and in Cicero's conversational interludes, the imagery, like the general atmosphere of courtesy and restraint, recalls that of Terence's gentlemen. But the language of Cicero's interlocutors is carefully related to their interests and social concerns: Scaevola's great allegory of Rhetoric as an illegal occupier prosecuted by the other disciplines (1.41) and Caesar Strabo's jests about his contribution as a *conlecta* and a *deversorium* (2.233–4) are examples of socially appropriate imagery. Yet Cicero could take a traditional image of Greek theory, such as *fontes* for intellectual sources, *supellex* or *ornatus* for rhetorical adornment, or the complex of aesthetic values associated with the health and beauty of style, and

adapt them to provide brief metaphors or full analogies for his recommendations on *inventio* and *elocutio*, and in all of them display a double concern to
respect the imagery of Greek theoreticians and the language of a Roman
literary predecessor (as in the case of *inhibere*, at 1.153) while retaining the
naturalism of dialogue. A dead or dying metaphor like *cursus* could be recalled
to life by a discreet reinforcement of words or phrases from one of three
contexts – the chariot race, the foot-race, or the voyage. Greek analogies are
sometimes kept unchanged, elsewhere given a Roman colouring, as in the
transference of *palaestra* images to military drill, or the illustration of beauty
deriving from utility by the gable of the Capitoline temple (3.180). But
Cicero shows a more positive attitude than Terence towards imagery with a
distinct national colouring; his landowning aristocrats draw analogies from
agriculture (pp. 145–6), and as wealthy connoisseurs are permitted allusions
to the fine arts and specific Greek artists. The latter would have been inappropriate to the bourgeois world of Greek or Roman comedy, but is legitimate
in characterization of these noblemen, and desirable as ornament and diversion from technical subject matter.

Besides the constant use of imagery for local, decorative purposes, the
two special developments are the thematic image (*fontes, regio, ornatus*, and
their derivatives) and the structural image. Scaevola's trespass motif (1.41) is
the challenge to oratory in book 1 which is finally answered by Crassus in
3.122 with a modification of the same analogy. The comparison between the
orator ignorant of jurisprudence and the would-be pilot unable to handle a
small boat marks Crassus' argument in 1.174, and Antonius' retort (1.237).
Major images with variations define the beginning and end of Antonius'
digression on *imitatio* and Greek oratory (2.88 and 97), his summing up of the
Aristotelian *Topica* (2.162 and 174), Caesar Strabo's digression (2.234–290),
Crassus' alternative analysis of *inventio* on Hermagorean principles (3.108 and
110; 122), and his catalogue of figures of speech (3.200 and 206). Less conspicuously they help the resumption of argument after dialogue from 2.70 to
73, and 2.294 to 303. Two basic metaphors, that of the orator as combatant,
and that of the speech as a body, run through the work and emphasize the role
of the orator in the courts, and the physical aspect of oratory as a performance
revealing health in action.

Syntactically the large scale and formal genre of *de Oratore* allows
imagery more freedom, and a given metaphor is not confined to the medium
of a single verb or noun, but allowed to develop its logic through a sequence
of words or phrases. It may be sustained through many paragraphs, as the

imagery of fire runs through the illustration of *movere* from Antonius' great defence of Norbanus in 2.188–205, maintaining the didactic message parallel to the narrative without the tedium of formal commentary.

Throughout this long and brilliantly orchestrated composition, metaphor and analogy are scored to promote the two aims of epideictic prose – to teach with clarity, and to delight with beauty. By their relationship with the argument and with each other the images contribute to the organization and unity of the whole work. In *de Oratore* Cicero has employed the highest level of artistry which he, and perhaps Latin prose of any period, could achieve, and the easy versatility with which he handles imagery is a fair illustration that Latin had reached the full powers of a mature and classical language.

Indexes

Latin or Greek words discussed for their figurative usage are listed in Index I (Latin) and II (Greek), including figurative technical terms of rhetoric. These and other technical terms are also listed in the subject Index IV, *Topics and Terminology*.

In Index III, *Passages Quoted or Discussed*, it has sometimes proved impossible to reconcile the alphabetical order of the abbreviated references used in my text with that of the full titles of works cited. I have sacrificed consistency of presentation where there is a conflict, listing references in the abbreviated form and the order it implies. In ordering references from Cicero, I have subdivided according to literary genre, listing the works in the alphabetical order of their abbreviations within five categories: I, Letters; II, Speeches; III, Rhetorical works; IV, Philosophical works; V, Poems. Thus the speech *post Reditum ad Quirites* is listed in II under *Red. Pop.*; *De Officiis* is listed in IV under *Off.*

Citations from Donatus' commentary are listed with the reference to the Terence passage upon which Donatus is commenting, but in the order of page sequence in Wessner's Teubner Text, not the alphabetical order of Terence's plays: similarly Menander references follow the page sequence of Koerte's edition, not the alphabetical order of play titles.

INDEX III PASSAGES QUOTED OR DISCUSSED

382/39, 79
439/56, 79
474/62
484/33, 63
491/69, 79
494/67
495/44
506/59, 77
515/61
543/29n17, 77
575/14, 16
628/69
682/51, 79, 103
690/17
695/14
718/58
744/87
780/59, 71, 77
821–2/14, 18, 79, 84
823/52
824/14, 18, 51
834/61
841–3/62, 79
856–7/44, 79
862/51, 182
874/67
897/50
943/67
964/28, 31, 77, 80
973–5/7, 60, 79
994/12, 13–4
1015/67
1026/67
1030/56, 79

THEOGNIS
994/54

THEOGNOTUS
KIII fr. 1/15

THEOPHILUS
KII fr. 6/20

TIBULLUS
1.2.11/86
1.2.98/88
1.3.64/90
1.4.81/89
1.5.5/89
1.6.4/86
1.6.74/86
1.10.53/85
2.1.82/87
2.5.109–10/88
2.6.17–18/86
2.6.51/86

VARRO
Menippeae
418B/154

VIRGIL
Eclogues
2.1/8n4, 87
2.68/86
2.69/86
3.66/87
5.10/87

8.41/88
10.10/88
10.22/86
10.60/86, 89
Aeneid
1.152/42
1.261/61
2.303/42
2.446, 464/117n4
4.4/123n14
4.478/70
5.176/36n24
6.353/36n24
6.462/61
7.790/61
8.307/61

XENARCHUS
KII fr. 2/20

XENOPHON
Cynegetica
8.8/51
Memorabilia
1.2.22/51
2.1.4/40, 51
3.11.10/51

Demetrius, *de Elocutione*: as evidence for
rhetorical terms 164; quoted 153n15, 155
Demosthenes: respected by Cicero 125n20;
his *de Corona* translated by Cicero 125,
125n20; difference of taste in fullness of
style, imagery 125; imagery in *de Corona*
126n21, 128n23; praised for his δεινότης
in metaphor of swordsmanship 153n15; his
emphasis on *actio* 160
deportment: the gentleman's deportment in
Cicero's *de Officiis*; the Roman attitude to
physical decorum, and its effect on metaphors of aesthetics 165
Dialogus: Cicero's use of the Greek word as
equivalent of *sermo* 138
dialogue: prose dialogue in Latin before
Cicero 139; verse dialogues of Lucilius,
ludus ac sermones 139
dice: life as a game of dice; history of the
Greek image 70, 182; in an analogy of
de Orat. 145
dignitas: as a Ciceronian aesthetic value 144,
165, 171, 174; equivalent to *ornatus* in
Rhet. Her. 167, 167n28; combined with
venustas as an ideal 144; as the male
principle of beaty, opposed to female
venustas, in *Off.* 165
digressions: framed by imagery in *de Orat.*
140, 145, 186; *deversorium* (Gk ἐκτροπή)
as rhetorical image for a digression 154–5
dining: the dinner ticket, *conlecta* 154; the
instructor convivi 124, 124n16
Dionysius of Halicarnassus: as a source for
rhetorical terms 164, 166n27, 173n35,
174n36; his analogy from the evolution of
sculpture and painting to rhetoric 141
Diphilus: his use of medical imagery 15–16
dispositio (arrangement) 165
disputatio: denoting philosophical argument
138
– *in utramque partem*, the Peripatetic practice
138
docere: one aim of philosophical writing 139
dogs: primarily associated with hunting;
implied by *odorari* in Cicero's letters 41n31;
hounds in Plautus 112; in Cicero, *Red. Sen.*
124n15; in *de Orat.* 143
– *Canis* as a vulgar insult 42; women as
bitches 56; whimpering, barking, and baring

of teeth 56
Donatus: his assessment of the tempo of
Terence's plays 72, 72n2; for comments on
individual metaphors. *See* Index III
Drama as a source of imagery: in Plautus and
Terence 33–5; in *de Orat.* 160–161; the
dramatic repetiteur 36–7
dreams and dreaming: as a metaphor for
folly in comedy 67
drinking: as a metaphor for the absorption of
knowledge in *de Orat.* 161; associated with
the imagery of sources and streams 160.
See also blood
dyeing: education as a steeping in dye, in
Plautus and Cicero 162, 162n24

eating: as a metaphor for extravagance in
comedy and Cicero's letters 46; the spend-
thrift as glutton 131; feeding as an image
of cruelty 133n35, but cf. 64
elegantia: as a critical term 3n1; a special
virtue of Atticist style 172
elegy: erotic imagery in Roman elegy 82–90;
relationship to comedy, direct or indirect
82–3; affinities in choice of imagery with
Terence, and divergence from Greek
erotic poetry 83
elocutio (diction and style): Cicero on *elocutio*,
critical principles and vocabulary 166–7,
167n28, 171
Ennius: relationship of *Ann.* 240-IV with Ter.
Eu. 401–7, 52; originator of phrase *fulmina
belli*, applied to Scipiones 118
epagoge 140, 144
Epideictic: Cicero's stylistic principles for the
genre 138–9; *de Orat.* as epideictic writing
138–40, 185; the aims of Epideictic and its
greater scope for imagery 138, 187
Eunuchus of Terence: frequency of imagery
72; Donatus' classification as *ex magna parte
motoria* 72, 72n2; relative frequency of
imagery in *senarii* and long-verse 74, 74n4;
metaphorical language of slaves, parasite,
and young Chaerea 75; opening scene
quoted in paraphrase by Horace 82;
portrayal of jealousy in this scene 83
evolution: evolutionary approach to art-
history and literary criticism in Cicero,
Dionysius, and Quintilian 141, 164

25 September 1982